W9-AXA-080

LIFE BETWEEN
THE TIDES

ALSO BY ADAM NICOLSON

The National Trust Book of Long Walks

Long Walks in France

Frontiers: From the Arctic to the Aegean

Wetland: Life in the Somerset Levels

Restoration: The Rebuilding of Windsor Castle

Regeneration: The Story of the Dome

Sea Room: An Island Life in the Hebrides

When God Spoke English: The Making of the King James Bible

Seamanship: A Voyage Along the Wild Coasts of the British Isles

Men of Honour: Trafalgar and the Making of the English Hero

Smell of Summer Grass: Pursuing Happiness –
Perch Hill 1994–2011

Arcadia: The Dream of Perfection in Renaissance England

Sissinghurst: An Unfinished History

Gentry: Six Hundred Years of a Peculiarly English Class

The Mighty Dead: Why Homer Matters

The Seabird's Cry: The Lives and Loves of Puffins,
Gannets and Other Ocean Voyagers

The Making of Poetry: Coleridge, the Wordsworths
and Their Year of Marvels

LIFE BETWEEN THE TIDES

ADAM NICOLSON

Animals and Heroes by Kate Boxer
Maps and Figures by Rosie Nicolson

FARRAR, STRAUS AND GIROUX

NEW YORK

Farrar, Straus and Giroux
120 Broadway, New York 10271

Printed in the United States of America
Originally published in 2021 by William Collins, Great Britain, as
The Sea Is Not Made of Water: Life Between the Tides
Published in the United States by Farrar, Straus and Giroux
First American edition, 2022

Grateful acknowledgment is made for permission to reprint lines from
"Wolves," from *Collected Poems* by Louis MacNeice (Faber & Faber),
reproduced by permission by David Higham Associates.

Library of Congress Cataloging-in-Publication Data
Names: Nicolson, Adam, 1957– author.
Title: Life between the tides / Adam Nicolson ; animals and heroes by Kate Boxer ;
    maps and figures by Rosie Nicolson.
Description: First American edition. | New York : Farrar, Straus and Giroux, 2022. |
    Originally published in 2021 by William Collins, Great Britain, as The Sea Is Not
    Made of Water: Life Between the Tides. | Includes bibliographical references and index.
Identifiers: LCCN 2021044058 | ISBN 9780374251437 (hardcover)
Subjects: LCSH: Tide pool ecology. | Seashore ecology.
Classification: LCC QH541.5.S35 N53 2022 | DDC 577.69/9—dc23/eng/20211013
LC record available at https://lccn.loc.gov/2021044058

Our books may be purchased in bulk for promotional, educational,
or business use. Please contact your local bookseller or the Macmillan Corporate
and Premium Sales Department at 1-800-221-7945, extension 5442, or by email
at MacmillanSpecialMarkets@macmillan.com.

www.fsgbooks.com
www.twitter.com/fsgbooks • www.facebook.com/fsgbooks

1 3 5 7 9 10 8 6 4 2

for Kate Boxer

Heraclitus on the shore.

CONTENTS

Contents

PART III: PEOPLE

LIST OF ILLUSTRATIONS

Picture sections: all photography author's own and all illustrations courtesy of Kate Boxer.

Sources of in-text photographs and illustrations not by AN or Kate Boxer

Sources for Rosie Nicolson's figures and maps

All from sketches by AN except:

INTRODUCTION

The marvellous

———

Sound of Mull, summer 2020.

The sea is not made of water. Creatures are its genes. Look down as you crouch over the shallows and you will find a periwinkle or a prawn, a claw-displaying crab or a cluster of anemones ready to meet you. No need for binoculars or special stalking skills: go to the rocks and the living will say hello.

In the 1850s, when Victorian Britain fell in love with the seaside, the rock pool became the heart of a kind of nature-worship which saw in its riches and calm a reassuring vision of

1

creation. Life in what Philip Henry Gosse, the great apostle of the pools, called 'these unruffled wells' was a gathering of goodness and even happiness. It was as if the pools came from a time before the Fall, when life was innocent and unthreatened. Gosse, surely half-remembering the children's rhyme, imagined 'Adam and Eve, stepping lightly down to bathe in the rainbow-coloured spray.' At just the moment Darwin was challenging the God-ordained vision of nature, and setting the whole of life adrift on chance-driven change, the rock pools looked to those Victorians like gardens of prelapsarian bliss, glimmering enclosures in which nature seemed to have enshrined perfection and permanence.

We have inherited some of that Victorian longing for calm. We still go to the seaside for consolation and simplicity. Demands and anxieties seem to drop away there; things still are as they were when we were ten. The rock pools still beckon, the blennies and gobies still shimmer beneath us. But there are ironies in choosing the shore as a theatre for reassurance. Even if its changes are dependable and rhythmic, it is thick with variability. A tidal coast is filled with that paradoxical quality: reliable unreliability, both closed and open-ended, both familiar and strange. Regularity toys with uncertainty there. Nothing is more predictable than the coming and going of the tide and yet nothing about it can be relied on: daily revelation and daily erasure, daily loss and daily reacquisition.

This book is about those multiple layers between the tides, the ways in which the simple overlies the less-than-simple there, the extraordinary mirroring of human and animal life on its shores, in pools that are silent and beautiful and as full of threat as any rats' alley or Roman circus. The intertidal is rich but troubled; as no coincidence, it is one of the most revelatory habitats on earth. Of all the great discoveries made in the science of nature, from a grasp of taxonomy, to the sequence of creatures through time revealed in the rocks, the adaptations of organisms to circumstance, the idea of natural selection – finally crystallising in Darwin's mind as he spent eight long years examining the inner structures of the barnacle – the working of ecological webs and the governing importance of trophic cascades – all these ways of understanding the pattern of life first emerged from studying what was happening to animals and plants between the tides.

It is where you can look beyond your own reflection and find the marvellous an inch beneath your nose. 'The soul wants to be wet,' Heraclitus said in Ephesus 2,500 years ago. That is the impulse this book follows.

It began for me in springtime, thirty years ago. I had not long known Sarah, who was soon to be my wife, when she took me to a place she had known since she was a girl. Her family had been coming there for years, far out on the west coast of Scotland, in Argyll where David Balfour in *Kidnapped* had found the sea 'running deep into the mountains and winding about their roots', an intercut geography 'as serrated as a comb'. Even on the map, land and sea there is as interlaced as the fingers of two hands.

We stayed the night about ten miles away in a small guest house on the shores of Loch Sunart. A polite atmosphere: cloths on the tables, charming, smiling service at dinner by the man who owned the hotel, a retired biologist, who dipped the end of his tie in the parsnip soup as he set it down in front of us. No one in the dining room said a word. The butter came on silver scallops, the oatcakes were in their own airtight tin and we whispered our secrecies over the venison and the crumble.

Next morning up early through the Atlantic oakwoods radiating their springtime green. Late May is the moment of perfection when the West Highlands start to acquire that burnish and glow which coats them for a few weeks at the beginning of summer. Cuckoos in the alders. Blackcaps in every other tree. Pied wagtails down on the wet rocks. The hollow notes of other, more distant cuckoos sounding as if they were calling through cupped hands. Everywhere the shadowed hyacinth blue of the bluebells and their scent.

Up out of the woods and on to the top of the hills. The whole riven province of Morvern, a mountainous fin of Scotland 80,000 acres wide and almost entirely surrounded by sea lochs, was laid out below us. We skirted the shoulders of the mountains and dropped to the pastures of a salmon river, past the freshwater loch at its head where the water slid out over the sandy beach, braided like silk, looking like whisky, and then along a heron-haunted shore to the sea.

Three miles to go. At last, we rounded a corner, past an eighteenth-century steading now used to shear and dag the sheep, and as the track turned, the bay appeared below, wide and tall, a world in itself, a half-circle of dark cliffs and wood-thickened slopes, the rim of those cliffs about 700 feet above the sea, water-falls dropping over them at intervals and through the woods to

The bay, looking south-east towards Lismore and the hills above Oban.

the rocky shore. A track hairpinned steeply down under the old lime trees.

It felt, as all good places feel, hidden from the world, enormous and strangely private. The bay looked out to the south, to the hills in Mull. To the south-east, seven miles away, the single white finger of the lighthouse on Lismore. Behind it, the hills above Oban.

This was the geometry: away from the wind, a cliff-backed semicircle of a bay, about a mile across and reaching half a mile in from the waters of the Sound, with strongly marked headlands at each side, the one to the west made of basalt, that to the east of limestone.

The head of the bay is lined with a dark beach, black basalt sand, the ground-down lavas from a volcano in Mull, lightened only with a scatter of broken cockles, an occasional bit of seaglass, the bottom of a bottle, some old limpets and mussels. Across it a small burn emerges from the flag irises of a bog and makes its way in zigzags that change with every tide and storm.

Even now, on each arrival, I go down to the beach. On the ebb, mounds of seaweed, most of it serrated wrack, lie about on the muddy-sandy surface. They look like piles of day-old salad. The sea extends away down the Sound in a perfect mirror. The abandoned shells lie on the drying sand. One half of a razor clam is out in the air, its gloss gone. There are some worm casts and a barnacle-encrusted rock, a bruised and battered lump of the ancient rocks brought here by the glaciers from further east.

I wade out into the shallows where, a foot deep and an hour before low water, the last of the tide is running between my calves. Little counter-whorls of current flicker in the surface just downstream of me. This is the world of flux and if I stand still in those shallows for a minute I am surrounded by the flitter and skitter of life. All kinds of resilient and defended creatures appear. Hermit crabs are suddenly busy on the sea floor in their winkles and whelks like porters with trolleys at a station. Everywhere I

Low tide and the serrated wrack on the beach at the head of the bay.

look, they are about their business. Some of those shells are encrusted with patches of the limy, self-hardening seaweed, the pink coralline. One has a sprig of wrack growing from its shell, an eighth of an inch tall. They scurry across the seabed, hurrying between the crumble-crusty, frilly-topped tubes of the sand-masons. There is a small greenish fish tooling around my feet, a common goby, less than half an inch long, its boxy body sprinkled with red spots, but with a bright green nose. I bring my hand down into the water beside and underneath it, a Gulliver presence in its Lilliputian world, and unlike any other fish I have ever known, it does not react but continues poking and looking, dark- and bubble-eyed, investigative at this intrusion, but not alarmed at the idea of an intrusion itself.

A flicker-spotted fish glides past, sweeping its fins back and forth as it goes, spreading them in half-made, embryonic fan-wings, and then landing in the mud at my feet, the fish itself slowly reappearing from the dispersing cloud and puff of sand its arrival cast up. I photograph it – half in the shadow of my phone, half in light.

A little juvenile dab, three inches from nose to tail, slides along the sea floor beside me, a ripple in every pore, moulding its body to the contours of the sand as if wedded to them, as close as possible to that miniature landscape, a creature as liquid as the sea itself, a film of life, but which, as it pauses, turns invisible, mottled like its surroundings, its greyness speckled with white, banking on a principle opposite to the hermit crab beside it: one almost stupidly visible but dressed in borrowed armour; the other soft, subtle and discreet, the diplomat of this half-world, unseen to the heron that stands now a hundred yards away from me, waiting intently and anxiously, ever-ready to bid.

In the ebbing tide, little fleets of grey, white and black shrimps suddenly appear – they are *Crangon crangon*, called brown shrimps but they are far from brown – hundreds of them, making their steady soldierly progress over the sea floor, spotted and marbled with the same mixture of white and brown dots as the sand, following the water as it goes, bounce-swimming, antennae alert, settling for a moment on their toe-tips beside me, tails spread behind them in painted fans, all of them heading out to sea away from the warming shallows. Nothing is coming the other way; only with the next tide will the inhabitants of the beach return.

I push a little further out towards the headland on the edge of the bay. The kelp fronds here come up above the water as if they were the fins of dead fish. Their outer tips are broken and beaten by storms. Beneath their dark canopy is a graveyard of ex-lives, of smashed and abandoned shells, a recycling centre for the whole intertidal. Primitive colonies of tiny animals – sea mats – make hieroglyphs and diagrams in lobed and scratched patterns on the sheeny leather of the fronds. In the air the sea mats are glamorous but inert. Push them underwater and within a moment they flicker into magical, frondy, animal life.

In the shade of these weeds, the most unlikely drawing-room colours erupt on a damp Scottish coastline. The coralline makes a vermilion mat where the limpets dig their nests. Venetian-striped top shells crawl between the dried-blood red of the beadlet anemones. Bright yellow and green sponges line the polychrome pools.

All this aquarium life becomes visible if you pull the overhanging weeds away but put your head in under the enormous, jungly, slimed canopy of the kelp and you find yourself in a different country: threatening, shadowed, dark and even haunted where pink fleshy starfish wear ghost-blue lines down each of their arms; where the purple-black dahlia heads of their tentacled mouths are all that can be seen of giant anemones half-buried in the bowls of sand. And where in these shadows, the king and dominator of this world, the green crab, blotched and mottled, with a whole night sky of spots and patches on his carapace, emerges as the terror-giant of a miniature, barnacled world.

There is a line from a Gaelic love song, written in Mull just across the water: '*Cha tàinig tràigh, gun muir-làn na dèidh*' ('A low tide never came that wasn't followed by a high tide'). Every ebb implies a flood, in a language where the word for ebb – *tràigh* – is the same as the word for beach. You will not find a beach without the promise of a rising tide. You may not love me now but love will come one day. An ebb tide is only a full tide in waiting. Trust your life to the turnings of the sea.

There is another side to it. The coming and going of the waters, their impermanence and unreliability, the sense in which the tide is a twice-daily catastrophe, has also played its part. In Applecross, on the west coast of the mainland of Scotland opposite Raasay, there is a bay called Ob'mhadaidh Ruaidh – the Bay of the Red Fox – from the story of a vixen that had been hunting on the shore who got her tongue deep into a large mussel, which closed on it, and held it while the tide rose and drowned her. Alexander Forbes, the early ethnographer who collected that story, also claimed that he had found a rat 'drowned with its paw under a large limpet and its body twisted up in a crevice whence it had been unable to free itself', while Alexander Stewart,

Victorian columnist in the *Inverness Courier*, found a 'dead kitti-wake, but perfectly plump and fresh, lying on the top of a mass of drift tangle … One of its feet was firmly held in the vice-like grasp of a large mussel, the mussel in its turn being anchored by its byssus to a tangle root (*Laminaria digitata*) of immense size.'

The rising tide is unforgiving. This fluxing and flexing is a landscape, a halfscape, that reverberates with the mutability of things. It plays in our shared memory, part of 'the challenge the ocean always poses', as the American cultural critic Steve Mentz has said, 'to know an ungraspable thing'.

Some of the most famous lines ever written, Ariel's song near the beginning of *The Tempest*, embrace that shoreline ambiguity of perfection and destruction, the beautiful and the strange, the 'menace and caress' of the sea. These early moments in the play are themselves full of uncertainty: Ferdinand, the young prince of Naples, thinks his father the king is drowned, but we know he is not; these kings and princes are now homeless vagabonds on a storm-blasted shore; Ariel himself, the soul of poetry, is disguised not as a creature of the wind but as a little sea god and, as that watery spirit, sings the most untruthful and enigmatic of songs:

> Full fadom fiue thy Father lies,
> Of his bones are Corrall made:
> Those are pearles that were his eies,
> Nothing of him that doth fade,
> But doth suffer a Sea-change
> Into something rich, & strange:
> Sea-Nimphs hourly ring his knell.
> *Burthen*: Ding dong.
> Harke now I heare them, ding-dong bell.

It is a hymn to the shore, afloat on 'sea-sorrow'; the king's body has become something like the floor of the sea. The colours of the shallow-deep waft over him. He is faded-rich. Encrusting jewels enshrine his head and his limbs transmute into submarine treasure. Everything that seems like threat and disaster is conjured here into masque-like glimmer. His corpse is a wonder of the wavering seas. And yet this is a song of death, an obsequy in which the elegance enshrines fatal loss, a drowning, a breaking of human connections, where the body is subject to the violence of the waves, and where sea nymphs ring the funeral bell. It is a place both of salt death and of scarcely imagined perfection. 'What care these roarers for the name of King?' the boatswain on their ship had cried as the winds had shrieked about them and now indeed the king has become treasure lying thirty feet down.

Sometimes, on a summer evening, when the tide is at full flood, and when, in the wonderful phrase Shakespeare used for this moment, it 'makes a still-stand', the whole of the bay outside the house goes quiet. Across the mile between its arms, a calm extends from headland to headland over what is, I reckon, about 300 acres of sea. If a fish moves anywhere in it, you can see that movement with your naked eye, the slightest stirring of its surface, a sleek molehill raised by the fish's tail and lit by the last of the sun. I have seen a sea trout on an evening like this, the best part of a mile away, reaching up out of the water, and thrashing back down on to it, in pure silence. Seconds later the sound of its arc and fall came over towards me. And magically, once, a basking shark cruised to and fro across the bay, twenty minutes to the east, twenty minutes back, lazy and easy, leaving behind it in that wide still sheet of water the triple wake made by nose, fin and tail, each dragging its own pink-lit pencil line across the calm.

I realised soon enough that I loved that stillness and that a rock pool would have it. I searched the bay but could not find one: only beaches and a wide rim of ragged stone in which there are no true hollows to hold the water. Then, I thought, perhaps I could create something like a stillness-cupping pool, a

Slack water high tide.

parenthesis cut out of the world of flux, an extension in time of what in the open sea is only a moment of calm. A pool, or even two or three: to make them at the beginning quite naked, exactly as the words say – a rock pool, a dish of rock on the shoreline, as if it were part of the earth before life had come to clothe it. And then, slowly, to allow the sea to bring life to that dish, to make it a living thing. It would be gardening the sea, providing not flower beds but life beds.

The foreshore in this bay is 'Presumed Crown Land'. Long debate filled much of the nineteenth and twentieth centuries over the ownership of 'that part of the land which is neither always wet, nor always dry due to the ebb and flow of the incoming and outgoing tide'. About half of the foreshore in Scotland was claimed by the neighbouring landowners, largely on the basis that their tenants, when gathering seaweed for fertiliser or to burn for its chemical residues, had paid the landowners rent for it. Scandalously, if rent was paid, ownership was implied. The relatively small amount of weed collected here meant that no rent was ever paid and so this bay went unclaimed. As Crown property, it is now administered by the Crown Estate Commissioners for Scotland.

Statutory public rights on the shore are thought to include (even if they are not yet enshrined in Scottish law):

swimming, sunbathing, playing games, going for a walk, having picnics, lighting fires and cooking food, gathering shellfish (except mussels and oysters, to which the Crown retains the rights), fishing (except salmon, ditto) and shooting wildfowl (as long as they are over the foreshore when shot), embarking, disembarking, loading and unloading a boat, drying nets, gathering bait and making sandcastles.

I wasn't sure if my pools would come under the heading of 'making sandcastles' and so I applied to the Crown Estate Scotland for permission. They paused to think but in the end, for a small fee, and with the agreement of Marine Scotland, the government's sea agency, I was allowed to make some pools on the edge of the bay at Rubha an t-Sasunnaich. A little wound-ingly, when I eventually sent some photographs of the work I had done, Tony Bennett, the Crown Estate Marine Officer for Argyll, said, 'I see no issue with them as they do not appear to be any different to anything built by local children during the holi-days.' All the same, the pools at Rubha an t-Sasunnaich are now marked on the general asset map of the Crown Estate Scotland website, with the CES reference number AR1-34-2.

He was right though. Making the pools, even if they each took days of work, was partly a way of playing with nature; partly to make good a lack, to create a still-stand of my own, a small piece of a sea world by which I and Sarah and the children could wait and watch; and partly so that I could learn what this nature was. The pools would be discreet. I would be careful to keep

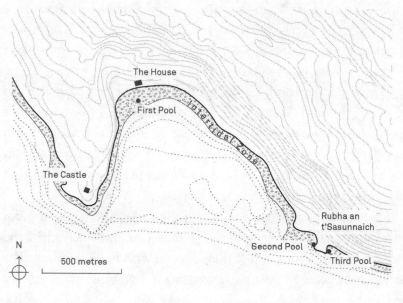

The bay and its pools. The Scottish Crown owns the speckled
land up to high-tide mark.

them almost hidden, or at least scarcely noticeable. By definition,
they would be invisible under the sea for much of the time. They
would be an invitation to life, an act, as I learned to call it, of
bio-receptivity, even bio-reciprocity, an enrichment of the habitat, not a subtraction from it.

The shore, as Seamus Heaney once wrote, is where 'things
overflow the brim of the usual', and that brim is at the heart of
this book. It is an Old English word that has slowly migrated
shorewards. Far back in its Germanic roots, the brim meant the
turbulence of a breaking sea, a place where the world roars, and
beyond that in the sea-less steppes of the Proto-Indo-Europeans
in Central Asia, to brim was to hum like a bee, to make the noise
of life. For the Anglo-Saxons it became the surf at the sea margin.
From there it moved on again to be the lip or edge of anything,
but one in which an *overflow* was always possible. A brim for us

now is an edge at which the limit is gently but slowly reached, a place for the overtopping of a tide or flood, where, as Emily Dickinson once dreamed, our 'Shoes / Would overflow with Pearl'.

There is something about a pool which – not to make too gross a pun on it – encourages the reflective, leads the mind not merely to transcribe the experience of the actual, to give it a topography, but allows the questions of why it means what it does, what its reality consists of, to what extent everything that confronts you is more than the local.

There are no boundaries here. The human, the planetary and the animal all interact, and all of them are inter-leaved in the realities of the shore. None makes sense without the others. The billions of acres of galactic time and the varying gravitational fields through which this planet swings count for as much as the daily actions of people and all the behaviours of the creatures in the intertidal. These categories blur: human life here, even human thought here, is identifiably animal; animals develop social and cognitive systems, means of attack and defence, hierarchy and cooperation, propagation and survival, that look strikingly like the ways human beings organise their lives and societies. Clans of prawns live in the pools; winkles can smell out their enemies; the pools are governed by the movement of the planets; philosophical understandings can be applied to the ecology of invertebrates; the life of the crabs is attuned to the tides.

This is not anthropomorphism – viewing the animal world according to terms more suitable to people – but its opposite: zoomorphism, recognising the continuities between animal and human consciousness, the continuousness of the spectrum that runs from bacterium and virus to scientist and poet. All can exist only within the overarching embrace of the world-as-it-is, each life driven by the need to be, each unaware of the significance of what it is that drives them. That unknowability is everywhere here and is part of what I mean to say: to know something, a person or an animal or a place, to become intimate with it, is not to know in any very conscious way but to dissolve the boundaries. To be with anything, life must overflow its brim.

'We stand, then, on the shore,' William Golding wrote in 1965, reviewing Gavin Maxwell's *Ring of Bright Water*,

> not as our Victorian fathers stood, lassoing phenomena with Latin names, listing, docketing and systematising … We pore [instead] over the natural language of nature, the limy wormcasts in a shell, 'strange hieroglyphics that even in their simplest form may appear urgently significant, the symbols of some forgotten alphabet …' We walk among the layers of disintegrating coral, along the straggling line of 'brown sea-wrack, dizzy with jumping sandhoppers'. We stand among the flotsam, the odd shoes and tins, hot-water bottles and skulls of sheep or deer. We know nothing. We look daily at the mystery of plain stuff. We stand where any upright food-gatherer has stood, on the edge of our own unconscious.

The first Greek philosophers experienced the world as what they called *physis*, a term that is famously difficult to translate but is somewhere close to the idea of 'growing'. Nature for them was something in the act of becoming, what Martin Heidegger, entranced by these early thinkers, called an 'upsurging presence', a 'process of arising', a 'self-blossoming emergence', a gift from nothing, the coming into being of being itself. That net of miraculous beginnings, in all dimensions, is what this book is about.

PART I
ANIMALS

1

Sandhopper

A bank of rolled and broken seaweed gathers at the head of the beach after storms where it lies for weeks in long dark bolsters. In the summer it can grow crusty on top, dried by sun and wind, with bits of driftwood and plastic caught in it, and the weed itself turning a mottled ochre, the colours of a fire that has burned down. But even then when you lift away its upper layers, something else appears, the semi-liquid slutch of rubbish and rot, every surface slimed, not the bright firm beauty of the sea itself but a world thick with decay, the microbial tide surging through the tissues of the weed.

Put your fingers in amongst its slipperiness and you can feel the nutrients being released back into circulation, no longer shut into their organisms but ready for another turn. It is the gift from the sea, delivered not by the beneficence of summer but by winter storms that have torn the wrack from the seabed and brought it ashore.

I begin now to poke into the mounds of weed. It is March, a cold dampish day with spits of rain hanging in the wind. The air between here and Rubha an t-Sasunnaich has thickened into a mist. The waterfalls are running but I cannot hear them for the gale. The grass is dead and brown and there is scarcely a sign of spring. It is the end of winter, everything reduced and bitten down, shut like a filing-cabinet drawer. The whole place feels bleached.

The tides have been up over the grass. All kinds of things are mixed in with the wrack: limpet shells, emptied of their inhabitants, upside down cupping the rain. There is most of a tree in here, an ash, its bark chewed by the deer, whose teeth have scraped furrows into the wood beneath. A huge grey buoy, torn away from a fish farm, is half-buried in the wrack. The carapace of a green shore crab has the double puncture of an otter's canines crunched into the lid as if through a water biscuit. There is a hazelnut here, still whole, but when I bite into its shell, the taste is of salt and rot. The sea has got in and the nut is pulp.

The oystercatchers and sandpipers are spending their day picking through the weed like shoppers in a market turning over the clothes for a bargain. There are opportunities to be had. Come closer – it is the governing instruction of life on the bay – and the rotting weed shows it is more full of life per square inch than anywhere on this late winter shore. Sink your hands into the slime and slither-gloop of the disintegrating mass and feel your way towards the creatures that make this place their home. There is a mass of them – millipedes and wrack-fleas – but what literally jumps out are the jumpers, the sandhoppers, the tiny crustaceans no bigger than the paring of a thumbnail that love the rotting weed.

I have seen them a thousand times before and never considered their existence, never named them, never caught one, never looked at one, never thought what they might be beyond something like the energy of rot, bursting up out of the sludge of disintegration. Now, though, the invitation takes me in.

There are two kinds of sandhopper on Scottish beaches. One is pale brownish called *Talitrus saltator*, the 'leaping knuckle jumper' – *talus* is Latin for a knuckle, *talitrus* for a finger-flick – which spends the day buried in the sand and emerges at night to feed on patches of wrack. The other, with which I am more familiar, is pinkish and called *Orchestia gammarellus*, the 'little shrimp-like dancer', named after the troupes in ancient Greece

20

who performed on the dance floor, the *orchēstra*, where the tragedies would also be played. *Orchestia* lives all the time in the wrack.

Both *Talitrus* and *Orchestia* are amphipods – the name means that they have several different kinds of feet – and every time you open up their world-in-dissolution, they go through the same wonderful three-part routine: leap; wriggle; play dead. Put the weed lid back on, lift it again and they do it again: leap, wriggle, play dead, finally curling up into self-protective balls in the shadows of the wrack.

Eighteenth-century naturalists had looked at them, often thinking they were a version of woodlice, but the first person to examine them carefully was one of the heroes of the shore, Colonel George Montagu (1753–1815), scholar-soldier, veteran of the American War of Independence, founding fellow of the Linnean Society, pioneering ornithologist, conchologist and mammalogist before any of those terms had been invented. He ran off with a niece of Lord Bute when he was twenty, but became bored by her grandeur and, after beginning as a pursuer of game, increasingly turned to the study of nature. In 1798, with his mistress, the Danish beauty Eliza Dorville, he abandoned his life and wife to set up with Eliza near Kingsbridge in Devon. Society was outraged. Montagu was disinherited by his family, court-martialled for creating a bad example and so turned with exquisite patience and assiduity to the creatures of the natural world. It was a model for shore-life: ignore society; attend to this.

Montagu spent his days poking about in the waters of Salcombe Harbour, naming species after species for the first time (including a hundred new molluscs), acquiring a Montagu's blenny, Montagu's harrier, Montagu's ray, Montagu's sucker (a kind of fish) and Montagu's sea snail. Eliza provided him with a stream of children – the two never married – and made the calm and refined drawings that illustrate his books of birds and shells.

Under these happy and freethinking hands, the sandhopper entered the annals of science. Having watched 'the multitudes which are seen skipping about in all directions upon our sandy beaches in a summer evening', Montagu looked patiently and admiringly at the little creatures. He was one of the first British naturalists to examine both preserved specimens and the living animal, and to make regular use of a microscope. Through his eyepiece Montagu saw that the sandhopper was 'oblong, sub-compressed, smooth, and extremely glossy. [Its] colour when alive corneous; when dried it becomes paler, and by exposure to the sun gains a tinge of pink; and the antennae partake of orange yellow. It is frequently found on the seashores bleached white.' They lived in vast abundance 'burrowing under the various rejectamenta of the sea, devouring both animal and vegetable matter with great avidity'.

If you can catch one of these mistresses of the rejectamenta and hold it by its legs, it does not, to be honest, look like an efficient design. A woodlouse and other isopods (which have, by contrast with the amphipods, only one kind of leg the length of their body) are compressed vertically, so that their bodies are low, wide and stable. These amphipods are

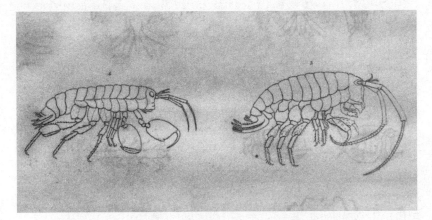

Orchestia gammarellus (left) and *Talitrus saltator* (right)
drawn by Eliza Dorville, 1808.

compressed laterally, so that they are tall for their width, with the same proportions as the trolleys that cabin crew push up and down the aisles of aeroplanes. You might think if you set an *Orchestia* on its feet, the high centre of gravity would mean it falls over. In fact it doesn't, and stabilises itself by spreading its legs wide, like the legs of a camera tripod. Why the lateral compression?

When either the *Orchestia* or the *Talitrus* is disturbed, all the animals that have been exposed start to jump at random, scattering as chaotically as the bubbles above a newly poured glass of champagne. Prey animals of all kinds do this, zigzagging, spinning, looping or bouncing away from the predator in what biologists have called 'protean flight', a storm of signals to confuse the killer, encouraging it to follow one then another and so allowing all the potential victims to escape. Mice, spiders, squid, fish and broods of young songbirds often 'explode' like this when an intruder threatens. If a single goal is sought, the offering of multiple options encourages indecision. Sandhoppers' genes have learned to overwhelm the processing capabilities of their predators.

23

The Soviet marine scientist A. I. Bulycheva very carefully watched an *Orchestia* hopping. She thought that it balances on a pair of legs in the middle of its body, draws its whole self tightly together so that its tail and enormously powerful back legs – they look under the microscope like the hams of a linebacker – are pressing into the sand, and then suddenly flexes its thorax so that it flings itself into the air, with no control over the direction it takes. The movement is astonishingly quick and effective. If you sit and watch them in flight, the impression is that each small animal is in one place at one moment and another a second later, with no catchable transition between the two, animal-quarks living in a strange quantum-crustacean universe. Those back legs act as shock absorbers when it lands (or so Dr Bulycheva says, even though they seem usually to land on their sides to me). Meanwhile Dr G. Bracht from the University of Münster has filmed the whole performance (at 1,000 frames a second) and found that an *Orchestia's* escape-jump lasts on average between a third and half a second, can cover a distance of eighteen centimetres and achieves an average acceleration on take-off of 300 metres per second per second. Within that time frame, *Orchestia* usually makes between four and six somersaults.

Be amazed. It is the fizz of life itself, the sand-jumpers and weed-dancers springing into spectacular rocket-fuelled survival. As they jump, the huge, supervising presence of the oystercatcher or sandpiper is confused. The final landing is a moment of vulnerability, when the predator can reorientate and find its prey, but the amphipod does not stand to be available once again to the hungry bird. It begins to wriggle on its side, like a rugby player caught in a tackle, all nine pairs of legs hard at work pushing the animal forwards and sideways down in between the crevices of the rotting weed. No woodlouse or leg-based isopod could do such a thing, or at least so easily. The amphipod slithers towards safety, entirely capable on its side, and with its relatively soft and shiny cuticle, far more pliable than the shells of the marine crustaceans, the shrimps and prawns, from which it is descended. The calcium carbonate that stiffens and hardens the shells of those sea creatures is not present in the exoskeleton of these weed-dwellers. They choose escape over armour. A lighter shell makes them sprightlier for jumping and also makes them supple, so that they can slip and wriggle away into the protection of the gaps between the rotting weeds. Hence the lateral compression.

Once there, they fake death, curled up into a seed-like ball whose sheer immobility is its camouflage. If you did not know they were there, you would not find them in the shadows and crevices of the weed. But poke about among these living dead and they will, quite literally, spring to life again, running through the gamut of their evasions.

Most of the nearly 10,000 amphipod species live in the sea, and these beach-dwellers are the descendants of marine ancestors that have come to an enriched but more difficult world, one in which flux both provides the basis for life and is its enemy. Bundled-up wrack is delicious for them but the temperature rises and sinks to greater extremes on land than in water, even inside the mounds of weed, and so desiccation, by definition impossible in water, becomes a constant threat. It is something life itself, the body itself, must defend against. That is one purpose of the semi-pliable, near-crunchy shell of these amphipods; if an *Orchestia* loses more than 25% of its body-water, it will die.

They do their best to avoid such a fate. *Orchestia* has a system of pores in its protective shell. A layer of wax is secreted through them, waterproofing the shell, making it like the waxed cardboard in which the fruit and vegetables of organic box schemes are delivered. The wax will keep the *Orchestias* damp inside. It has a melting point of about 37°C, which means the sandhoppers cannot go wandering about with any safety in full summer sunshine. If they did, their protective coat would melt and they would die of dehydration.

Large-scale catastrophe can strike. One very warm May, when sunshine hung over the West Highlands of Scotland for two full weeks, the weed on the beach dried to the consistency of dark, wrinkled, uncooked pasta, not only in the upper layers but deep down into the bulk of it. I went looking for the *Orchestias* and lifting the weed away in stiff plaques found crowds and crowds of them lying there on the gravelly sand, dead and pink as if they were a plateful of cooked shrimps, the victims of drought and unseasonable early summer warmth.

Normally, though, the wet weed is both hiding place and restaurant. If you remove the top layer of weed, but shade the *Orchestias* as deeply as you can, they feel they might still be in something like the dark and they begin again to lead the normal hidden life of the cryptozoic. They feed, nibbling on the weeds, and from time to time they also start to look after themselves, their little hands and feet feeling over the surface of their own shell-coat for any grains or fragments that might be abrading it, breaking the glossy seal that Colonel Montagu noticed and so putting them in danger of drying out. *Orchestia* must groom to stay alive, in particular picking anything out of the joints in their legs where a speck of dust or sand could damage the connecting membranes and allow the precious wetness of what biologists call 'the internal milieu' to escape.

To sit and watch them about their business, their multiple limbs flickering and pausing over their own bodies, keeping house, keeping themselves proper, ensuring their own continuity, is a challenge to any pre-existing idea of animal consciousness. They must know and feel where there is a speck of grit to be removed. They must know how to use the multiple tools of their various limbs in a way as effective and as complex as a multi-bladed penknife. They must be making decisions. They must have minds at work.

Most of this was known in the nineteenth century but from the early 1950s onwards some astonishing discoveries started to be made about these tiny crustaceans, largely in the hands of the Tuscan zoologist Leo Pardi. He was born in 1915 in a small town near Pisa and in 1937 graduated from the university there. From the start Pardi emerged as 'the most acute observer of movements and expressions, both in animals and men'. With unforced lucidity and soon becoming a brilliant teacher and talker, Pardi transformed the study of animal intelligence.

All through the war and up until 1953, at the Zoological Institute of Pisa University, he examined the habits of the paper wasps, in particular the ferocious struggles between a new colony's would-be queens, who bit and clasped and clashed their antennae until one emerged triumphant (called marvellously the *Nestmutter*, the 'nest mother', by Karl von Frisch, the great Austrian biologist and bee expert who had guided Pardi towards this study) while the others either left or retreated into a subsidiary status, called by Frisch the *Hilfsweibchen*, the 'little help wenches', which were organised in ranks below the *Nestmutter*. Wasps it seemed had as much of a status hierarchy in their colony as hens or wolves. What Leo Pardi discovered, through hundreds of dissections, was an extraordinary interaction of that social status with the body form of the wasps. Somehow, the alpha wasp, perhaps by some kind of hormonal signal, was able to inhibit the development of ovaries in her rivals. She became fertile and her hormonal winds blowing over the colony ensured that her rivals remained barren. Pardi found that if a beta wasp was removed from the presence of the *Nestmutter*, the beta's ovaries were able to develop quite normally and she could think of becoming a *Nestmutter* herself, hormonally depriving in her turn the gamma, delta and epsilon wasps of their chance to procreate, at least until they too were removed to their own colonies.

A mental and social life usually associated only with hens, wolves and people had been found in the insects. Pardi published his discoveries in several international journals, encouraged by the great Dutch animal ethologist Niko Tinbergen and others, but in March 1950, his ideas were brutally attacked at a seminar in Paris by a French entomologist and Pardi, hurt and exhausted, withdrew from wasps to something he could make his own: intertidal creatures, in particular the sandhoppers which he found on the beaches of the Tyrrhenian Sea to the west of Pisa. In a pattern that repeats again and again in these stories, the edge of the sea was playing its part as a psychic refuge.

Both *Orchestia* and *Talitrus saltator* usually live above the high-tide mark, hidden either in the sand or in patches of wrack, which is damp and where predatory birds have trouble finding them. At night, they leave their hiding places. *Orchestia* tends to stay up at the top of the beach but *Talitrus* goes on major expeditions, coming down towards the strand line and browsing there on whatever they can get in the rotting weed. As the tide floods again, they make their way back up the beach to safety.

From left to right: the Austrian biologist Karl von Frisch, Leo Pardi's
pupil Floriano Papi and Pardi himself observing orientation behaviours
in sandhoppers on the beach at Gombo, Tuscany, 1952.

How do they do this? It is the question any of us might ask
but Pardi's asking it began a slow unravelling of the extraordinary
capacities of these creatures. He and his co-workers found, first,
that *Talitrus* responded to damp: if they were wetted with seawater they would head inland; if they were threatened with dehydration, and were hot and thirsty, they headed for the sea. The
direction of travel was reliably at or near ninety degrees to the
axis of the beach, as nearly as possible either towards or away
from the water.

How did they know to go in those directions? Pardi's first
discovery was that the sandhoppers on the Tuscan beaches had
an internal sun-compass by which they could work out where to
go. The compass was combined with a clock so that at any time
of day *Talitrus* could adjust its orientation and make either for
the sea or the top of the beach. Pardi captured some of the

sandhoppers from a west-facing beach, took them back to his lab in Pisa and put them in a small 'arena' twenty centimetres in radius with pitfall traps all around the circumference. The floor of the arena was kept dry, Pardi allowed the sun to shine on it and the sandhoppers still headed off westwards in the direction of what would have been the sea if they had been back in their Tyrrhenian home. If the apparent position of the sun was altered by using mirrors, the sandhoppers adjusted their escape paths to account for it. He then took some of them out to sea on a boat: they still headed west, or what they thought was seawards. Another group were carried over to the east coast of Italy, on the Adriatic. Still the sandhoppers in their enclosed arena headed west, in the direction of the sea they had known all their lives.

What about at night when most *Talitrus* journeys were made? Astonishingly, it turned out that *Talitrus* could use the moon for the same purposes, and that it had two clocks running independently of each other, one remaining aware of the timetable by which the sun came and went, the other the moon. If *Talitrus* was kept in constant dark for many days, both clocks continued to run without interruption and it would resume its sun- and moon-guided walks as soon as allowed.

As Pardi and his students continued to observe and experiment on *Talitrus*, its celestial vision of sun and moon and the day- and night-attuned life-rhythms became increasingly clear. Further experiments were made when sun or moon were hidden by clouds. Pardi found that even then *Talitrus* could read the landscape and orientate itself accordingly, particularly if there were large buildings or cliffs above the beach to distinguish landward from seaward views. It could also tell the difference in colour between the long blueish wavelengths of light coming from out at sea and the redder and browner colours from the land. On top of that sensitivity, experiments revealed that they could read the difference between an up-slope and a down-slope. Thirsty sandhoppers tested in the dark would always head for the lower (i.e seaward) end of a tilted box, at least when the sand beneath them was dry. If it was wet, they would head to the upper end.

In 1962, Pardi moved to the University of Florence, to become director of the Zoological Institute there. He and his co-workers collected sandhoppers from beaches on both the western, Tyrrhenian coast and the Adriatic and bred from them in the Florence laboratory, keeping westerners and easterners quite separate. All four sets of *Talitrus*, expert adults and inexperienced Florence-born offspring from both west and east, were set to work in the laboratory arenas, making sure each time they were in full sun.

Not surprisingly, the adult sandhoppers from the Adriatic, placed on the dry bed of the arena sand, headed east; and those from the Tyrrhenian, west. Amazingly, though, their progeny, which had never experienced anything except life in the Florence laboratory, followed the same directions as their parents, if not quite with the same degree of accuracy. Pardi and his team had discovered that orientation in the *Talitrus* was not something learned in life but embedded in their genes, heritable from one generation to the next.

At Porto Ercole, the summer resort for chic Roman families, two beaches reaching out to the peninsula of Monte Argentario face in nearly opposite directions: Giannella just north of west and Feniglia just east of south. The Pardi team collected sand-hoppers from both beaches and back in the Florence laboratory bred them together. If sea-orientation, guided by the sun- and moon-compasses, was heritable, in which direction would the offspring of these contradictory impulses choose to go? The answer was clear if extraordinary. Whether the mothers came from north-west-facing Giannella or south-east-Feniglia, the result was the same: the progeny chose on average to go almost precisely south-west, within a few degrees of halfway between the two parental directions.

Deep down at the genetic level, *Talitrus* had inherited its compass, but the organism was no automaton. After a while on an east-facing beach, a *Talitrus* with western-orientated genes can learn that it is not in its homeland and change its way of life. As the form of the beach shifts under tide, storm and wind, they can change their routes to and from the water. If they are kept in captivity for many weeks and then returned to the beach they once knew, most of them have forgotten what it was like and make wrong or uninformed decisions about the direction they should take. And when exposed to the realities of a beach for a few days, they can begin to learn what it is like and make much better-guided decisions about where to go when the tide is up or night has come or dawn is breaking and they need to return to the safety of their burrows in the sand.

Pardi and his colleagues in Florence and Pisa changed the way I see these hidden creatures. Each time I walk the beach and kick open, if only by chance, a pile of gathered wrack, I see them jumping at me as an example and epitome of everything this book is about, a fragmentary illumination of the layers of understanding, skill and volition in the most unconsidered corners of life. These half-soft, semi-elastic, glossy-shelled bodies shelter a decision-making, life-perpetuating, ingenious set of selves that has evolved over the aeons.

'What reason may not goe to schoole to the wisdom of Bees, Ants, and Spiders?' Thomas Browne asked in *Religio Medici*. If he had been in Pardi's laboratory, he would surely have added *Talitrus saltator* and *Orchestia gammarellus*.

Ruder heads stand amazed at those prodigious pieces of
nature, Whales, Elephants, Dromidaries, and Camels; these I
confesse, are the Colossus and Majestick pieces of her hand;
but in these narrow Engines there is more curious
Mathematicks, and the civility of these little Citizens, more
neatly set forth the wisedome of their Maker.

There is one further alarming aspect to their life. The sand-hoppers' habit of chewing on what they find stranded on the beach means they are the great disassemblers of anything that is there – including human rubbish. Scientists at the University of Plymouth have found that if a normal plastic shopping bag is exposed to sandhopper shredding, it will be turned into about 1.75 million pieces of microplastic, the tiny toxic fragments that easily spread across the sea and which poison and pollute all forms of life from plankton to whales. That is one reason to pick up the mess: it is not beach- but sea-cleaning.

2

Prawn

It is the spring equinox, early in the morning; the tide has yet to pull down and I am here to dig a rock pool. I am dressed for it: a thick hat, three padded shirts, thermal underlayers, neoprene waders, heavy-duty gloves and a pair of roofer's knee pads. The air temperature is just above freezing but the wind makes it colder. I have a chisel and a set of bolsters, a steel bucket, a geological hammer with a pick on one end, some steel bars and

Digging the first pool.

club hammers – 'suitable for wrecking, dismantling and prying' the sales blurb had said – a mallet, a spade, a full-size pickaxe and a long simple steel spike with which to lever away the rocks in which the pool will rest.

For three wet cold days, leaving when the tide rose, returning when it fell, with my chisels and wrecking bars I dug down into the early Jurassic rocks, seeing things that had not been seen for 200 million years, becoming as familiar with them as with the soil in my own garden. It was hard, slow and dirty, as sloppy as a Flanders trench, the process as graceless as the churning of a concrete mixer, until, finally, I was done. After one tide had washed it clean, the new pool looked serious but lovely, grey and stony but a place of calm, framed by its basalt lumps and Jurassic sandstones, a bright window away from the world of flux.

All I had to do was to wait, impatiently, for something to happen. I read. I tidied the house. I filled a small aquarium with seawater for the moment I might find some creatures to put in it. I split some logs and did the laundry. Nothing happened. One

The first pool filled with its first tide.

tide brought in a piece of bladderwrack, but it was loose, a bit of flotsam, not integral to the life of the pool. The next tide floated it away again.

The frenzy that had gripped me over the three preceding days, that muddy exhaustion, felt like an irrelevance, out of synch with the way things are. This nothing-doing was more like the nature of reality: steady, unbroken, the long-form music of the patient world. The cosmic and planetary rhythms were playing the music of the spheres, but their pattern is too long for any single life to recognise them. What do they translate into? Only the *longue durée*, the unbroken lastingness of repetitive being.

The high and low tides moved on in their fifty-minute progress through the days. The moon shrank and grew. The curlews cried their love-weep morning and evening. I read the life of Virginia Woolf by Hermione Lee in which she quoted Woolf's diary from 8 September 1918: 'I remember lying on the side of a hollow, waiting for L[eonard] to come & mushroom, & seeing a red hare loping up the side & thinking suddenly, "This is Earth life". I seemed to see how earthy it all was, & I myself an evolved kind of hare; as if a moon-visitor saw me.'

That is what this first pool was giving me, this long gaze at being.

I sat on the bench in front of the house reading Professor Lee's book: the surface of the bay looked like slit silk – dark but with slips and eyelets of brightness all the way across it where the light was catching the incoming seas and – thanks to Woolf and her biographer – life seemed for a moment then to be what Woolf took it for: a pattern of eddies and back-turnings, an endlessly shifting density-field in which identities and truths come and go.

Woolf was entranced by liquidity, which could embody realities that solids could scarcely address. Water as a source of ecstasy, 'sheeting the body like an eel', 'pouring down the wall of the mind'.

Virginia Woolf.

In her hands fluidity attaches to more than ordinary liquids. Existence itself can dissolve and soften so that 'It seems as if the whole world were flowing and curving – on the earth the trees, in the sky the clouds.' The source of this entrancement lay deep in Woolf's memory, of the room in Talland House in St Ives in Cornwall where her family went on holidays when she was a girl, of which the memory, as she wrote, stood at the foot of her life as the base of a bowl stands beneath it, holding out its open cup. The memory

is of lying half asleep, half awake, in bed in the nursery at St Ives. It is of hearing the waves breaking, one two, one two, and sending a splash of water over the beach; and then breaking, one, two, one, two, behind a yellow blind. It is of hearing the blind draw its little acorn across the floor as the wind blew the blind out. It is of lying and hearing this splash

and seeing this light, and feeling, it is almost impossible that
I should be here; of feeling the purest ecstasy I can conceive.

Then again from a draft of *Jacob's Room* written in 1920:

The blind was thin yellow; curved out, for the nursery
window was open. It curved fuller, & then was sucked in. At
the same time the sea made that dull noise; then the water
was drawn back; then it made the dull noise again. Now the
blind was filled with more yellow; and the dull noise
sounded further away … The little trailing noise that the
knob on the blind cord made as it was drawn across the floor
made him open his eyes.

Life is tidal, full of loss and arrival, a thing that makes and ebbs,
of that wooden button dragging on the floor to and fro, full of
things half-present and half-forgotten, in which the truth
of experience goes beyond the material or biographical fact, a
set of dissolving realisations that come more easily on a shore
than in the other places, perhaps because of the constant under-
music of the waves and the coming and going of the tide.

An evening came when the moon was full and the tide was
down. The mud-sand of the bay was skinned in moonlight,
which the surface of the pool concentrated in its own bright
mirror. I went down with a torch and knelt beside it. There in
front of me was all I needed: five common prawns, pool life,
glimmer-still, with points of white electric light, pure and
pin-like, scattered over them. Sparkled lines of those chromato-
phores were dotted along their legs and bodies, marking the
plates of their armour, in their fore-claws and up the long wavering radio-masts of their antennae. Here were some cohabitants,
life where there had been none, companions in the desert of the
rocks. This was the first time things had lived on these rocks and
sands in 200 million years. Common prawns – they were

Palaemon elegans, named after one of Jason's argonauts by the German zoologist Martin Heinrich Rathke in 1837 – may indeed be the commonest of creatures and every child catches them at the seaside but it felt like a sort of de-extinction. I had made a place where life was welcome.

I knelt and watched them: minuscule adventurers, at home in this world, with pitch-perfect neutral buoyancy, floating in their stillness neither up nor down. With the slightest movement of their swimmerets, the paddle feet below the centre of the body, they send themselves from headland to headland across the micro-ocean I have made. Each scoots past the others as if they were aerial taxis, something like the fleet in *Blade Runner*, inhabitants of a liquid universe just deeper than their bodies.

They are very nearly transparent, glass-beings, and can look like the specks that float in the surface of your eyes, semi-seen presences, with no more than a hint of inner organs glimpsed beyond the grisaille of their armour. They drift towards the invisible. If the sun is shining, they are spotted most easily not directly

The Common or Glass prawn.

but through the shadows they cast on the floor of the pool, like the images of aeroplanes projected far below, sliding seamlessly over rock and leaf and sand.

It is the exoskeleton that defines them. They are toy-like because that is usually how our toys are built: hard on the outside, even metallic, with the workings protected. But these are toys that Fabergé would have made: enamel brooches that scud beneath me; the dark eyes on each side of the head on stubby little stalks, independently, constantly and even feverishly alert and looking; the little forelimbs, the maxillipeds, endlessly gathering microscopic detritus from the rocks and pushing it into mouths on the underside of the head. The swimmerets paddling, while the long walking-limbs in front straddle across the pool floor, bracing the body, less architectural than engineered, struts for life. One of those limbs now and then reaches up and over the back of the carapace, cleaning and sifting there like a man scratching the baldness on his head.

The prawns are just longer than the top joint of my thumb but as intricate as a space station, a machine for processing life, a micro-engineer's fantasy of applied brilliance, as indifferent to sleekness as the most inner part of an engine or computer, all purpose, no appearance, articulated, tooled up, strange.

The complexity is bewitching. I feel assailed by the absolute singularity of things. 'Hardly a natural historian,' Stephen Jay Gould once wrote, 'has failed to locate his chief delight in the lovely puzzles … of actual organisms in real places.' These, for this morning, are my lovely puzzles, and I want to unravel them. And so, first, I see that they are like me. For all their strangeness, I can see my body in their symmetry: a trunk with its appendages, its orifices, its sensory mechanisms, its means of movement, of finding and consuming food, of perceiving and understanding the world, all arranged around the same one central axis.

We are balanced like each other but if lateral symmetry is in both of us, there is also a longitudinal asymmetry in both of us:

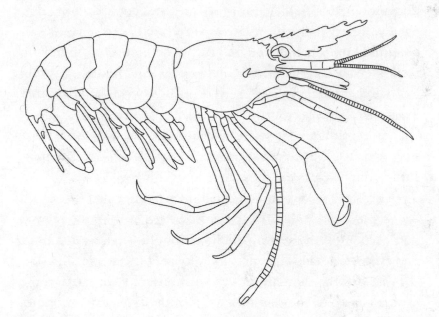

our fronts differ from our backs. Like me, the prawn is arranged in a hierarchy of engagement, with sensing first. I have forward-reaching eyes and ears and nose; he has those whisker antennae, the finest of fly-casting rods, amazingly equipped with smelling and tasting and desiring organs at their tips, which put the prawn's self far out in front of its body, so that the animal does not wander into closeness with another but will always approach carefully, sensitively and perhaps anxiously.

Behind that delicacy of arrival come the limbs with different functions – manducatory, for chewing, ambulatory, for walking, natatory, for swimming, and finally, within the hinged plates of its glamour-armour, the thrusting escape mechanism, the big muscle which in crisis the prawn like many other crustaceans can rapidly contract to give itself a fast backward and/or upward thrust, using the big flattened fins on the tail, accelerating away from threat.

There, it is true, we differ. It is difficult for a human being to leave a room in quite such a hurry as a prawn but in both of us this combination in the body of lateral symmetry and longitudinal asymmetry is the formative architecture of our selves, vertebrate and invertebrate as we are, with something like 700 million years of evolutionary difference between us. Our bodies construct our worlds. The prawn and I live in the different universes that our physical beings create for us, but what we share is this: knowing there is a difference between us and not-us. We are not what surrounds us. We are not the world in which we live. The presence of our selves is the most enormous thing we know.

The irony of the prawn's life is that the very thing that is designed for its safety – the giant escape muscle, triggered by the prawn's startle reflex – is the reason 7 million tons of them are eaten by us every year. That tail is the meat in every prawn sandwich.

I think of the thousands of these animals I have eaten: those meaningless bits of sweet meat, the stupidity of my encounter with them, a mild maritime delicacy, salted and peppered. How blunt I am compared with what they are. This drift and skitter in front of me now, the courage of their lives, that quiver-touch sensitivity of the little being, with all its purposefulness and manoeuvrability and fineness, set against my motorway lunch, the mayonnaise-slather between the butter and the bread, the Brobdingnagian me-ness of me dumped over the precision beside which I am now kneeling.

Not that I am unique. The English language flicks carelessly between the names it gives to shrimp and prawn without attention to anything they actually are. Gaelic is worse; these animals can be identified either as *carran* or *carran-creige*, meaning 'sea eel, conger eel, shrimp, prawn or stickleback'; or *cloidheag, cloimheag* or *cloitheag*, meaning any 'small fish found under seaweed; the prawn, shrimp, small lamprey'. The language tells you what you had already guessed: we scarcely care to know about the reality of these intricate lives.

Prawns live in a world of threat of which we are a part. As I watch, a shore crab, a lovely Bentley green, mottled with black

42

spots on its back, darkening towards the eyes, cratered with those spots like a map of its own planet, suddenly manoeuvres on the floor of the pool, a single multi-leg step out from the shadows and then tucking itself back in under the lean-to roof of some basalt. In the scale-shift of being with the prawns, the crab looks large and threatening. The prawns' cool, liquid swimming turns suddenly to a frenzied jackknifing, each of them tail-flipping back and away from the crab, the power-flex thrusting them into clear water. One prawn flings itself by mistake into a dark place, from which it thrashes back out again – perhaps another crab in there – making for the shadows under a flake of limestone, a refuge into which it shoots its body, disappearing like Mephistopheles in a burst of fear.

Is it too much to think that the prawns have *panicked* at the appearance of the crab? Melanie Challenger, the English philosopher of animal life, has compared her own panic attacks to these startle-responses in other creatures. She was on a walk one winter's day:

> I felt happy enough. But, in less than a moment, a shade cut across. My heart began to beat like crazy and my palms began to sweat. It was as if the uncontrollable elements of the outside world had passed into me and obliterated my sense of self.
>
> This kind of sudden terror is an animal shadow sweeping over the human form ... While the brain's language-centres work at any narrative that might assist, other regions of the body bang out norepinephrine and serotonin to prepare for an imaginary threat. Legs become twitchy and ready to run like hell.

These are the signals from what Challenger calls 'the mysterious and disconcerting regions of selfhood' where the terror, as she says, of being physical, of 'being trapped inside something that will die', overwhelms the steadier, metronomic patterns and habits of life.

The prawn's startle reflex is not far from that human experience of the spectre of death. Much of its life is predicated on fear. Its many tools are designed both to accommodate and to avoid it. The body is both armoured and half-visible, coated with the dazzle-markings that make its outline uncertain. Between its eyes its carapace stiffens into a yet-harder, serrated rostrum which is surprisingly stiff and acts like the nosepiece on a Greek or medieval helmet, defence against the hammer blow or sword cut. And the animal can run from trouble. How much nearer that is to us and to the commotion of human existence, with its tides of love and fear, and all the dysfunctional transmutations of that fear into paranoia, hypochondria, obsession and anxiety, than to the rocks and sands among which it lives. We and the prawns are cousins, however distant, in a way basalt or granite can never be.

These little creature-puzzles look delicate and in some ways they are. They are up here in the pool not far from the top of the beach because they like it here and choose it, tucked away from the turbulence of the sea. They are not as good at standing up to waves as their slightly more robust cousins *P. serratus*, which live in the deeper waters and as a result form a larger proportion of the commercial prawn catch. And so *P. elegans* and *P. serratus* divide the sea between them. It may be the stronger and bigger *serratus* outcompetes *elegans* in deeper waters. But how does the elegant one find the ideal niche for its existence?

It has recently been discovered that these inshore prawns smell their way towards the best places. When some rock-pool prawns from New Zealand (close relations of *elegans*) were put in experimental tanks and given a choice of swimming up a channel filled with water taken from pools in which there was no seaweed or a neighbouring channel flowing with water taken from weed-filled pools, they consistently chose the weedy water, reading the chemical signals given off by the wracks, telling the prawns that there was a place of greater safety.

Weed both hides them from predators and provides shade in which they can stay a little cooler than in the warm and salty water of a rock pool exposed to the sun between the tides. It may have been the odd piece of detached bladderwrack washed in by the tide that drew them in here the other night.

Nevertheless, life in a rock pool is tough. Temperatures can slew from freezing to 30°C or more. I have often at the end of a summer afternoon put my hand into a shallow pool late on a rising tide, just before the sea reaches it, and found the water as warm as in a tepid bath. For as long as the tide stays down, the pool water continues to evaporate, salinity climbs and its oxygen content falls. *P. serratus* does not do well in these conditions, soon dying, but *P. elegans* can cope with those daily tidal shifts, lasting up to four hours in water with no oxygen at all (a single hour does for *P. serratus*) and returning to normal much more quickly when the newly oxygenating tidewater comes in. Not that the experience is without stress. Lactic acid, felt by us as the burning in the muscles when running or rowing, also builds up in the prawn's muscles and blood when exposed to these low-oxygen waters. That can be imagined: the tide drops, the pool starts to warm up, the prawn begins to feel the stress of an environment in which it is increasingly difficult to breathe. The water around it becomes the equivalent of thin air. More water needs to be breathed through the gills than when it is cool and oxygenated. Life has turned hostile. And only then, at last, after as much as twelve hours of exposure for a pool high on the beach, is the twice-daily trial over and cool, newly aerated and life-giving water floods in from the sea.

When a group of prawns is introduced to a new pool, they fight. Females almost always win, because they are larger than males for the good reason that a big female can accommodate more fertilised eggs in her breeding pouch and more eggs increase the chance of survival. For males, no such argument applies and it is better for them, in pools and shallows patrolled by the predatory cod, pollack and blennies, to be as discreet as possible. If we look down into a pool, this size difference is clear enough: some big confident prawns paddle contentedly around their world. They are the dominant, breeding females, the queens of this terror court. They may be winning but because they are big, tasty and fat, they are eaten by their enemies more often than the males and so in any population there is always a higher proportion of males than females. In a well-developed pool you see it: beside the relatively rare and handsome queens, often tucked into the best hiding places, little male courtiers flit to and fro, shadows looking for shadows.

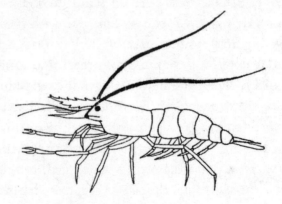

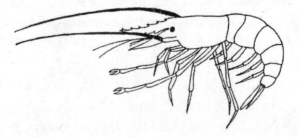

Above, when approaching a rival or enemy; below, when in sudden retreat, the escape muscle flexed.

For all this inherent antagonism and rivalry, the pool is not a place of anarchic violence. The very opposite: a certain orderly calm seems to prevail between them, disturbed only when some outside presence – my own shadow, the quick single gestures of a crab – disrupts the established order, producing the panic-struck jackknife thrashing of the escaping bodies.

Only when they first meet, can there be something of a face-off. Both prawns approach each other with their long whiskery antennae held aloft and out of the way, risking no damage to them. In front they project aggression with a pair of their walking legs protruding forwards like double spears, ready to encounter the enemy. This is a war-face. Actual fighting is rare; somehow the signals are read and the likely loser usually retreats in front of the likely winner, but even this virtual confrontation is relatively uncommon. They seem to know how to cohabit without hate or fear. Why this calm?

In 1999, a group of scientists at the University of Graz in Austria, led by the neuroscientist Robert Huber from Bowling Green State University in Ohio, conducted an experiment with some relatives of the prawns, the crayfish *Astacus astacus*. Huber and his colleagues wanted to measure what happened to the relationships between a set of potentially fierce and mutually destructive animals when first introduced to each other in a closed space, the aquarium equivalent of a pool.

The crayfish were between twelve and eighteen months old and for eight weeks were kept in perfectly comfortable mutual isolation, fed every second day with fish food and live mealworms. Small plastic numbers were glued to their backs so that they could be identified. An aquarium was built, three feet long and two feet across, with water pumped continuously through it at a depth of about four inches. Every day at nine o'clock in the morning, five successive groups of four crayfish each were put in this observation pool to see how they would behave. The situation was not unlike the conditions in which crayfish can be found in nature, where they often live together like this in small pools.

The crayfish fought and over five days Huber and his colleagues observed 2,452 'agonistic encounters':

> As the interaction progressed, maximum intensity was noted according to the following criteria: (0) *no fighting*: neither animal attacked its opponent or one animal consistently retreated from the advances of the other; (1) *threat postures*: both animals contested the interaction using threat displays or ritualised fighting without resorting to the use of their claws; (2) *claw lock*: both animals contested the encounter and at least one animal used its claws to grab the opponent; (3) *strike and rip*: both animals contested the encounter and at least one animal made unrestrained use of the claws in an attempt to rip or tear off appendages. The fight ended when an animal turned or walked away from its opponent, increasing the distance between them to more than one body length.

At first the fighting was brutal and unconstrained, the crayfish never hesitating to engage in combat, struggling with each other for a long time and often at frenzied pitch in strike-and-rip mode. But as the encounters went on, a pattern emerged. Any crayfish that had recently won a fight became less likely to retreat in the next. Winners thought they could win again. After they had won several times and knew they were strong, they became 'increasingly likely to escalate to higher intensities early in the encounter'. Dominant players knew they could brutalise their opponents with little risk. Victory suggested victory and defeat defeat. Winning enhanced further success and losing drove individuals further and further down the social hierarchy. Slowly and steadily, this expectation of victory and loss began to shape the world of the aquarium so that towards the end of the experiment, it grew increasingly calm. Every crayfish started to learn its place. It came to understand, from experience, which of its companions it could dominate and which would dominate it in turn.

Although no one has yet done this experiment with the prawns, the neural structure of the crayfish is similar to theirs, and it is more likely than not that what seems to be the perfect calm of prawn life in the pool is in reality a version of rigidified terror. Unlike crayfish, *P. elegans* don't often have physical fights but threaten each other with close-up, face-to-face encounters, from which one blinks first and the other is left in command of the field. It means that individuals are less likely to get hurt and perhaps establishes a genetic benefit for the population, as the biggest and most powerful female prawns have access to the best food resources and the best hiding places.

But there are prawns and prawns. Daniel Maskrey, of the University of Liverpool, has recently conducted a pair of experiments with some *P. elegans* he caught in rock pools next to Gyllyngvase Beach, on the southern edge of Falmouth in Cornwall. In small populations, like the four groups of forty prawns Maskrey and his colleagues collected, there turns out to be an entirely predictable variation in their personality. First Maskrey put prawns into a tank which had a shelter at one end, marked each animal individually and recorded which prawns spent most time in the shelter and which liked to go out adventuring. He then put the same group of prawns in a tank into which he lowered, as a tasty morsel, a 'fully defrosted 5 g cube of brine shrimp' and recorded which prawns were able to dominate the food resource and which came further down the pecking order.

Maskrey was able to show that what looked like shyness in a prawn, and a timid desire to remain within the shelter, was in fact a sign of dominance, since it was the apparently 'shy' prawns that consistently monopolised the cube of brine shrimp. Those which, just as consistently, had been apparently 'bold', going off exploring the experimental pool, out into parts of their world which might have concealed extra sources of food, but were also likely to be filled with unseen danger, did not get such good access to the brine shrimp.

Bold prawns, which might have been thought of as the Walter Raleighs and Francis Drakes of their world, were in fact the victims of dominance, *forced* to go exploring by the tough and exclusive behaviour of their more powerful, shelter-dwelling, stay-at-home and food-dominating cohabitants. All the prawns Maskrey chose to use were of the same size and so there was no question of big prawns dominating the others. This was a question of character. Some were tough, home-dominating winners; others were slightly diminished survivors on the edge of society.

There may be a beneficial effect of this on the population as a whole. If a group of prawns has both resource-controlling power-brokers and foolhardy/courageous seekers of new horizons, the population as a whole has some elasticity and resilience built into it, a flexible response on which the next generations might have to rely if there are storms to be outlasted and changes to be weathered.

Maskrey called his paper 'Who dares doesn't always win' but he could have called it 'Conservatives need adventurers in a crisis'. 'We speculate that alternative strategies for acquiring limited resources,' Dr Maskrey concluded soberly, 'might thereby contribute to the maintenance of personality variation observed in wild populations.'

Natural selection is at work in the pool, sifting multiple traits from one two-year generation to the next, creating hierarchies and allocating roles. Some prawns can benefit from a position low in one of those hierarchies; others have the skills to become the dominant queens, monopolising the best of shelters and the food supply. It is not absurd to say that the prawns had organised themselves into little, self-perpetuating, territory-defending and resource-maximising clans. Survival is not a given. The chief dominates his or her immediate followers, who dominate those below them, and who dominate those below them in turn. Like chiefs in their defended castles, the big and powerful females in their shelters, where they guard the next generation in their brood pouches, can be seen to hold the stored capital of the little clan, on which their shared future relies. At the other end of society, the poorest and weakest, for whom dominance is no more than a distant dream, are the creatures that can be cleared and evicted at will from any shelter they might claim as their own.

A berried female soon appeared in the centre of my pool, steadily occupying the space between two fronds of channel wrack, while the others, presumably the males, continued to scud around the margins. Do these creatures have personalities? Constant behaviours can be detected in different prawns – the powerful are slow and stable; bravado is evidence of impotence – but the idea of a personality goes beyond that. Personality requires intention and decision-making, a mind at work beyond purely instinctive or inbuilt reactions. Otherwise a computer might be said to have a personality – helpful, neat-minded, responsive – or a stone: solid, slow and uncooperative. Is it possible to say that a prawn, or its larger and more easily examined relative the crayfish, ever actually *decides* to do something?

Many experiments with these crustacea have shown that they have two different, if connected, nervous systems: one for ordinary life and one for crises. With the first, they seem to make decisions, to paddle to and fro, to go adventuring, to have a face-off with a rival. With the second, it looks as if the body, the neurons and the muscles they drive, is making decisions without the animal itself being engaged in the process. But there the language breaks down. In what way is the prawn not the body of the prawn? How can a prawn's body make decisions in which the prawn is not involved? Or does the prawn exist – inevitably you want to ask 'Do I exist ...' – on two levels, one involving merely the body and the other the prawn's vivid, vital self?

Giant nerve fibres are gathered in a fat cord that runs along the under-surface of both crayfish and prawn, bundled together like cabling in a duct, one set transmitting information from the front of the animal, its rostrum and antennae, the other from the sensitive hairs on the abdomen and all over the shell of the tail. Other smaller nerves – the non-giants – are gathered alongside them, controlling the ordinary functions of life.

If you take a big prawn, remove the shell and very carefully cut down into it from above, pinning back the muscle on each side, it is perfectly possible to find that nerve cord running down the length of the body from the little cluster of ganglia in the head, branching and then recombining around the oesophagus, and reaching all the way to the tail. With very careful picking apart, you can also find the little side-branches that deliver information to the muscles.

The giant nerves are so thick in relation to the size of the body because a prawn in crisis needs huge bandwidth. If its sense

The nervous system of the prawn, distributing nerve stimuli to the limbs attached to the body and above all to the massive muscles in the tail which allow it to thrash into its sudden escape manoeuvre.

organs have detected a threat, that information must be communicated with lightning speed to the muscles of the tail that will jackknife it away from danger. And the response is dazzlingly fast: from five- to fifteen-thousandths of a second elapsing between the stimulus being given and the big abdominal muscles contracting into the escape flex. It is a flash of electric impulse surging through the connecting axons between the nerve cells, with very little delay at the synapses, what is in effect an electric hotline from sensors to escape muscle.

Over many years, and with degrees of invasive maltreatment, scientists have investigated in great detail the way in which these giant fibres work. They are not stimulated by anything, however brutal, that happens slowly, not, as one paper expressed it, 'by gradual pinching, even to the point of breaking sternal ribs, by prodding, even to the point of piercing the ventral cuticle, by making extensive incisions of the belly, or by mashing, cutting, or pulling off appendages'.

At first, it was thought that only an intense stimulus would trigger the giant fibres into the tail-thrash response. But in 1972, Jeffrey Wine and Franklin Krasne of the University of California implanted electrodes into freely swimming crayfish and discovered, by measuring the currents in the giant fibres, that 'intensity is not as important as suddenness. Very light taps are often effective, and since the [giant nerves] occasionally fire just prior to actual contact, it may be that even the pressure waves in advance of a rapidly approaching object can be an adequate stimulus. In free animals the lightest touch of an antenna or antennule may elicit [giant nerve] responses.'

That finding confirms everything you might have guessed from looking down into the prawn pool. The first nerve system continues to govern everyday life. Make no sudden movement and cast no sudden shadow and the prawns will coast about their world, framed by the hierarchy they have established between themselves. But stand up suddenly, or even move an arm that throws a shadow on the water, and the jump reflex kicks in.

Experiments have shown that the sudden escape surge does not originate in the cluster of ganglions in its head – the central processing unit of the prawn, what non-scientists might call its brain – but is communicated directly from the animal's sensors to the muscles in the tail, bypassing any thinking mechanism. The jackknife escape is involuntary, the equivalent of our jumping away from a flame before we know that it is hot or that it is burning us.

By contrast, everyday movement in prawns originates in the brain. These 'non-giant reactions' are essentially voluntary in nature. 'Animals very much appear to choose their own moments to respond.'

That process of choosing how to behave is up to ten times slower than the millisecond thrash of the giant nerve response. This latency, or tendency to delay, is significant. 'We believe,' Professors Wine and Krasne wrote, 'that the longer latency of these reactions provides time for the animal to adjust his response to the situation.' That difference is apparent in the rock pool: a certain slow deliberation in the trawling prawn, a pausing to consider, sometimes turning this way, sometimes that, thinking what to do next, evaluating the state of play. These movements, as Jens Herberholz and Gregory Marquart from the University of Maryland have written recently, should be 'considered, in a way, "voluntary" because the animal "chooses" to activate certain patterns of flexor muscle groups'.

Herberholz and Marquart put scare-quotes around both 'voluntary' and 'chooses' because the idea that a crustacean has a will is still thought questionable.

It seems to me, anyway, that the implications are clear. Like us, the crustacean has non-conscious escape reactions alongside a whole set of behaviours that are entirely conscious. The crayfish or prawn usually considers its next move, at least until danger threatens, and only then is all thought banished. These are two ways of being, structured at the level of the neuron, and not entirely unlike ours. In peace there's nothing so becomes a prawn as modest stillness and humility: but when the blast of war blows in his ears ... he changes radically, jetting away from danger faster than his enemy can get him. We and the prawns are alike: both careful, thinking and resource-maximising; and sudden, instinctive and threat-reacting. I look at the prawns in this pool I have made and I am looking at an aspect of myself.

One thing these crustacea don't do, it has been long thought, is to plan ahead, nor practise any vigilance, looking out for enemies that might hurt them. They have been said to rely entirely on the nerve-burst of reflex response when a sudden threat appears. It was long assumed that it was a fixed response to fixed signals, so that as Herberholz and Marquart have said, 'The decision to escape is made at individual decision-making neurons; if the predatory signal is sufficient to activate them, escape will inevitably follow.' No mind was involved; the sensors and nerves, and the muscles to which they are connected, controlled the behaviour.

Recent research has changed all that. Suddenness may be what a prawn dislikes most, but the tail-flip is not always the response to it. Exposed to the sudden arrival of underwater noise from boat engines in a busy harbour, prawns do show the clearest signs of distress. If they are killed and dissected afterwards, the brain and blood contain high levels of stress hormones. But when this situation was repeated experimentally, the prawns did not try to escape as the noise went over, but went stock-still, 'freezing' *in situ*.

Herberholz and Marquart investigated this conundrum. If the jackknife response was purely instinctive, why did the crayfish not make it whenever they were threatened? Was mind somehow involved in the choice between freezing and flipping away?

They put some crayfish in an artificial stream and exposed them to fast-moving shadows which, critically, came from the same direction as the smell of food. In response, the crayfish did one of two things, either flipping away (from both food and shadow) or freezing and remaining motionless until the threat had passed.

How did they choose? Freeze or flight? There were certainly character differences: some crayfish were habitual freezers, some habitual flippers, whatever the circumstances around them. More interestingly though, as Herberholz and others had found in previous experiments, the speed at which the shadow approached the crayfish tended to govern the response. Shadows moving at one metre a second summoned more tail-flips than freezings. As speed increased to over two metres and then to four metres a second, crayfish tended to freeze in front of the threat.

The water flowing past the crayfish was full of the smell of food, '1 gram of crushed medium-sized shrimp pellets (Ocean Nutrition Formula One, Aqua Pets Americas)'. The crustaceans had to decide which was the better option, to run and probably abandon the chance of shrimp, or to freeze, hoping perhaps to be invisible, and as soon as the danger had passed happily resuming their foraging? In a third experiment, it was found that very fast-approaching shadows were considered inescapable, as the shadow overwhelmed them before they could generate a tail-flip. It clearly made what the scientists call 'economic' sense not to flip in those circumstances. Because it was too late to get away, a late flip would not save it and if it flipped, in natural circumstances with very mobile food, the crayfish would lose the chance of catching its prey. So their neural systems have been selected over time to freeze when food was near and the threat was fast. The Maryland scientists found that the stronger the smell of food, the more likely the crayfish were to freeze. 'Crayfish calculate the costs and benefits of different behavioral options and they carefully weigh predation risk against expected reward, eventually selecting the most valuable behavioral choice.'

This makes the picture complicated. It seems as if the power to choose is an aspect not only of the everyday coasting around the pool but is there within the lightning-fast reactions that might lead to a tail-flip. In times approaching six-hundredths of a second, the crustaceans make the decision to flip or freeze. The usual neural pathways used for poking around the pool are not in play. The flip is activated – or not – by the giant fibres in the nerve bundle running the length of the animal's body.

So the response is not, as was previously thought, entirely stereotypical. It can vary. Even at this speed, and even using the neurons in the giant fibres, the crayfish is capable of making a choice. No one understands this yet, but somehow, in response to a particular combination of terror and hunger it can decide. But is the crayfish making the decision? Or its body?

It is an odd and repeated experience that unless you know to look for something, you are blind to it. Only after reading these papers by the Maryland biologists did I see the behaviours they had described: the low-level ordinariness of life conducted with all normality between the rocks; the jerk-flipping away from my shadow; and then the freeze, the absolute stillness of the alert body, as I tried coming up at them quickly, moving my hand and its shadow as fast as I could (four metres a second is about nine miles an hour), and seeing how under it the tiny crustaceans paused like dancers, as if the film had been stopped, until the threat diminished and normality resumed. It was all there in front of me, the unseen genius of the prawn body and mind revealing its layered abilities to think, evaluate and decide.

It would not be difficult to program a robot to be like this. Instructions: in everyday life, swim about the pool. If a sudden movement is detected, flip away. If too sudden, stay where you are. If the smell of food is in the water, grade your response: the stronger the smell, the less likely the flip.

Here, then, is the strange philosophical question of the prawn in the pool. It has skills and habits. It behaves with the consistency of a coherent being. It can detect its surroundings and move towards places where life is better and safer. It recognises its superiors and its place in a hierarchy. It makes choices, on at least two neural levels. Is it a machine? Or does it have a self? Is the prawn more like me or my phone?

A prawn always floats the right way up. It arranges itself like that through little organs called statocysts that sprout from near the bottom of its short antennae. They are small round sacs, only about one millimetre wide, covered with a flap and filled with liquid. The floor of the statocysts is lined in little sensitive hairs on which there is a small heap of sand grains (which are lost when the prawn moults; it gathers up a new set for its new shell). If the prawn tips to the left, the sand grains press a little harder on that side and the prawn corrects its position until the pressure equalises. In some pools I have found prawns in which the statocysts are clearly not working properly and a prawn, otherwise complete and perfect, moves through its life tipped slightly to one side, like a boat whose ballast has shifted, or a cow with one leg shorter than the others. It is the tenderest of sights, a prawn, disabled either from a genetic flaw or from damage in life, nevertheless persisting in its life purpose, somehow accommodating what has happened to it.

These statocysts are shared among all the invertebrates, and have their equivalent in vertebrate animals too, from fish upwards. Is the process mechanical? Or to do with being? Colin Klein and Andrew Barron, both philosophers at Macquarie University, Sydney, in discussing what they call 'the hard problem of consciousness', think a key element in this question is precisely the sense of being in the world, of an organism orientating itself in a set of circumstances that are clearly not part of what it is. Klein and Barron are convinced that invertebrates such as these prawns 'are aware of the world (including the state of the mobile body within the world), and that this aware-ness feels a certain way to the organism that has it'.

Not only does the tipped prawn know that it is out of balance. Klein and Barron think that its need or desire to be in balance gives it a certain feeling, a feeling bound up with its existence as a prawn. That sense of getting itself right in the world is virtually indistinguishable from the feeling of selfhood. It exists, it knows that it exists and it knows that it should exist in a certain way. The prawn has no pilot. It is itself. It is making its own choices. It has its own feelings. It provides its own fuel. It generates its own progeny. Does all of that imply it is not a machine?

Charles Darwin looked carefully into the ways fear, anger and affection were emotional experiences that seemed common to the animals we know well and decided it was obvious that non-human animals had feelings. 'The lower animals, like man,' he wrote in *The Descent of Man and Selection in Relation to Sex*, 'manifestly feel pleasure and pain, happiness and misery. The fact that the lower animals are excited by the same emotions as ourselves is so well established that it will not be necessary to weary the reader by many details.'

Can invertebrates have emotions? The European Union's Animal Health and Welfare scientists concluded in 2005 that 'The largest of decapod crustaceans [a term which includes prawns] are complex in behaviour and appear to have some degree of awareness. They have a pain system and considerable learning ability,' and so 'all decapods should receive protection'. Other scientists fought that idea and the crustaceans were not protected under EU animal welfare legislation. Almost alone, Switzerland has included lobsters and crayfish in their laws for the humane treatment of animals.

The difficult question was whether the crustaceans were capable of feeling pain. Many attempts have been made to see if they do: electric shocks to mantis shrimps, ghost crabs, crayfish, hermit crabs and green crabs; acid on the antennae of prawns and crayfish; formaldehyde, ink, quinine and caffeine painted on green crabs; peppers, wasabi, a soldering iron at

54°C and dry ice at −78.5°C all applied to the most sensitive parts of crayfish.

The animals often reacted to these treatments and clearly they have means of perceiving something that is harmful to them, the capacity known as 'nociception'. But do they experience that sensation as pain? The question is bound up with the problem of consciousness because pain is an emotional response to physical hurt. It is the difference between our sudden and unconscious pulling a hand away from a hot plate – nociception – and a second later feeling something – pain – which needs rubbing and looking after. Nociception does not need a mind; it can work like a smoke alarm. Pain requires the kind of consciousness in crustaceans that has been suggested by Colin Klein and Andrew Barron and is in some ways analogous to ours. But do they have it?

There are many who deny it. Dr Ben Diggles, a Queensland aquaculture and fisheries consultant, makes the point that 'electric shocks used by some research groups to generate behavioural changes in crabs … could represent an "irritation", "stimulus", "unpleasant sensation", "buzz", "itch", or "tingle" if applied to human skin under similar circumstances'.

Dr Diggles asks us to consider that the ways in which other invertebrates are so radically unlike us – 'insects … eating their own innards and continuing feeding while being eaten' – mean that any extension of the idea of 'pain' to them would be absurd. It may be that the running of a big brain is an expensive option for an animal and invertebrates are under heavy selective pressure to reduce the cost and size of their brains. Brainlessness and painlessness may, on the level of a population as a whole, be an effective choice in a brutally competitive world.

This may seem depressing. The prawns I have come to be so fond of in my pool may be irredeemably distant, way down the far end of evolution's long road, as foreign to me as anything I might ever encounter as an animal. But all is far from lost. Some subtle and recent experiments with freshwater crayfish made by Pascal Fossat, a young professor at the University of Bordeaux, have transformed the discussion.

Fossat and his colleagues fished some *Procambarus clarkii* out of the beautiful marshes in the Marais de Bruges just north of Bordeaux. *Procambarus* is a fearsome-looking creature, an American invasive, dark red and formidably armoured, known to a million diners in the southern United States as the Louisiana crawfish or mudbug.

Crayfish and prawns are naturally exploratory. They will hide in dark, sheltered places when threatened but will also go looking around their marshes and pools by day and night. Fossat wanted to know if these crayfish could ever feel anxious, not during fearful moments or when calm but after they had been exposed to stress. Would they adapt their behaviour because of what they remembered?

Modelling his experiment on previous trials with rats and mice, he built a very simple underwater maze in the shape of a cross, where two arms were kept dark and two brightly lit. The aim was to put a crayfish at the central crossing and make it choose between its innate curiosity for new places and its dislike of anywhere that was over-bright and threatening, with nowhere to hide.

Fossat kept all the crayfish for three weeks in a state of well-fed calm and then divided them into three groups: one he exposed to a set of mild electric shocks (to which they responded with tail-thrashing) and one group he left unmolested. The third, he exposed to the electricity and then gave them an injection of benzodiazepine, a powerful anxiety-reducing drug.

When unstressed crayfish were placed in the crossing, they set off to explore the whole maze, including the bright, white arms. Those that had been given the electric shocks stayed only in the dark arms and if they wandered into the beginning of the bright arms, paused, considered and rapidly left them. The stressed

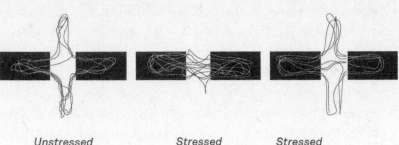

Unstressed   Stressed   Stressed
                                      + anti-anxiety drug

Pascal Fossat's record of crayfish tracks in the dark and bright arms of a
simple underwater maze under different psychological conditions.

crayfish that were later injected with the anxiety-reducing drug
behaved in ways indistinguishable from the unstressed animals.

It was an astonishing discovery. For the first time in a crustacean, Fossat had witnessed the kind of anxious behaviour only
previously seen in vertebrates. Anxiety is distinct from fear,
which is a response to present danger and generates the instant
behaviours: escape, freeze or aggression. Anxiety is more subtle

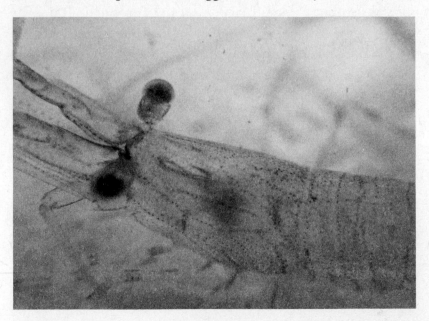

than that because it occurs when the danger is either not there or at least not known to be there. It is what Fossat calls 'an anticipatory fear' which allows the animal to deal with danger more easily when it comes.

Fossat's discovery introduces a complexity into the character of the crustacean which implies a vivid and layered self: to behave like this, it must have a memory of past fearful events; be capable of a carefulness which involves projecting its existence into the future. If an animal can be anxious, it must know about the passage of time. An anxious prawn or crayfish has both a past and a future. In that sense, Fossat revealed that a crayfish had an imagination, a mind in which possibility could take its place alongside actuality and in which decisions could be made not in the face of what it saw or smelt or otherwise perceived, but what it thought or dreamed or feared might be there.

'In this context,' Fossat wrote in *Science*, 'the crayfish represents a new model that might provide insights into the mechanisms underlying anxiety that have been conserved during evolution. Our results also emphasize the ability of an invertebrate to exhibit a state that is similar to a mammalian emotion but which likely arose early during the evolution of metazoans.'

A 'metazoan' is the word a professor of biology will use to mean anything that has lived since the great extinctions at the end of the Permian 252 million years ago. With the formal modesty usual in scientific papers, Fossat was making the great and beautiful claim that virtually all animal life on earth knows what it feels like to be alive.

3

Winkle

The rock pool had acquired a slightly ambiguous, amphibian identity. I had made it but it was making itself, a micro-Arcadia, a self-creating fragment, the opposite of one of Jean Tinguely's famous self-destroying machines that tore themselves apart in a juddering frenzy, conducting a war on their own bodies until they lay in ruins around themselves, the remains of a party to celebrate their own dying.

The pool would run that film in reverse: a self-gathering organism, a self-enriching thing, with the layers of significance and connection building in it over the weeks and months, and in that way turning into a model of the growth of life itself. In the world at large, a huge diminution is underway. In the seas and on the shores around Scotland damage has been done and will continue to be done. But here, in the smallest of gestures, something could perhaps turn the other way.

All kinds of ideas came clustering in. The pool seemed, in fact, to generate associations and implications. First, from reading some essays by Tim Robinson, the writer, cartographer and mathematician, who mapped and wrote about wild and treasured landscapes on the far western edge of Ireland. He was an outsider to those places, and had gone to the Isles of Aran in 1972, working as an artist, but with a background in mathematics at Cambridge and a sense that on that far western edge of

Europe he might find his life's work. The maps he made were subtle, exact, speckly, light-veined things, as precise as a leaf. He walked every yard of every lane and boreen he could find, tracing as far as he could every stretch of cliff and shore, marking not only the changes since the Ordnance Survey made their maps in the early twentieth century but adding the Irish names and the hidden, valuable places, the sacred stones and wells, the secret corners, the overgrown paths and causeways, which had not mattered to the British surveyors but were the grain and weft of the place for the people who had always lived there.

Partly through this close and repetitive attention to the country and partly through his training in mathematics, Robinson came to realise that our relationship to anywhere in the world, and above all to a coastline, is governed by one particular aspect of its geometry: its *fractals*.

He had been alerted by a short paper published in *Science* in 1967 written by the American mathematician Benoît Mandelbrot. 'How long is the coast of Britain?' Mandelbrot had asked, drawing on the work of the English geographer and meteorologist Lewis Richardson, a specialist in the measurement of turbulent phenomena. Richardson in the 1930s had established the strange and counter-intuitive fact that the length of any irregular line – a coast, a path, a fallen thread, the outline of an eruptive cloud – expands or contracts according to the scale at which you measure it. Use a large, coarse-grained ruler and you will get a rough – and short – idea of its length. Use a micrometer, and the line will begin to stretch towards infinity.

Mandelbrot systematised Richardson's empirical observations and proved, as Robinson wrote, that when mapping a coastline 'the idea that one gets a better and better approximation to its length by measuring it in finer and finer detail is false; the series of approximations does not converge to an answer; it just gets bigger and bigger'.

Mandelbrot gave the name 'fractal' to these infinitely lengthening lines, from the Latin *fractus*, meaning broken or irregular, and in doing that created a new realm of mathematics and geometry which stepped beyond the standard Euclidean certainties, but could be applied to all sorts of phenomena in nature. The concepts of point, line and plane, the primary elements in school geometry, work for ideas or conceptual forms but not for the wriggled, convoluted shapes of reality. Euclidean certainties cannot describe the swirl of water into a hollow, or the plume of a volcano, or any kind of turbulence, a flowing stream, the branch-pattern of lightning, the growth of trees or corals, the alveoli of the lungs, the wrinkles in skin, the shape of a shore or the growing and ebbing of grief or love.

This unmeasurability means that the Mandelbrot world is a set of dizzying spirals. The closer you look, the deeper it dives. Any examination of anything becomes an ever-growing, ever-inward plunge into the indefinable. The slower you go, the more there is to your journey. Pause for a moment and a place will pool out around you, not as an illusion but as a fact, in details it would not have had if you had not stopped to look.

This means that in the real world, outside the classroom shapes of a straight line or a perfect sphere, nothing is measurable. For every inch on a straight line, there is indeed a single inch. But most shapes in nature are longer than you imagine. The place itself becomes the only possible measurement of what it is. Seamus Heaney wrote of *The People of the Sea*, David Thomson's beautiful exploration of the place of the seal in the imagination of the Scottish and Irish margins of the Atlantic, that his book was 'luminously its own thing'. That is true of the shore itself: it is its own book, the only full account of itself, its own luminosity. Its existence is the only true light it has.

Robinson had first been drawn to mapping the coast of Connemara because of its 'strange geography, like a rope of closely interwoven strands flung down in twists and coils across an otherwise bare surface'. But Richardson and Mandelbrot had shown that picture to be false. You could never straighten the rope. However taut you pulled it, more twists would emerge. A coastline would be equally wriggly if you examined it at the scale of a continent, a rock pool, a sand grain or an atom.

Like all discoveries, Robinson wrote, Mandelbrot's realisation 'surprises us yet again with the unfathomable depth and texture of the natural world; specifically it shows that there is more space, more places, on a seashore, within a forest or among the galaxies, than the geometry of common sense allows'.

Vertigo comes with that. Reality must outstretch any understanding of it and as Mandelbrot wrote, 'coastline length turns out to be an elusive notion that slips between the fingers of those who want to grasp it'.

The fractal is a kind of mind-cuckoo. I was wanting in my rock pool to see in detail the reality of things. The fractal pushes aside any hope of certainty and, once that doubt has taken up residence, it cannot be dislodged. Everything succumbs. Fractals are everywhere: in the way that winds blow, each gust a curved outgrowth of the trend, each gust-within-a-gust mimicking the wind structure that folds out across oceans and continents; or the way a river will run past a rock or tree root and twist into spirals beyond it; or in waves breaking on a beach; even in the way natural populations develop; or markets shift; or the boundaries of growing cities push out into the surrounding country; in the shape and formation of the universe. Look at an image of the surface of the sun and it boils with infolded possibility, turning in all three dimensions, inhaling as much as dilating, a dance of nuclear, magnetic and gravitational flux, spirals at the source of everything we can see.

This turbulence is embedded in the workings of the physical world. And not only the physical: allow your mind to wander in its thinking and ideas do not follow in a predictable, clarified, linear, Euclidean path, but bubble up like this, within themselves, emerging as the children of the ideas that preceded them, growing within the wombs of those parents, and then becoming parents themselves of the ideas that succeed them, a rippling involution and evolution of successive and successively nested thoughts, as if the mind were a breaking wave or a river disrupted by the bed in which it ran. 'Every atom belonging to me as good belongs to you,' Whitman said, and that is a fractal recognition, the cupping of reality in successive layers of itself.

The shore is filled with infinite regressions from ocean to channel to bay to pool to bay within the pool, to an inlet in that bay, to a micro-pool, an inlet within it and so on and on into the microscopic. The whole sequence is a frozen – or in fact exceptionally slow – kind of fractal turbulence, the sea imposing on the land a form of shaping which if taken away from our own time-perspective and given its planetary due, would bubble and break, in time as well as in space, an endless overturning of the substance of the world.

To make a rock pool was in fact to make something no less complex than the ocean itself. But here is the dizzying part. Fractal theory suggests that the closer you look at something, the more it remains unknown. Knowledge cannot embrace whatever it seeks to know. It can only sit alongside the world, contingent, touching it, maybe, at one or two points but shrinking beside the unaddressable and limitless actuality of things.

One of the applications of the theory, as Tim Robinson wrote,

is to estimate the number of habitable niches available to creatures of different sizes on a given surface. Here a small area of shore, say an acre, when examined in detail discloses a huge variety of holes and crevices, of a total surface area hundreds of times greater than of the acre, and within those holes and clefts are smaller ones sheltering smaller creatures, who enjoy areas hugely greater still – and so on, to the well-nigh infinitesimal, the single-celled.

The rock pool was not going to be a tiny, graspable fragment of the universe. It was going to be as unknowable as the universe itself.

This is one of the oldest of conundrums. Plato knew it. 'May a man not "possess" and yet not "have" knowledge?' Socrates asked in his usual taunting way. The question was not whether a man may have the knowledge – which is obvious enough; we all know things – but whether the knowledge can 'have' the thing it knows. The habitual Socratic interrogative is a fractal form, doing no more than revealing the questions within his questions, as if the world were a series of Chinese boxes each one labelled 'Uncertainty'. 'Suppose someone has caught some wild birds,' Socrates asked, 'doves or any other birds – and is keeping them in an aviary which he has made at home. We can say of him, in one sense, that he has them because he possesses them, might we not? ... And yet, in another sense, he has none of them.'

It is the most subversive picture of knowledge. Look at a wild creature – even hold it in your hand – and it is obvious that you do not 'have' it. You hold it but everything it is stretches far beyond your enclosing fingers, in time and space and through its own interior existence. You may possess it, even for a moment, but it is not yours. Plato's understanding was to see knowledge in the same way. Whatever it is that is to be known remains outside the grip of our knowing it. The knowledge can scarcely embrace the irredeemably wild and unconstrained facts it hopes to know. We might make an aviary of our ideas but the birds we shut inside it have their life and being far beyond its walls.

When I first heard the story of Socrates's aviary – which is the nub of Socratic wisdom: the acknowledgement that fractal depths lie within any known or measured surface – I whooped with the pleasure of recognition. It confirmed everything I had been instinctively feeling about the pool. What is a tidal pool but a cage, an aviary, with permeable walls? A volunteer zoo into which life will come if the conditions are congenial, but leave when the tide floods and the walls become irrelevant? Not a place that preserves what is already there, but a frame to encourage the assembling of life, in whose linkages and interstices the functions of life might find a home. Nothing in it would be mine. Its boundaries would be both open and closed, alternating with the tides, twice a day, breathing like that, drawing organisms in, holding them, releasing them, depending on the sea to give it life. Making the pool was a kind of gardening, but one in which the gardener merely built the enclosure, or a half-enclosure, an enclosure that twice a day melted and dissolved, only to reappear as the tide dropped, and brought no plants and weeded no weeds.

It represented a curiously true relationship to the natural. Making it would be a human act but with a natural outcome. It could both enclose and fail to enclose; its fractal spirals could spin off into the sea itself. It would be a model of Socrates's aviary and in that inadequacy – the explicit transience of its containment – would be a kind of perfection, perfect because imperfect.

April came. The grass was still as brown and low as ever. The sycamores were just coming into leaf, or some of them. Individual limbs of particular trees were fronded green; others still in winter. Different parts of one branch were in different seasons. The spears of the flag irises were up in the marsh above the shore, no flowers yet, but under the trees, celandines and big pansy-sized violets were scattered in the grass. Wild strawberries and prim-roses flowered at the foot of the trees where the trunks curved out in little buttressed hollows towards their roots.

The first pair of house martins had arrived. Their nest was tucked up under the bargeboards at the west end of the house. Every minute of the day they flew up to the eaves and out again, from life to nest and nest to life. They sometimes picked bugs from the strand line, perhaps quick enough to catch an *Orchestia*, then flew in low over the grasses, scarcely avoiding the bright points of the irises, before cutting and slanting in among the trees, thread-weaving past the trunks.

I made a map of the pool. The prawns were in evidence but otherwise it was in the same planetary condition as when I had dug it. Photographs underwater looked like a scene on Mars: a stone universe, with mineral shards of this and that lying there. Some disconnected bits of wrack had floated in on the tide. There was nothing growing except a few filaments of bright green gutweed – close-up it looks like a string of neon sausages – but that is not a good sign. Gutweed likes fresh or brackish water, which means the salinity of this pool was not high, the saltiness of the sea probably overwhelmed by the rain that had fallen into it.

Nothing had failed here yet because nothing had happened. The pool was full of sand and sticks, a leaf or two from the trees,

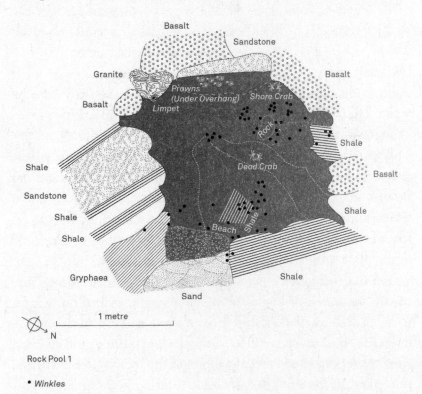

Rock Pool 1

• *Winkles*

The otherworldly conditions of the first rock pool before visible
life had begun to colonise it.

the shell of two dead crabs, gone white and orange, their
ghost-bodies dusted with the sand. It is what the sea would be
when life had come to an end, a picture of one of the great
extinction catastrophes. Inert and finished. No drama.

Then one morning, in this nothingness, I found some inhabitants, about sixty dark grey, bulbous common winkles, *Littorina
littorea*. They tend in the first days of spring to come up from the
lower parts of the tide where they have been sheltering in
the winter from the cold. And so they had arrived here now
in the pool, another marvel in this shrunken world.

These are the edible winkles – their Latin name means 'the
shorey shore-things' – picked in their uncounted millions from
these coasts now and exported largely to France. Clumps of the
big round bodies of their shells, narrowing at the top to pointed
spires, were gathered here and there on the rocks and on the fine
mud-sand in the centre of the pool. I thought at first they were

still, but watching each cluster showed that gently, at about a move a minute, they were jostling and bustling, a slow-motion stirring like a stately and patient dance. It was a Dickensian scene: a 'social conference', in silence but with the look, if you could have heard it, of much muttering and murmuring, Stilton and Wensleydale for all comers, no one here without his watch-chain. Winkles have the dignity of corpulence, a cigar in one hand, a glass of port in the other and I sat in the sunshine counting this happy party of grey-frocked beadles.

They are the commonest of things here and they played their part in the metaphorical life of the people. A miser, it was said, was the sort of man who would count the periwinkles on a rock. Numberlessness was their condition; they became the very bottom layer of life on which the poor could rely. A broth made with them was said to be good for nursing mothers. If strained and drunk, it would mend the gravel and the stone, a form of sympathetic magic: a soup of these pebble-like little creatures, sieved so that only the liquid remained, might in pure sympathy ease any stony concretions from the body.

James Macpherson, the eighteenth-century collector, editor and translator of the songs of Ossian, which he thought fragments of a Gaelic epic based in Morvern, full of warring, sighing, grieving heroes, calls one beach at which the heroes landed the *tràigh na faoch* – the periwinkled shore. It was a phrase Macpherson's critics thought 'inconsistent with epic dignity'. Would Achilles or Odysseus ever have landed on a shore encrusted with sea snails?

But adjust your scale and the winkles are full of epic dignity. They were now engaged on their various rolling, stage-coach journeys across the sand and they soon dispersed. One, very pale with variegated stripes to its shell, started to make its way slowly eastwards over the sandy floor, its pair of flat antennae feeling the way out before it. As it moved, there was a slow, slight wobbling of the house on its back. The burdened creature was making its way across its world. There was no prawn-like flitting here. The massive shell declared the principle on which the winkle's life is based: not quickness but armour, a slow and protected seriousness which does not leave much room for spontaneity. The prawn may like and need its refuge, in the way of any high-strung, flickery thing, but the winkle carries its well-being with it and no need of a rock under which to hide. Its mode is to trundle. The music of its life is slow and deep. In five minutes, it moved about two inches, leaving its track as a shallow groove behind it in the sand. Only then did I see that the entire floor of the pool was criss-crossed with those tracks, woven in and out of each other as much as the flight of the martins had made a warp and weft between the trees.

Some got all the way to the beach (three feet away) where they settled next to a piece of limestone. Others migrated a yard to the various spots on the eastern shales, and one or two a couple of feet to the north-western lump of basalt where they stopped on a patch of old, greyish coralline. I made a map of their paths, a joint biography of the winkles' morning since the tide had last been in.

Where they crossed the fronds and hanks of kelp that had floated into the pool, they left their tracks on the surface of the weed. It was clear that the marks were more than just the drag of their passage. The winkles had removed the layer of indeterminate stuff that had settled on the kelp, in fact grazing on it, harvesting this scurf known to biologists as 'biofilm', which is the foundation of life on the shore.

Julian Cremona, one of the great coastal biologists of Britain and for many years head of the Dale Fort Field Centre on the edge of Milford Haven in Pembrokeshire, has described how these 'biofilms are found on any surface where there is moisture, from swimming pools to the top of a mountain range, from the surface of a moss to the film that covers your teeth before you brush them clean'. That clogging tooth-film on waking up is the foundation of rock-pool life. The wet surface of your teeth, as of these blades of kelp, attracts bacteria which within minutes begin to secrete sugary chemicals, the polysaccharides, that start to pullulate and fold over on themselves, making a matrix of layers that soon, in Cremona's words, 'becomes a complex 3D structure of holes and tunnels'.

This microscopic sub-world, with its underpasses and flyovers, refuges and public squares, the throughways and piazzas into which life can funnel and crowd, becomes a growing city for all sorts of beings: diatoms and other micro-algae that float in their hundreds of millions as plankton in the seawater; strings of connected life; all types of ancient photosynthesising bacteria, the cyanobacteria, among the oldest of living things on earth. The infolding mesh of these new arrivals, suburbs and colonies of vitality, climbing above the original surface, will trap any detritus falling through the water column of the pool, fragmentary pieces of broken or dropped algae from seaweed torn by the waves or eaten by tiny single-celled animals, the protists.

Unseen by us, too small for us, but fundamental to the life-workings of this place, an entire ecology and economy develops within layers that are no more than a few microns thick. The complexity and local variation is unaddressable. I can see only the periwinkles mowing their swathes through the biofilm as if through the grass of a field, or more like the earth-moving machines that create new cuttings and embankments for roads and bypasses. They use their radulae, the raking and rasping cheese-grater tongues, fitted with a complex of small and renewable hooks, to file away at the bacterial sludge and at the bodies of the softer green seaweeds, the gutweed and the bright green fronds of the sea lettuce, recycling the nutrients, making them, for a moment, their own.

You can see this, and watch this and observe the relationship of gastropod to its algal and bacterial food, but the sense of vertigo, of the layers of life disappearing away from sight down into the tunnels of the microscopic, is inescapable. Every part of the world is an otherworld.

These winkles like a rock pool because they can only happily feed when immersed in the seawater and their surroundings are wet. They are able to spend time out of water, stuck to a dry rock with some of their own mucus and with their damp body shut inside the shell with a little, carefully fitted lid, an operculum, that protects them from desiccation and from predators, but that is unproductive time. The result is that those winkles that are immersed in seawater for only a brief period at the top of the beach must eat their microscopic food more quickly, scraping away at the biofilm with their radulae up to thirty-five times a minute. Those that live at the bottom of the shore and are immersed for longer can afford to spend their lives chewing away more slowly, the radulae usually harvesting the biofilm at between five and ten times a minute, less than a third of the rate of their cousins at the top of the beach.

Why, if life is more difficult here, are there any winkles at the top of the beach? Why are they not all down at the more consistently productive levels where the world is usually wet, and where temperature, oxygen and salinity are all more constant and more easily dealt with? The answer is the unkindness of strangers: competition from others and the threat from enemies. The lower shore may be richer but it is more dangerous, filled with rivals and predators. The upper shore is poorer but it is also safer. Having to eat quickly may be a price worth paying if it is less likely you are going to be eaten in return.

The shore is a Darwinian laboratory in which the sculptor of life is the threat of death. These periwinkles, like any other being, are the outcome of an arms race between the ingenuity of their predators – largely crabs, but also shorebirds, fish and whelks – and their own defences. An animal's existence is what it can get away with, the room to which their predators are denied access.

Sea animals rely on chemical senses to detect their enemies. They know to escape when they get the taste or smell – the two senses are indistinguishable in water – of the predator itself, usually its urine. Some species take this a step further. Minnows, tadpoles, sea urchins, sea anemones and many sorts of snail, including these periwinkles, are able to tell when one of their own kind is being hurt. They will start to escape as soon as they sense the telltale signals of periwinkle flesh being cut or crushed.

In 1980, the distinguished marine scientist Robin P. Hadlock, now based at Cornell University's Shoals Marine Laboratory on the Gulf of Maine, conducted a classic experiment investigating this ability of the winkle to sense trouble. Dr Hadlock began by crushing some periwinkles and dropping their juice into one or two rock pools on the Maine coast. The winkles in the pools responded as one might, 'by moving to sites ... where they were less visible to a human observer', crawling into crevices, in between seaweed fronds or under rocks. As soon as the smell of the juice reached them, the winkles speeded up from about an eighth of an inch a minute to about half an inch a minute, running for the hills.

Robin Hadlock then took some winkles to artificial rock pools in her lab and, with considerable sangfroid, watched, step by step, exactly what happened when they met up with a green shore crab, *Carcinus maenas*, the European crab, the commonest crab on British shores and a destructive and invasive introduction to almost every other temperate coastline on earth.

As soon as a crab senses a periwinkle nearby, the pair of short antennae between its eyes start to flicker quickly, apparently searching for the source of the smell, their orientation ranging across the pool in front of it. The maxillipeds, the pair of plates on the underside of the crab in front of its mouth, which are used to shovel food in towards its chewing parts, start to sway from side to side, in a set of movements which look as though the crab is licking its lips. The predator has yet to make its move and may continue like this, quite still, for a few minutes before going into the attack.

Only after it has settled on the target, does the crab begin to walk towards it. As it approaches the prey, it sweeps its legs and claws across the floor of the pool, in 'a semicircular swiping motion' while the fingers of the claws, the moving parts, open and close in 'a dactyl snap'. What role is played by the theatricality of this crab behaviour, no one has yet established.

Once the crab has come into contact with the shell of the winkle, either with its walking leg or its claw, the violence begins. It may simply pull the shell of the winkle from the floor of the pool and bring it to the attack position in front of its mouth. Or, more dramatically, the crab can suddenly pounce, using its own body to pin the winkle to the pool floor and then, using its legs, push it forwards towards its mouth.

Once the winkle is in position, the crab turns it over with its claws, going quite slowly and delicately pushing the dactyl of its claw into the periwinkle's opening, probing for the flesh of the animal inside. This is an exploratory gesture, perhaps to check that the winkle is worth killing. The crab then removes the dactyl from the opening and starts turning the shell again, stopping occasionally, with one claw around the spire end of the shell and the other holding the bulk of the winkle from below.

Death is not long in coming. If the winkle is small, the crab crushes the shell with a claw or breaks off the top of its spire. If the shell is too big to crush, the crab either chips away at the outer lip of the opening until the winkle's little lid is no longer tightly sealed against the shell and then pushes a claw into the opening where it grabs the body of the winkle. The other claw tugs the shell in the opposite direction or, if the winkle is recalcitrant, continues to chip away at it. The outcome is never that neat and the crab always has to perform more cracking of the shell before it can get hold of the bulk of its victim's body.

Once it has the soft parts exposed, the crab holds the shell up to its mouth with its claws and begins to eat. A small cloud of fluid appears around the mouthparts. Bit by bit, the whole of the winkle is eaten, after which the crab sits quietly and either resumes searching for another winkle or grooms itself, brushing its eyes and antennae of any crumbs that might remain.

The dynamics of this terrifying relationship are mysterious at first. Winkles, even with their lives at stake, when they quadruple their usual speed, are not fast movers. A shore crab can easily outrun them. How is it then that any winkles survive the presence of a crab in their pool?

It turns out that the timings are critical. Dr Hadlock found that within about four minutes of the crab being placed in the pool, it had located and started attacking any winkles that were stranded out in the open. If they were small, they were crushed and eaten in about two minutes thirty seconds, which meant that the crab could quickly move on to another victim.

If the next target was a large winkle, more than three-quarters of an inch long, the crab could not usually break its shell and it would survive the attack. The sheer bulk and shell-strength of large individuals is 'a size refuge'. Medium-sized winkles were always eaten, the shell cracked and tissue gradually torn away but it took time, on average nine minutes fifty-four seconds before the crab had finished with it.

Crucially, Hadlock also found that individual winkles, alerted by detecting crushed winkle juice in the water, and then running for cover, took on average about ten minutes to find a crevice in which they could hide. Once in there, the crab took longer than sixteen minutes to discover the winkles and start its attack. It knew winkles were in the pool equally quickly (judging by antennae-flicking and maxilliped-licking) whether the winkles were in the open or in a crack but had much more difficulty finding the winkles when they had managed to hide. Even then, the crab found attacking a winkle in a crack with its claws much more difficult and slower. A rock crack is a genuine refuge for a winkle.

The implications of this experiment are fascinating. Large winkles are big enough to survive crab attack. Medium and small winkles have no chance once caught. But the ability of the winkle to understand that other winkles in its pool are being attacked is its saving. Small victims serve no purpose to the general population; they are killed and eaten too quickly to make a difference. But in attacking medium-sized winkles, the crab buys the other winkles time to escape and find a refuge. The shells of those medium-sized winkles, in other words, do not protect those individuals but, through the chemical signals their lacerated flesh sends out, the shells do protect the others. In the time the struggle buys the other winkles in the pool, they can escape to hiding places, continue to grow and eventually develop the thick shells that will protect them in the future.

Each winkle population will have multiple victims among the young, a protected older strand of winkles and a band within the population of medium-sized creatures which are effectively killed for the others, a temporal buffer that buys the general population some safety and a continuing life.

This biological community structure, which is entirely consistent with Darwinian principles, looks oddly like the roots of something else: the clan civilisation of the Highlands. In a pattern shared with many other pre-modern Indo-European societies, from the herder-warriors of Central Asia, through Homer and the European Bronze Age to the knightly culture of medieval Europe and even to the nineteenth-century rekindling of chivalric ideals, there is a curious continuity with this winkle world. In all of them, young adults suffer so that others do not. Their death guarantees the safety of most. Their resistance is both a communal good and a mere prelude to their own dying.

Can it be that a population of winkles, here in this pool, as in all others, has, merely through the forces of natural selection, developed a means of survival that relies on the death of young heroes? Does it mean that Achilles, or Oscar, Ossian's son who in the tales was brought back here to Morvern dead from battle in Ireland, carried on his shield, are nothing but members of a biological category, which any population of any animal subject to predation will also have among them?

The periwinkle has more secrets to reveal, in an environment of more complex interactions. Its preferred seaweed food is soft green algae such as gutweed – its Latin name *Ulva intestinalis* tells you what to look for: long strings of intestinal weed, bright green when growing, turning white when dead and dried in summer – and its cousin *Ulva lactuca*, the equally bright green sea lettuce which has flat, lettuce-like leaves. Both of them, at least in sheltered places on the upper shore, will outcompete other seaweeds and, left unchecked, will come to dominate their pools. Further down the shore, where conditions are rougher, they do not survive so well and are outcompeted by the tough brown perennial seaweeds such as bladderwrack and egg wrack, which can take over in summer when the sea lettuce dies back.

A beautiful pool on the upper shore full of that greenery will look (or smell) attractive to a winkle but it will also contain an unpleasant secret. Shore crabs like pools full of gutweed and sea lettuce because the weed hides them from gull and otter predators. As the marine ecologist Jane Lubchenco revealed in her groundbreaking PhD at Harvard in the 1970s, those three organisms – winkle, crab and green weed – perform their own revolving dance around each other in a set of interlocked and cyclical changes on the upper shore.

The first stage in spring is a green pool. The crabs hide in the weed and eat the small newly metamorphosed periwinkles as they come in from the sea, where the young proto-winkles have floated as plankton, spreading around the shore. The green weed thrives because it has no consumers and it outcompetes other seaweeds.

Then the balance changes. Enough periwinkles move in to outlast and outgrow the effects of crab predation and they begin to make inroads into the gutweed. The more winkles there are, the more the weed shrinks and the less hospitable it becomes for the crabs.

Few crabs can survive there now because there is nowhere for them to hide and the gulls take them. All the gutweed in the pool is eaten by the winkles and it becomes dominated by other seaweeds, particularly the hard, scarcely edible pink encrusting coralline and carragheen, or Irish moss, the beautiful red seaweed whose fronds glitter with the blue shimmer of their reproductive spores. The few winkles that remain survive on small young algae which are eaten as quickly as they sprout.

It is a system of exquisite and jewel-like ecologies with two alternative positive feedback loops – green pools remaining filled with green weed, dark red pools with scarcely a sprig of green. You can see this on rocky shores: some pools thickly weedy and green, often when some fresh water gives an advantage to the *Ulva* species; others, usually further down the shore, dominated by the red and brown seaweeds, particularly the carragheen, that can grow only when the green weeds are kept in check by the winkles. Both are stable states, kept going by those two positive feedback loops: green weeds mean crabs mean no winkles mean green weeds; winkles mean no green weeds mean no crabs mean winkles.

More recently Geoffrey Trussell at Northeastern University in Boston has taken those Lubchenco findings and refined them. In the same shallow pools as she studied, on the so-called 'tied island' of Nahant, east of Boston – it has a narrow spit connecting it to the mainland – Trussell and his co-workers topped up the natural population of periwinkles so that they were at the solid density of one hundred winkles per square metre.

They also put green crabs into some of the pools, two per square metre, which was the natural density. In others, they put the same density of green crabs, but with a difference: these crabs

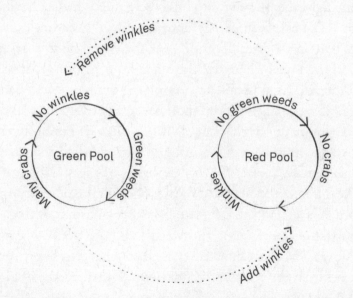

If you add enough winkles to a pool, they will eat the green weeds, the crabs that had hidden in the weeds will disappear and red seaweeds will come to dominate. If you take the winkles away, the green weed will return, crabs will again hide in it and you will have a green, winkle-free pool. Each state is stable until the conditions are changed.

were shut inside perforated plastic tubs that were anchored to the floor of each pool, so that the crabs would not be able to escape and prey on the winkles. From time to time these imprisoned crabs were fed mussels and winkles. In a third set of pools, equally full of winkles, the biologists made sure there were no crabs at all.

Trussell covered each pool in vinyl-coated netting, with a thirty-five-millimetre mesh, anchored to the rocks around it. The bigger crabs were kept either in or out of the pool by the netting, but the team checked every week that no small crabs had crept in to disrupt the experiment. If they had, they were removed. Importantly, though, the netting allowed light into the pools so that the seaweeds could grow and the mesh was big enough to allow winkles in and out.

Six months passed and the winkles were counted again. Not surprisingly, the number in pools where the crabs had been able to catch and eat them was significantly down, from one hundred per square metre at the beginning of the experiment to seventy-one. In the pools where the crabs had been kept in their plastic tubs and had been unable to prey on the winkles, the reduction of winkle numbers was even more severe: no more than sixty-six per square metre. In those pools where there had been no crabs, tubbed or untubbed, the number of winkles had increased to 159 per square metre.

The difference in winkle numbers had a dramatic effect on the seaweeds. The pools that had crabs, either in or out of tubs, had at least three times more gutweed than the pools where the winkles had been unthreatened. And so what had happened? It was clear that the winkles did not need to smell crushed or lacerated winkle flesh to start their escape manoeuvres. The mere presence of a crab was enough for them to leave. The gutweed had proliferated because the winkles had smelt a crab in their pool and got out.

Trussell had shown that Lubchenco's conditions were not fixed. A migrating crab can drive winkles out of a pool and so change its ecology. Its arrival could turn a red pool green through winkle fear alone. Predation did not need to occur for its effects to be felt. Fear of abuse was as potent a motivator as the abuse itself. The winkles could understand at a distance when their lives were under threat, act to escape it and abandon a pool to a new, green, crab-filled future. Just as easily, though, the winkles could work on crab fear, turning a green pool red by stripping it of its green weed and exposing the crabs to the threat of gull predation, from which inevitably they would also run.

There are three sorts of winkle in this bay: the smooth-shelled, grey edible ones; the tiny, beautifully named *Littorina neglecta* which lives on the upper shore in cracks and the empty cup-cases of barnacles; and their slightly larger cousins, the flat periwinkle called *Littorina obtusata*, meaning 'the blunted one' because the twist of its shell does not come to a spired point like the others. This flat periwinkle usually lives a little further down the tide on the fronds of the serrated and bladderwrack and they come in a variety of colours and chequered patterns, often brownish or greenish but most sparklingly a bright canary-primrose yellow, visible ten yards away on the beach.

The winkles of the bay, from left to right: *L. neglecta*; two colour forms of *L. obtusata*; and *L. littorea*, the edible winkle.

Why such yellow in this world of browns and greys? It is almost certainly another form of hiding. If you wade out into the shallows and look down on to the serrated wrack, bladderwrack or grape wrack on which these smooth winkles tend to live, nearly all of them disappear from view. In the shadows and branchings of the weed, with the movement of the sea and the glinting of the light, the little brownish nodules of the winkles become indistinguishable from the bladders and bumps on the seaweed itself. They are hiding from the birds – or at least the brown ones are. What are radiantly prominent to the eye are the yellow winkles, sprinkled over the mid-tide landscape like sequins. The answer to this oddity is that not all the winkles' predators look at them from above. The green shore crabs, like the blennies that also prey on them, are – at least in part – visual predators. From below, in sunlight, the weeds are pale, near-yellow, brightly lit and in those conditions, it is the yellow winkles that are difficult to see. Their brown cousins stand out as all-too-visible packages of prey. Yellow *Littorinae obtusatae* survive by hiding in the light.

Not that anything is fixed. A decade after completing her doctorate, Dr Hadlock, now at Cornell and married to the bee scientist Thomas Seeley, turned her attention to the evolution on the American coast of this little blunt winkle. Its enemy, the European green shore crab, had arrived north of Cape Cod only in about 1900, but its coming had brought a revolution to the world of the winkle.

Robin Hadlock Seeley measured and analysed all shells of the smooth winkle that had been collected in New England before 1900 and then measured shells of living populations from the same places. It was clear that the form of the winkle had entirely changed in the century it had been exposed to the green shore crab. Before 1900, the blunt winkle in New England was not very blunt at all, with a taller spire and a thinner, more elegant shell than its European equivalents. Smooth winkles collected at the same places in 1982–4 were shorter, blunter and with thicker shells.

The hundred years it took for the American smooth winkle to change its form is a blink in geological time. In any fossil record it would appear as an instantaneous shift from one state to another. A palaeontologist would consider this the arrival of a new species. It wasn't, but a measure of flux in the persistence of life, the arrival of a new predator distorting the forms of the biological field around it, in the way that a heavenly body bends and tests the gravitational field through which it passes. The European crab had, in effect, changed its prey into the shape it has in European waters.

The winkles are living in an increasingly hostile world. Everywhere in the North Atlantic outside Europe, as the Dutch evolutionary biologist Geerat J. Vermeij has written, an increase in shell thickness has been taken as a response 'to the spread of the introduced European green crab (*Carcinus maenas*), but these changes may also have resulted from an overall increase in the abundance of native shell-crushing crabs (*Cancer* spp.) and lobsters (*Homarus americanus*) as the predators (including cod) of these crustaceans were overfished'.

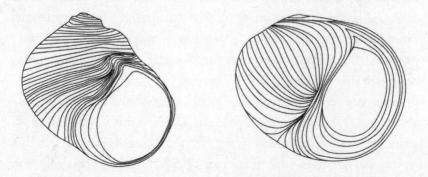

Drawings made from Robin Hadlock Seeley's photograph of American *Littorina obtusata*: left, spired and thin from 1871; right, blunt and thick in 1982.

The destruction of the cod and the collapse of their position as an apex predator in the Atlantic has led to a growth in the abundance of shrimps, lobsters, and crabs throughout this ocean. It is now a sea of claws. That hugely increased claw count, and competition between the clawed animals, has risen to the point where the shell-dwellers are feeling the pressure and have responded as shell-dwellers and shell-wearers must: by thickening their defences and toughening their lives.

But modern life has provided them with one more hurdle: the acidification of the world ocean.

It is recognised now that winkles and other sea snails only need the flavour of a crab in the water around them to react defensively. Nor is the reaction a spur-of-the-moment event. Ruth Bibby, from the University of Plymouth, raised some young periwinkles she had collected from pools on the Devon coast. When the aquarium she grew them in also contained a crab (the periwinkles were enclosed in perforated plastic pots so the crab could not attack them) the periwinkles increased their usual shell thickness by about 30%. Somehow, in ways that are not entirely clear, the young winkles knew their survival depended on thicker shells.

The acidification of the ocean plays havoc with this defence mechanism. One-third of all the carbon dioxide that has been emitted since the beginning of the Industrial Revolution has been absorbed by seawater, turning it acid. It is still being absorbed, at a rate which is about a hundred times faster than any period in the last 650,000 years.

The way in which animals make their shells and skeletons, drawing calcium carbonate from the water, is more difficult in an acid sea. Shells dissolve in acid. When Ruth Bibby raised the young periwinkles in the presence of a crab but in seawater that was acidified by bubbling CO_2 through it, the shells did not thicken but remained as thin as those of winkles that had grown up with no crab in their tank. An acid sea will make winkles vulnerable to crab predation, with all kinds of ripple effects spreading from that: more crabs, fewer winkles, denser algae and a disruption of the entire coastal ecosystem.

The effect is more than purely chemical. When seafish are exposed to acid water, their senses of smell and hearing are both disrupted. Young fish find it more difficult to learn, become less frightened by danger and are even attracted to the smell of predators. The chemical mechanisms of their nerve systems are in this way fatally disrupted by the acid water.

The same effects have recently been found in marine snails such as the winkles. The spectacularly named seaweed-eating conch, the *Gibberulus gibberulus gibbosus* and its specialist predator, the cone shell *Conus marmoreus*, live in sandy areas around tropical coral reefs. The conches have a special foot and operculum, the hard lid on top of the foot, which they use both to flick themselves upright if they find themselves upside down and to escape their cone-shell predators, which can shoot them with a poisonous dart. Once the conch smells the cone shell in the water, it kicks out and dramatically leaps away from the enemy, the jump usually being about one shell's length away from danger.

Sue-Ann Watson and her colleagues from James Cook University in Queensland collected conches and their cone-shell predators at Lizard Island Lagoon on the Great Barrier Reef, wanting to know what happened to this response if the water was acidified.

A single conch was put in an aquarium ten millimetres in front of a thin transparent plastic barrier. The seawater could flow across the top of the barrier but it was designed to stop a successful attack if the conch did not manage to escape. A cone shell was put ten millimetres away from the barrier on the other side. Predator and prey faced each other and Dr Watson observed.

In normal seawater, 65% of the conches jumped away. In acid water, only 33% jumped at all, taking twice as long to react to the danger and, when they did jump, choosing to leap not so directly away from the cone shell. In nature, without the barrier, most of them would have died.

There was no change in the physical jumping ability itself. Even in acidified water, the conches could easily turn themselves upright. What the acid seawater affected, in Dr Watson's own term, was the 'decision-making' of the conch. The toxic sea was distorting its mind.

4

Crab

___

As the year pushed on into spring, I realised the pool in the rocks in front of the house was not right. It was too high up the shore and out of the sea for too long between each tide. When I put a thermometer in there at the end of a sunny afternoon, it read almost 60° Fahrenheit, over 15°C. As soon as the tide came in and filled it, the temperature dropped to 40°F, just more than 8°C. That zigzag graph was too much for most life to cope and for weeks now nothing had come to grow here. The super-tolerant prawns were still in evidence and the periwinkles were still going about their business but otherwise it remained a place of rock and water.

I would have to start again, further down the tide, and not like this at the head of the bay, but out on one of the headlands, exposed to wind and water, a place in which there was a chance at least that life could come to meet me.

I walked the mile over to Rubha an t-Sasunnaich. A pair of curlews by the shore were 'trailing bubbles of music', as Norman MacCaig once said of them,

Music as desolate, as beautiful
as your loved places ...

They left as I came down to them and the gulls bounced and beat away crosswind.

The point itself is a knuckle of very late Triassic limestone, just older than the rocks at the head of the bay. At the shoreline this featureless stone is hard, sharp and intractable, chemically dissolved by seawater into inch-high spicules and hollows, the whole place stripped by the storm waves to a platform on which geese roost and leave their droppings in the rain pools. On a grey day, it can be a sombre place.

The rock is riven every thirty or forty yards with dark basalt dykes. At the west end of the headland, there was a place that looked right: one of the narrow trenches from which the sea had prised the basalt away opened out into a triangular gap in the limestone, about thirty feet long on each side. At high tides, the sea poured in through the little gateway and filled the triangle to the depth of three feet or so. Once the tide withdrew, this pool drained away through the narrow ditch, leaving only a shallow and rather sludgy puddle in the centre of the triangle in which nothing much occurred. If I could dam the gap, keeping the seawater in the pool, I could make somewhere better than the pool I had dug at the head of the bay: larger, in a more energetic environment, further down the tide.

The dam would have to be substantial. The pressures were large. But I was worried that if I built a solid dam, it would fill only at the highest of high tides. The pool would be refreshed with new water only twice a month, when spring tides over-topped the wall. Between those moments of renewal, the water would stale. I needed something that would let the sea in at neaps but then hold it there. I had seen something like it on the Somerset Levels: one-way exits that opened to allow the rivers to run into the Bristol Channel but stopped the rising tide coming in to flood the Levels themselves: a flap-valve. If I could use that in reverse – allow the tide in, not let it out – I had a chance.

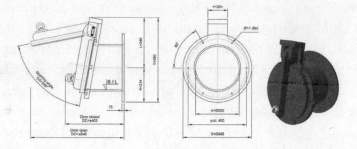

Althon's flap-valve for the dam at the second pool, designed to admit
neap high-tide water and keep it there.

When I rang Tim Gates, director at Althon, outfall engineers
of Norwich, he was completing a contract for the rebuilding of
Inverness Airport and another for the main drainage system for
the city of Doha. I told him something twelve inches wide might
do for me. Would I be happy with an Althon 300 mm HDPE/
SS316L Flap Valve with Square Back? he asked. Its hinges were
in Grade 316L stainless steel so would not rust for fifty years. I
would.

Bringing the dam materials in.

For the dam itself, I needed mortar that would cure in the sea. Gilbert Cox, managing director and concrete chemist at Rockbond Special Concretes in Essex, had in the past supplied more than 4,000 tons of underwater and tunnelling materials for the Channel Tunnel. I told him my dam was four feet long and three feet tall and he thought I could use Rockbond Underwater Mortar. 'Maybe 0.3 tons,' he said. The mortar had been used to seal and waterproof the walls of the restaurant under the House of Lords. All importantly, it would not contaminate the sea, contained no poisons and was safe.

Flap-valve and mortar in 25 kg bags soon arrived by courier and I took them across the bay by boat. The dam building began, hard, long and dirty, no machinery, using the rocks from around the pool and plenty of the mortar mixed, bag by bag, in a bucket. The rain never stopped but it was a kind of happiness, not unlike bread-making: stirring the mortar and seawater to a putty-like consistency, oozy and caky under my gloved hands; picking up and dumping hummus-like patties of it on to the limestone; rubbing it in, as Gilbert had said, to make a good bond with the surroundings; settling the rocks into its soft and yielding

The second pool dam completed.

cushions; watching the mortar easing from underneath them in rounded grey Buddha bellies, or like one of those squeezes of stone, the *torus*, at the foot of classical columns.

It took three days between the tides. I embedded the flap-valve in the concrete sludge and built a channel for the water to enter. Then a roof for the channel with a big slab on which I could stand.

I chose some final rocks for the dam that had channel wrack and spiral wrack growing on them. And then it was done. I took the boat and all my tools and the empty mortar bags the mile or so back to the head of the bay where I hauled everything ashore, left it at the top of the beach, dropped into the house and fell asleep in front of the fire for nine hours straight.

The ebb was to begin the next morning after ten. It was early summer and the bay was more beautiful than I had ever known it. The light was bouncing up into the wood off the sea. In a place which is so often grey and wet, mornings like this overbrim with colour. Even a distant sail, tipped like a feather on the Firth of Lorne, looked washed and perfect. The trees were like lettuces, every leaf with the light in it.

I had been reading some of Iris Murdoch's early philosophy. 'One might start from the assertion that goodness is a form of realism,' she wrote, and repeated what Rilke had said of Cézanne: he did not paint 'I like it'; he painted 'There it is.'

Murdoch's governing idea was to look to the real on a day like this, to fuse Rilke's categories. I like it here in the wood above the sea because it is here. It is here and so I like it. In her 1970 masterpiece, *The Sovereignty of Good*, she wrote of these 'occasions of unselfing':

I am looking out of my window in an anxious and resentful state of mind, oblivious of my surroundings, brooding perhaps on some damage done to my prestige. Then suddenly I observe a hovering kestrel. In a moment

Iris Murdoch (1919–1999).

everything is altered. The brooding self with its hurt vanity has disappeared. There is nothing now but kestrel. And when I return to thinking of the other matter it seems less important. And of course this is something which we may also do deliberately: give attention to nature in order to clear our minds of selfish care.

It is not that nature itself is valuable. There is no more value in it than there is in us. But the opportunity it provides to amend our consciousness, to remove the unending claims of the self, to deny the primacy of the self as anything more than a ripple in the general flux of the world, is a moment of education in what she called the 'intolerably chancy and incomplete' nature of being. 'We take a self-forgetful pleasure in the sheer alien pointless independent existence of animals, birds, stones and trees,' she wrote, and then repeated, without attribution, her version of Wittgenstein's great saying: 'Not *how* the world is, but *that* it is, is the mystical.'

> The self, the place where we live, is a place of illusion. Goodness is connected with the attempt to see the unself, to see and to respond to the real world in the light of a virtuous consciousness. This is the non-metaphysical meaning of the idea of transcendence ... Virtue is the attempt to pierce the veil of selfish consciousness and join the world as it really is.

Diminish the self; feel the reality of things; accept the facts of mutability, including the fact of death; allow the other a valid and vivid place in your mind; do not think of the self as a dam against the flux, but allow the flux to flood through you; see beauty in the realities of the world, the quivering of the kestrel, the blurring of the tide; and in the wake of that, a kind of happiness, the happiness that comes not from absence or self-abnegation, but from openness, from seeing existence as a pool into which the sea can come and go, has a chance of flooding in. 'Love,' Iris Murdoch once said, in the tenderest, gentlest and most honest sentence she ever wrote, 'is the extremely difficult realisation that something other than oneself is real.'

I was down at Rubha an t-Sasunnaich as the tide was starting to pull away. I could see the dam I had made still a foot under-water, its rocks liquid and out of focus with the movement of the sea over them. The flap-valve was opening and closing as the pressure of each new wave pushed at it and withdrew. Half an hour to wait, watching for the leaving of the tide. A gannet was fishing in the bay, in from St Kilda, down the Sound to the castle and back up again, cruising half a mile a minute, beating to windward, then, seeing something, turning and sweeping down, before climbing again. Then its dive, which it began and partway through pulled out, the fish gone, a dive *interruptus*, now only the glitter of the sea beneath it, as it flew off away to the west, joined by another, both searching, nothing perfect.

It was 10.26 in the morning and the bay was turning stony as the ebb pulled eastwards. The ochre-orange of the wrack started to coat the fringes of the shore. Above it, a band of the black verrucana lichen, which tolerates salt spray but not regular immersion; above that, the white of the limestone speckled with the green-and-pink buttons of thrift; and above that, among the grasses and the eggs-and-bacon vetch, the pink wind-torn petals of ragged robin. It is a world of layered niches in which the vertical gradations are fine, these changes occurring in steps above the sea no more than nine or ten inches high.

10.42: the tide drops and the water is now only three inches above the top of the dam.

10.46: as the flow steepens, the sea rolls out over the dam in a smooth shampoo curl across its upper rocks, the whole structure under it bellying and shifting in the lens of the ebb.

10.48: one of the rocks in the dam comes out of the water for the first time.

10.54: the broken surface of the sea means that its level changes with every wave and I cannot judge if the dam is holding.

10.57: at last, and still only intermittently, the calm of the pool starts to grow like the closing of an eye. Outside all is chop and motion; inside, momentarily, stability, the still-stand. The pressure difference between the two is now holding the flap-valve shut tight.

11.01: the sea has dropped away and the pool lies in its cup of rock, clear and perfect. The wind makes a slight ripple across its surface. The dam is holding.

The enclosure felt huge. I could look down into it from the little cliff on the south side as if into a giant aquarium, about 2,500 litres of sea held in there, two and a half tons of water. Some of the creatures that had previously been surviving in the

The dam is working and the second pool appears at
Rubha an t-Sasunnaich.

small puddle in the centre now found themselves at home in the
deepest part of the pool. My friend Tom Hammick came for a
day or two and with long steels we manoeuvred rocks into those
deeps to make shade and shelter for the animals.

When I put my head in, or dipped an underwater camera in
there, I met a parkland of beauty, a sudden access to 'the world
as it really is'. Beadlet anemones, some of them bright new-blood-
red when seen against the wavering sunlight, others auburn and
copper, the colour of my daughter Molly's hair, all in the pale
filter of the clean water, with winkles and prawns around them,
a common goby and a narrow, elegant fish, half hidden inside a
sprig of weed, hanging there, two and a half inches long, a sharp
snout, the tail unseen, a gilded eye, with grey mottled top and
pale yellowish underside, not making a move: a fifteen-spine
stickleback, waiting in the way that predators wait.

I watched a tall green parasol-ribbed limpet making its slow
way across one of the boulders that Tom and I had put in there,
dragging its track through the biofilm and leaving in its wake a
dark line of the cleaned-down basalt, the mark of a steady and

A 15-spine stickleback, in the second pool.

purposeful morning, in which it had gardened its rock, farmed its country, and understood its world, mowing the meadow in the laborious, careful way of those who are attached to their places.

I soon saw that this was to be a crab pool, their own little theatre in which the dramas of crab life could be played out. There are many different sorts of crab in the bay and in creels I have caught them all: the pie-crusted lid of the edible or brown crab; the pink of the swimmers; the dark, furred mystery of the velvets. Those are largely found away from the shore but here, this pool was now to be the stalking ground and manor of the green shore crab, *Carcinus maenas*, whose Latin name sounds as if it describes its maleficence but signifies only that it likes to eat a little fish, a *maena*, now and then. The French call it *le crab enragé*, from its habit of approaching in fury with open claws held aloft.

I put a small crab trap in there, baited with bacon. Within a few minutes, a green crab was manoeuvring towards it, from about four yards away, the smell communicated through the water. It was big, about three inches across, and walked directly towards the trap and then up over its netting, soon finding the inward-reaching, cone-shaped mouth that led towards the bacon. The crab paused there for a good minute, as if questioning the

100

Limpets crawl through the biofilm thickening in the second pool.

idea of entering this strange, food-rich, unaccustomed place. Was it a trap?

The smell of bacon must have overcome the wariness and it pushed further in. Six minutes after I had first seen it moving, the crab had fallen down into the trap's belly where it would get to the bacon but from which there was no escape. As it started to touch and hold the bait, two other crabs could be seen approaching from the far side of the pool. The first went past the entrance and in under the trap to the point where it was next to the crab that was already in there. The two of them began to

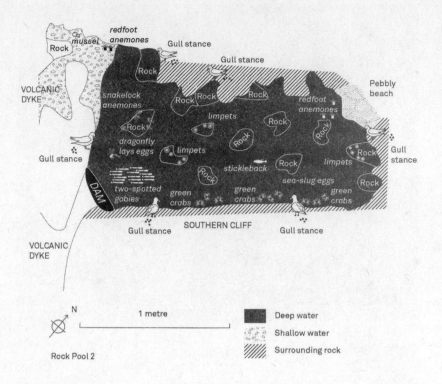

The second pool and its inhabitants. Deep water is in grey, the dam black,
shallow water speckled and surrounding rocks in diagonal hatching.

grapple with each other through the net, one with access to the
food but trapped, the other with no bacon but free.

The third, a little pale green one, bundled itself fast across
the floor of the pool, climbing and semi-buoyant, with slightly
less than neutral buoyancy, looking as if it had about as much
gravity in water as an astronaut on the moon. Without pause,
a fool rushing in, it flipped down into the trap already occupied
by its bigger rival, which now looked suddenly enormous.
Perceiving the entrance of the small pale crab, the older one
neglected its rival outside and turned towards the newcomer.
Young crabs are all green but old ones, or at least crabs which
have not moulted for a long time, are flushed red, particularly

A green crab lurks under the southern cliff of the second pool.

in the joints of their legs and claws. This beautiful old thing had a grey-green carapace, black at the front and with pale, almost moth-like patterning on its lid, white constellations of dots fanned out like the eyes on a peacock tail. Carefully it stirred its bronzy legs, each joint glowing orange like a set of eyes, and greeted the intruder.

The drama lasted a few minutes. The little crab retreated to a corner and held its pitiable pale, lime-green claws up towards the enemy. For a moment the big crab picked up the little one in a claw and walked back sideways with it, crabwise, down into the depths of the trap, past the bacon, to a point at the far end where the little crab was held there in its attacker's pincers, delicately as if it were a teacup in a pair of fingers and thumbs, while the young crab's legs flicked and stirred at its undoing.

I waded in and collected the trap, released both big and little big crab and watched the third walk away quickly past the ochre anemones, heading for the shade of the south wall and a protective stand of bladderwrack.

It does not take much to see that these animals are brutally successful: efficient and voracious, eating worms, other crustaceans, including their own conspecifics, and many molluscs. They will dominate and transform any coast they find. As aggressive opportunistic predators, with the ability to tolerate wide extremes of heat, salinity and even drought, they have been carried inadvertently in the holds of ships across much of the world, and are now a destructive and alien threat in Japan, Australia and Tasmania, South Africa, Argentina and both coasts of North America, from Newfoundland to Virginia and California to British Columbia. Their only enemy is warm water and although they have often been found there they have yet to colonise the tropics.

There is something in us which dislikes the successful and prefers the rare and endangered, but you have to admire the chutzpah of the green crab. In October 1991, Dr J. P. O'Connor of the National Museum of Ireland was telephoned by Dublin's environmental health inspectors to be told that some 'crab-like creatures were infesting a domestic premises in Dublin City'. The owner of the house, an elderly lady, had complained to the Health Board that something wicked was emerging from the drains and besieging her.

They had crawled about on the floors of the kitchen and the living room. She was frightened and had killed one of them with a telephone book. The same creatures had entered the house on two previous occasions but the lady had been too ashamed to report these incidents to the Health Board.

Inspectors arrived and found dead green crabs outside the house, on the pavements of Manor Street, more than two miles from Dublin Bay and about 800 yards uphill from the River Liffey where it flows through the city. Dr O'Connor was then informed of another green crab that had been lost somewhere in

Crab Distribution

Green shore crabs have thrived in temperate waters (black lines) but
failed to colonise warm water harbours where shipping has transported
them (black dots with dates of arrival).

the city, only to be rediscovered forty-two days later in a damp
garage. 'When found,' Dr O'Connor reported, 'the crab (a fully
grown male) was dusty and thrust out its claws aggressively. It
recovered fully from its experience and was returned to the sea.'

The adventurousness and adaptability of *Carcinus maenas* may
explain its world-straddling success, but it is far from cavalier.
These crabs approach life with impressive displays of delicacy and
discrimination, clearly recognising that only by looking after
themselves will they survive. One might imagine that the most
economic of crab strategies is to find the biggest mussels and
crack them open for food. That is largely the human approach to
eating other animals but it turns out that in common with other
shell-focused predators – such as oystercatchers, which usually
choose to open the smaller-than-average cockles, wanting to
protect their bills from harm – that is not the case. Nature is not
red in tooth and claw, but a constant and careful evaluation of
the risk-reward ratios in every transaction. The greedy die young;
accountants get rich.

The two claws of green crabs are of different sizes, the bigger one a crusher, the smaller a cutter. Usually, when presented with a small or average-sized mussel, the minor claw steadies the shell while the crusher does the work. With bigger mussels, whose bodies present the prospect of a large amount of meat, but whose shells are too strong to crush, the crab changes tactic and uses the smaller claw to snip along the leading edges of the mussel, where the two halves of its shell meet, and get access that way. There seems to be a universal rule of thumb which shore crabs follow: if the width of the mussel is more than a quarter the length of the crab's crushing claw, the crab will be forced to cut its edges rather than crush the whole animal.

But cutting is not popular. The Dutch biologists Isabel M. Smallegange and Jaap Van Der Meer investigated the eating habits of green crabs on the western coast of Texel, at the southern end of the Frisian Islands in the North Sea, and found, first, that the crabs much preferred crunching to snipping, probably because it was quicker; and, secondly, that the mussels they decided to crunch were always well below the horizon at which crushing would not work. 'It would seem,' Smallegange and Van Der Meer wrote, 'that crabs prefer to crush in the safe zone, to prevent damage and wear to the claws.'

Instinctive calculation, a capacity to measure, a sense of proportion, in the relationship of mussel width to claw length, and the understanding that life needs to continue beyond the attractions of the immediate moment: all of this is in the mind of *Carcinus maenas*.

After a few days, entranced by the life in the new pool, looking into all its corners, finding the refuges of the crabs, the gatherings of anemones, I came across a huge and beautiful mussel which had clearly lived a long time in the edge of the pool, perhaps in one of the minor folds in the rock which had held some water before I had made my dam. It was well settled in, too defended and too much of a prospect for any crab to nail. It sat handsomely in its tight corner, near an anemone, encrusted and ancient, rimmed in coralline and with a leaf of channel wrack on its shell, the bivalves just open, showing its inner body, like lips just apart, filtering the water for microscopic food, living a rich old Miss Havisham life which no crab could disturb. It was the only mussel I could find in the pool. There was a total absence of smaller mussels around it. I could only guess at its age; mussels stop growing when they are about six years old but individuals can survive until they are about twelve, as I am sure this one had; but it was clear that if this old mussel-matriarch was producing offspring, the crabs must have been dealing with them one by one as soon as they came to life.

This reduction in mussel abundance was the product of an arms race. The toughening and enlarging of the mussel was up against the toughening and enlarging of the crabs that were out to kill and eat it. As with the winkles, the only way of winning the race was to escape predation until you were too big to kill, or at least so big that killing you would cost too much in time, risk and effort.

At the same time a full-on arms race is also underway within the population of the crabs themselves. Claws are the necessary instruments not only for eating but for establishing a crab's place in its world. Meet a green crab with your fingers and it will fling both claws out above it and to each side, holding them high above its face with pincers apart, as much like a stag and its antlers as any marine creature. It becomes in an instant *le crab enragé*.

Male crabs fight hard over access to females and at those moments, a big pair of claws is a better predictor of breeding success than a big body. But there are subtleties here. When a claw is damaged, the crab has the ability to sever it from its own body, a form of self-amputation known as autotomy, after which a new claw grows in its place, if only slowly and over the subsequent one or two moults. When the crab is old, it loses completely the capacity to replace the missing limb.

The Norwegian ecologist Gro Sekkelsten investigated the effect of missing claws on the mating success of green crabs, with an intriguing result. Among small young males, those with a missing claw were no less successful in mating than those with both claws, not because missing a claw did not matter but because small young crabs had little success in mating, clawed or not. The handicap did not materially affect the outcome. Little male crabs do not on the whole win in the battle for mates.

In medium-sized males, the negative effects of clawlessness were obvious. Properly clawed-up males found mates and were able to breed with them. Males with only one claw or none were left mateless. There was a third stage, when among the largest, oldest males – it is impossible to age a crab, but they also might live until they are nine or ten – the negative effect of losing a claw was again small, but for a reason opposite to the failures of the smallest crabs. Big males, two-clawed or not, were just as able, literally, to grab and hold a female as normal males. Once females were in their possession, the big males were able to mate with them. Age and strength, even if you carry the scars of ancient battles, are the route to sexual success in the world of the green crab.

In the pool on Rubha an t-Sasunnaich, looking in there one summer morning, when the air over the Sound and the water in the pool were of equal stillness and clarity, Sarah saw just beneath the little southern cliff a big green crab holding a smaller one in its arms. We had never seen such a thing before. It looked like a heraldic emblem, an escutcheon demonstrating the facts of dominance, but this was not another killing. It was the very opposite, the protection by a big male of a pre-moulting female in preparation for crab sex.

The whole phenomenon is dependent on the life choice represented by a shell. The crustacea have found armour as their principal means of defence. But armour makes sex difficult if not impossible and female crabs are receptive to the male only after they have moulted their old shell and for the day or two until it

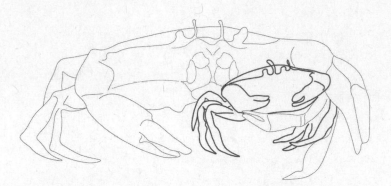

The (paler) male gathers up the (darker) female in a 'pre-copulatory embrace' while waiting for her to moult.

hardens again. They must be soft to have sex. In the crab-eat-crab world of the pool, that moment of procreation is filled with danger and so the male gathers her up, even before she has moulted, into what is called 'a pre-copulatory embrace'. That is what, entrancingly, we had seen in the pool: big male with smaller female held in his arms, protecting her from other crabs that might have wanted to eat her in her softness, while also guaranteeing that he was the sole male parent of the brood she would bear.

The timetable is not rushed. In aquarium experiments, there was a lag of up to twenty days between the first introduction of male and female crab and the male scooping her into his arms. She sends out pheromone signals to him in her urine, suggesting this might be a good idea, and in some experiments, she walks towards the male and touches him with one of her claws, repeating the gesture many times. Some biologists have seen, very occasionally, at this tender moment, the male crab eating the outstretched claw of the female, to which she responded by continuing to stroke and touch him with her other, single remaining claw. It was thought, maybe, by the Floridian scientist who observed this horror, that the male crab was

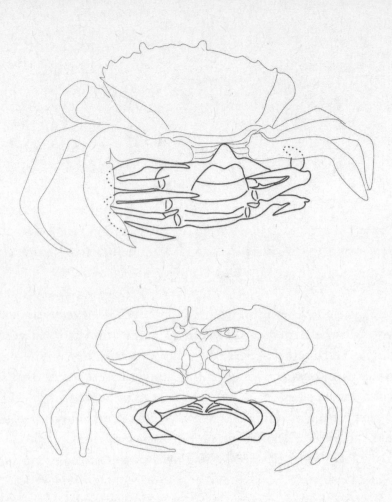

At copulation, the female moves beneath the male and each opens their
ventral flap to accommodate the other.

immature and did not understand the offer the female was
making to him.

Such a catastrophic outcome is not usual, though, and once
she is in position, he carries her around, holding her with one of
his walking legs against the underside of his abdomen, the female
cooperating by not resisting and by keeping her walking legs and
claws at least partly folded. They are both the same way up, her
back pressing against his abdomen.

This holding-while-walking can go on for more than two weeks, but usually lasts less than half that. He is perfectly able at this point to fight off other males who come too close.

Finally she moults underneath him and copulation begins soon afterwards, him helping to turn her carefully over so that they meet abdomen to abdomen, folding out the abdominal underflaps so that he can 'insert his copulatory stylets into the female's paired vulvae', while she hangs on to him with the tips of her legs for two or three days until copulation is over. Afterwards, she turns the right way up again and they embrace, staying like that for two or three further days before separating and moving off to their different places in the pool.

Is this not unlike anything you might have imagined for a crab? The patience and delicacy of it, the reality of communication between the sexes, the sense of choice that is implicit in every one of their steady and careful moves?

I knew from a later study by Gro Sekkelsten that green crabs were deliberate and careful shapers of their submarine world. Once a week over two summers, on the rough and stony beaches of the island of Herdla, about twenty miles north of Bergen, she snorkelled across an area of nearly four acres, just offshore, looking to see how the green crabs were behaving. In a small part of that area, she found that the crabs had established 'a mating ground', which she visited every day, following their lives by marking them with wax crayons and by (painlessly) branding numbers on to the carapaces with a soldering iron.

This mating ground was, objectively, nothing special, with no particular resources nor any protection against bird or fish predators. But it did occupy a striking geographical position, at the tip of a small headland in the very centre of a bay, between that headland and an offlying skerry. It was not unlike the places where the chieftains of medieval Argyll chose to locate their castles and display halls, crowning spots which could be recognised as hinge-locations in that part of the sea.

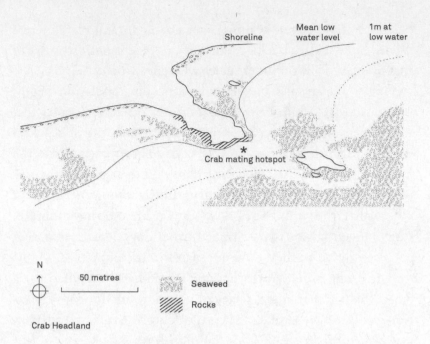

The crab mating ground at Herdla, Norway.

A site of male prominence, dominance, violence and theatrical display is exactly what Gro Sekkelsten discovered in the green crabs' mating ground. It became what she called a 'hotspot'. The big, old powerful male crabs gathered there and females knew that was where they could find them.

As a crab shell ages between each moult, it moves over from green to yellowish, orange and finally red, not equally over the whole surface of the shell but in a beautiful mottling, as if each stage in a crab's life had within it a spring, summer and autumn, finally reddening like a maple leaf before the shell is cast. When young, they can moult several times a year, the body enlarging by something like 20% each time; as they age, the rhythm slows, and by the time they are six or seven, they have ceased to moult at all and have settled on growing old in their skins, putting more energy into reproductive strength than the growth of their own body. These old breeder males are the endpoint of that process:

bigger, redder, more aggressive, with a larger 'master claw' and a thicker carapace than all the others. They are also, in the way of grand old autarchs, rather touchy and set in their ways, less able to tolerate changes in temperature, salinity and oxygen content in the seawater than their younger, slighter and greener rivals.

Female crabs were not usually found in the hotspot, but were discretely dispersed around the coast. They came to the mating ground only when they were ready, visiting it to seek out one of the big old males. The competition between those old males was violent and ferocious, a life-struggle to get hold of the visiting, sex-ready females. Young, agile little males had no chance of fighting their way in there. The group of dominant old reds monopolised the visitors, choosing mates freely, 'taking over a female from subordinate males without much cost' as Dr Sekkelsten observed and fertilising them one after another as they arrived at the tip of the peninsula. 'Sequential polygyny' was the prerogative of a dominant male and the group of them dictated conditions in the hotspot, each remaining in his particular zone within the patch.

What is a young male crab to do? They can achieve little reproductive success by competing for mates in the same way as those reds. And so should they not compete at all and invest instead in growth, rather than in endless failed attempts at reproduction? Did they have to wait and, as Gro Sekkelsten expressed it, 'run the risk of not living long enough to reach dominant size'? Even when death was ever-present and postponing sex might mean never having sex at all?

Those questions are real for young male green crabs and they have an answer: don't confront the big old tyrants but sneak in where you can. All around the peninsula on Herdla, Sekkesten observed a positively Shakespearean set of dramas unfolding. The old despots found the softening, pheromone-broadcasting females coming up to them in their hotspot territories as if it were their due. The female crabs were choosing to come not to the big crabs themselves but to the mating ground where fierce competition guaranteed that only the strongest could survive there. It was a way of using geography to ensure high-quality progeny.

If a small male tried to grab one of the females in the hotspot, he would always have her snatched away from him by an old male. Nevertheless, in the suburbs of that mating ground, small, young males would roam or even wait in hiding, hoping to ambush the pre-moulting females making their way to the big crabs at the tip of the peninsula. Unseen by the big reds, the young Turks could occasionally get away with it. The anxiety can only have been enormous and once they had collared their pre-moult female, the young crabs made sure to take them somewhere safe. 'All small crabs were found mating in places almost inaccessible for the largest males and distant from the mating ground,' where whatever gratification a crab can have was had not in power-driven, establishment copulation but in secret, no-doubt fear-filled trysts hidden among the rocks.

I am not sure yet, because it is early days and these geographical patterns may take time to develop, but I hope that the pool on Rubha an t-Sasunnaich might become one such hotspot. Certainly, at least one big green-going-on-yellow-orange-and-red crab had taken up position there and a pre-breeding female had found him and offered herself to be gathered up in the protective hold of his pre-copulatory embrace, from which future generations will no doubt emerge.

In the late eighteenth century, as the imperial enterprise of the European states spread out across the world oceans, the scientists accompanying the naval expeditions started to examine the creatures of the deep. As John Vaughan Thompson, the great hidden hero of these studies, wrote in 1828, strange and unknown creatures had been found.

The bay in high summer, with the castle on the point and the Sound of Mull beyond.

On the path to the castle in springtime.

A midwinter sunrise.

With the dried seaweed lifted away, the sandhoppers that had been sheltering there are revealed in midsummer as desiccated, pink and dead.

Pool 1, dug in among the basalts and the layered sandstones of the Jurassic.

The 15-spine or sea stickleback.

A common prawn in Pool 1 at night.

The common prawn *Palaemon elegans*.

The newly made Pool 2, held in by its dam, with the Sound, the bay and the castle on its headland beyond.

In Pool 2, snakelocks anemones occupy a newly submerged basalt boulder.

Beadlet anemones, limpets, barnacles and various tube worms colonise a boulder.

A beautiful bronze morph of the beadlet anemone, *Actinia equina*, in Pool 2, the pale blue beadlets just visible at the edge of its tentacles.

A big old green crab, *Carcinus maenas*, at the foot of the southern cliff in Pool 2.

A hermit crab.

Professor Slabber in a Dutch Work entitled *Natural Amusements and Microscopical Observations* published at Harlem in 1778, has given us a description and figure of the species which has been since designated *Zoea taurus*.

Bosc, one of the most judicious naturalists of the French school, in a voyage which he undertook to America with a view to Natural History, discovered a single individual in the Atlantic Ocean, 5 or 600 leagues from the coast of France; and justly conceiving it distinct from all the other Genera ... first instituted that of *Zoea* for the reception of these anomalous animals.

Mr Cranch, in the course of Captain Tuckey's Voyage to the Congo, discovered the curious and singular species which Dr Leach has named *Z. clavata*, from the club-like shape of its dorsal and lateral spines.

These zoeae – meaning 'living things' – by which Slabber, Bosc, Cranch and Leach were so intrigued, were a class of animal which would not receive their collective name until almost a century later: the plankton, meaning 'the floaters' or 'wanderers', those creatures which did not seem to move with any direction given by themselves.

Thompson himself had been born to an English family in New York in 1779, but the family soon removed to England after the loss of the American colonies and Thompson was educated as a doctor in Edinburgh. He became an army surgeon, in the Caribbean and Mauritius, and in his spare time made careful studies of plants and birds.

In 1816, he returned on half-pay from Mauritius to Cork, the port-city on the south coast of Ireland. On the long voyage, 'the luminosity or sparkling of the sea by night' entranced him. The sea was full of those glittering presences and his focus turned to 'the more minute and invisible inmates of the sea'. Wherever he was, Thompson would always 'throw out a-stern a small towing

net of gause, bunting, or other tolerably close material, occasionally drawing it up, and turning it inside out into a glass vessel of
seawater, to ascertain what captures have been made'. It was a
plankton net and Thompson is the first person known to have
used one regularly.

This 'towing for luminous animals' had discovered strange
beings. They seemed to be related to shrimps, prawns and crayfish but as Thompson wrote, it was 'no matter of surprise, that
all the leading Naturalists of the present day, should have been at
a loss, how to dispose of *Zoea* in their arrangements of the
Crustacea'.

The breakthrough came in 1822. Thompson, now married to
his Irish wife Martha and with the first of their six children born,
'to his great surprise' found '*Zoeas* in the harbour of Cove, and
that in considerable abundance'. The following year, when he
threw out

> a small muslin towing net on crossing the Ferry at Passage,
> such a capture of minute animals was made as furnished a
> treat which few can ever expect to meet, and could hardly be
> excelled for the variety, rarity, and interesting nature of the
> animals taken. Some of them never before met with but in
> the great Ocean … others previously seen by a solitary
> observer … and almost lost sight of by Naturalists and
> excluded from their works.

Among them was a particularly large zoea and Thompson
managed to keep it alive in a jar of constantly refreshed seawater
from 14 May until 15 June,

> when it died in the act of changing its skin, and of passing
> into a new form, but one by no means similar to that
> expected, as appears evidently by its disengaged members
> which are changed in number, as well as in form, and now,

correspond with those of the Decapoda, (Crabs, &c.) viz. five pair, the anterior of them furnished with a large claw or pincer.

No one until that moment in Thompson's study in Cork had imagined that a crustacean could undergo metamorphosis. Insects were known to go through various distinct stages of grub and pupa before emergence as an adult, but it was the accepted wisdom that the lack of metamorphosis was what distinguished crustaceans from the insects.

Four years later, the final link was made. In the waters of the Cove, Thompson had caught an edible crab that was 'berried', or thick with clustered eggs, stored on its abdomen. He removed some of the eggs and kept them in an ever-refreshed jar of seawater. One or two of them soon hatched and 'presented exactly the appearance of *Zoea taurus*', the 'bull-horned life-thing' found and named fifty years before by Professor Slabber. Thompson was justifiably excited at what he had seen: 'the *Crustacea Decapoda* then, indisputably *undergo a metamorphosis*, a fact, which will form an epoch in the history of this generally neglected tribe, and tend to create an interest which may operate favorably in directing more of the attention of Naturalists towards them'.

He had found that crustaceans undergo metamorphosis; that the distinction between the Crustacea and the Insecta was invalid; and the strange presence of zoeae in the ocean had been explained. A year later in 1828, he published a paper announcing his discoveries with the appropriate punctuation: 'On the Metamorphoses of the Crustacea, and on *Zoea*, exposing their singular structure and demonstrating that they are not, as has been supposed, a peculiar Genus, but the Larva of Crustacea!!'

No one believed him. The biological establishment in Britain and Europe poo-pooed the revelations from Cork. The *Zoological Journal* cast aspersions on his methods. In 1835 J. O. Westwood, secretary of the London Entomological Society, published a

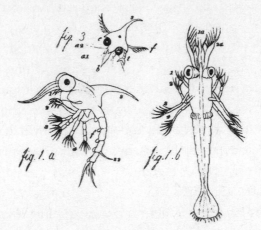

J. V. Thompson's drawings in his *Zoological Researches* of the zoea (left) and megalops (right) of the crabs he collected in the harbour at Cork in the 1820s.

paper in the journal of the Royal Society 'On the supposed existence of Metamorphoses in the Crustacea' which rubbished Thompson's discoveries – 'It is the received opinion among naturalists that the Crustacea do not undergo metamorphoses, properly so called, and that the transformations they exhibit consist merely in the periodical shedding of the outer envelope' – and hinted, obliquely, at fraud, referring to Thompson's '"supposed" *Zoeae* and "supposed" metamorphoses'. French and German biologists, including the great Prussian Heinrich Rathke, thought crustacean metamorphosis impossible. Rathke had witnessed young crayfish that had emerged from the egg microscopically small but indistinguishable in form from the adults. If crayfish were born as recognisable, why not crabs?

It was a brutal and painful exclusion, inescapably reminiscent of the big-clawed reds in their hotspot and the little greens dancing hopefully around the edges. Thompson was right and the grandees wrong but he was poor, publishing privately in Cork and they rich, with all the resources and influence behind them of the great scientific institutions in London, Berlin and Paris.

Nevertheless, heroically, he persisted. On 1 May 1826, he collected in his net 'a small translucent animal one-tenth of an inch long, of a somewhat eliptic form. When in a state of perfect repose it resembles a very minute mussel and lies upon one of its sides at the bottom of the vessel of seawater in which it is placed; at this time all the members of the animal are withdrawn within the shell.'

Thompson had no idea what this creature was but as an experimental scientist, with his discoveries in mind of metamorphosis in the crabs, he was prepared to watch. He put these tiny, withdrawn ellipses 'in a glass vessel covered by such a depth of seawater that they could be examined at any time by means of a common magnifying glass'. At night a week later, 'the author had the satisfaction to find that two of them had thrown off their exuvia, and wonderful to say, were firmly adhering to the bottom of the vessel and changed into young Barnacles such as are usually seen intermixed with grown specimens on rocks and stones at this season of the year'.

As the larval, swimming form of the barnacle metamorphosed into its fixed and sessile state, it lost its eyes and began to build around it the calcareous plates that would protect it for the rest of its life. Thompson had made a second discovery as amazing as the realisation that the zoeae were young crabs. Until then, everyone had assumed that barnacles were relatives of limpets. Thompson had seen they were closer to prawns. 'Thus then an animal originally natatory and locomotive, and provided with a distinct organ of sight, becomes permanently and immoveably fixed, and its optic apparatus obliterated and furnishes not only a new and important physiological fact, but is the only instance in nature of so extraordinary a metamorphosis.'

The zoological establishment was again slow to accept his findings. Not until the 1850s was Thompson's genius recognised, when Charles Darwin, by then the king of barnacle studies, called Vaughan Thompson's work a 'capital discovery'. Rathke, Westwood and the others all came round in the end but too late for Thompson to feel celebrated or even vindicated.

Martha Thompson had died in 1832 and, dismayed at the reception of his discoveries, her husband was left alone with six young children and shrinking funds. He wrote to the treasurer of the Linnean Society in London, describing

the pecuniary loss sustained by the publication of my Zoological Researches & the great expense incurred by the prosecution of those discoveries, by being obliged to keep up an establishment on the sea-side during a great part of the period, & the disbursements consequent on Boat hire travelling back & forward.

It could not continue, and in June 1835, he took a desperate new position in Australia as chief medical officer to the army and to the convicts in New South Wales, as bleak an occupation as could then be imagined. A portrait was made of him, wearing the handsome and epauletted uniform of the army medical man, but in whose eyes and pursed mouth it is just possible to detect the sensitive, clever, bruised figure he had become.

Communicating with the scientific community in Europe was not easy. Isolated and disappointed, Thompson died at home in Sydney in 1847, aged sixty-seven. This great and pitiable man was buried in the city two days later but when in 1901 Sydney Central Railway Station needed an extension, Thompson's grave and its stone were both destroyed.

There is something unworldly about the mathematics of marine generation. Female green crabs can breed two or three times a year, carefully keeping the male spermatophores in copulatory pouches, where the sperm remains viable for four or five months,

J. V. Thompson painted by M. D. Roux in London on the eve
of his departure for Australia, wearing the military uniform of
a chief medical officer.

until the time has come to fertilise the eggs. Each time, they will
carry up to 185,000 of them. If they breed for five years, each
female crab will produce almost 3 million fertilised offspring.
They are not like us; but they are scarcely in the race when it
comes to other sea organisms. A single oyster can broadcast
between 15–115 million young into the seas around it. Starfish
pump out 200 million spermatozoa each breeding season. And
the predators are waiting: every day a large mussel can filter-feed
on up to 100,000 larvae of various creatures.

So many progeny, so few survivors, in a ratio of making to
living that seems almost mad, not like the fine-tuning of natural
selection but a blanketing of the sea space, proposing almost
infinite numbers of candidates for life, for each of which the

121

chances of individual survival are within one or two microns of zero.

And yet the fine-tuning is there. Unknown to Thompson, and not fully realised until the 1990s, the early life of a green crab is meticulously fitted to its world. First, while the eggs remain attached to the female, the embryos within, waiting until they have grown to a point where they can survive independently, become 'entrained' – both habituated to and familiar with – the comings and goings of the tide. Perhaps through changes in water pressure that rises at high tide and drops with the ebb, a tidal consciousness is embedded in them by which they will govern much of the rest of their lives. 'These tidal clocks are set in phase with local tides before zoeae are released.' Microscopic animals learn to grasp the essential pattern of their world.

The mother is equally aware and, controlling release of the eggs, she ensures that the newly hatched zoeae emerge into the water at the very moment of a night-time high tide, the dark still-stand when the ebb will begin to flow and draw the tens of thousands of young vulnerable creatures away from the shore and out into the deeper sea. Crab larvae have been found in one of these early planktonic phases thirty miles or more out from the coast, protected by the scale and volume of the sea, which is not a salt desert but a giant refuge, where tiny vulnerable beings can hide in its immensity.

They do not get there by chance. In the summer of 1994, the Chinese crustacean zoologist Chaoshu Zeng was researching his doctorate at the School of Ocean Sciences in North Wales. He collected the zoeae of *Carcinus maenas* with a plankton net in a series of slow, 2.5 knot tows behind a small boat in a sheltered bay at the mouth of the Menai Strait.

Looking after them as carefully as he could, he put them into a set of little perspex aquariums, each tank fifteen inches high, six wide and two inches from front to back. They were made that narrow to isolate a particular form of behaviour and fitted with two infrared beams, one at the bottom and one at the top. Zeng filled them with seawater and populated them with the zoeae. A computer recorded every time a zoea crossed a beam.

This beautiful experiment, for which the Zoological Society of London gave Dr Zeng their Thomas Henry Huxley Award for original contributions to zoology, revealed something that had never been shown before: the crab larvae swam up and down the tank at completely predictable intervals of twelve hours and twenty-five minutes. These vertical journeys were timed so that the larvae were at the top just after high tide and at the bottom just after low tide. The larvae, in other words, swam up into the ebb tide so that they would be carried out to sea, and down below the levels at which there was any appreciable tidal flow when the tide set the other way and would have carried them in towards the shore.

This 'endogenously controlled tidal vertical migration' means that the young crabs 'are preferentially transported seaward'. They use the tide to go out to sea in order to grow in safety.

The larvae are released into an independent existence at early stage of development and do not yet have all the body segments and appendages an adult crustacean needs for life on the shore. During their life out at sea, they gradually and successively add new body parts and limbs until the required number is reached.

As it makes its way towards adulthood, the young crab goes through four of these zoeal stages, each lasting up to a week, until in the end, in its final larval transformation, it turns into what has clearly become a proto-crab, still only an eighth or a quarter of an inch long but without the defensive spike on its back and now called a megalops, meaning 'big eye', as it has acquired proportionately enormous eyes alongside a full complement of legs, claws, maxillipeds, antennae and tail.

Here Dr Zeng made his second great and connected discovery. He had revealed how the young zoeae escape offshore. How did megalops return to begin the shore-based life of the green crabs you can find under any stone on nearly any beach in Europe and, increasingly, the temperate world?

Zeng trawled for the megalopses and found them crowding in towards the shore at night, towards the end of the flood tide and within a day or two of their final metamorphosis. They had clearly swum up into a flood tide which had brought them inshore. But the situation was complicated. The zoeae had simply used the ebb tide as a conveyor belt to take them away from the land. The megalopses, when they were in the laboratory aquariums, swam to the surface at times that coincided with *both* the ebb and the flood. Why was that? If they needed to use the flood tide to come ashore, why not stay down at the bottom during the ebb?

Zeng's answer implied a subtle net of ideas in the mind of the young animals. They would have sensed they were within a few days of metamorphosing into a true crab. Every one he caught was approaching that change. They would know that, 'notwithstanding the advantages of flood-tide swimming in bringing [them] inshore, such swimming would also put them at considerable risk of premature stranding intertidally if metamorphosis was not imminent'.

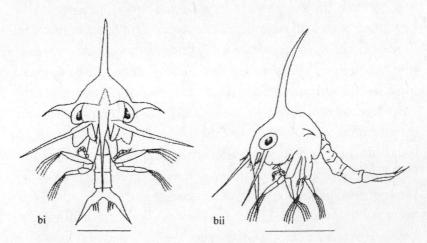

J. V. Thompson's crab zoeae.

His theory was that two processes were at work. The megalopses retained from the zoeal stages the instinct to swim in the ebb. They had also developed a desire to come inshore on the flood. For a brief and critical period in their lives the two instincts were in balance. They would live just offshore, even in the surf-zone, until the moment they were about to moult and become true crabs, and then they could choose to come ashore on the high tide, swept in by the sea, arriving at the beach as they had chosen, just at high-tide mark, where they would moult and as shore crabs, still only a few millimetres across, begin the rest of their lives.

It is not hard to repeat what Dr Zeng had done. Most of the plankton in the sea by early summer are different forms of crustacea and they bloom each year from early June on into July and August, feeding on the vegetable or phytoplankton that erupted in the spring.

Now in summer evenings, the animal or zooplankton make a vertical migration into the surface waters. There, with the fine-mesh muslin net trailed behind a slowly rowed boat and a small jar tied to its tail end, I fished for some, before carefully decanting their seawater into lidded jars.

I brought the gathered seawater back to my microscope and in the eyepieces in front of me found a set of beings which looked as if they came from another world. The sudden recognition of forms: some like a length of data or computer code; others spiral, a chromosome of light and dark repeating around their twisted cycles, like the heavy springs from the suspension of a car, but all too small to be seen with the naked eye; some like small translucent glass animals; others with horns and spikes, protected by their lances both fore and aft, and every one of them an instrument of almost unnecessary precision, as if the smaller the animal, the less sleek it could be, the more openly laboratory-made, unlike the sheeny, cosmetic and hermetic enclosing skin, say, of a mackerel or a salmon. The world in the microscope looked like a world without skin. These millions of beings which flood the bay each year, at such enormous expense to their parents and themselves, have no need of sleekness. They are the ingredients of the unseen soup of life. Pure vertigo, limitlessness beneath my feet, looking down into this other universe.

I tried at first to examine them without killing them but it was no good. They zipped away from the eyepiece of the microscope at speeds for which the level of magnification made it impossible to track them. I had no industrial alcohol and so they were embalmed for my studies in eighth of an inch of Finnish vodka, whose fumes came sifting up past me as I peered into their remoteness and complexity. They floated below me in a kind of inner space, the imagined creatures of a vodka cosmos.

Among them was the megalops of a green shore crab, in reality about one-third of a millimetre across, just visible to the naked eye, but in the microscope revealed in its magnificent strange-

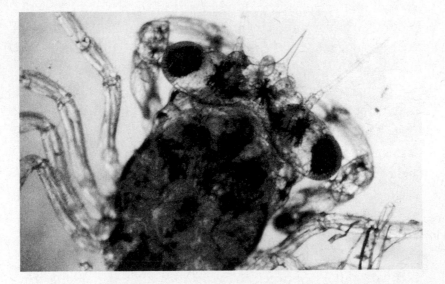

The green crab megalops collected with a plankton net from the bay, preserved and then consumed in Finnish vodka.

ness: vast-eyed, frail-limbed, spiculed, green but semi-transparent, its organs visible within its shell, the claws of the adult already in evidence, an organism on the verge of life ashore.

After I had made my attempts at photographing them with a camera that slotted into one of the eyepieces of the microscope, the least I felt I could do was to drink the vodka, a little salty with its admixture of seawater, mildly proteinaceous with the infant animals it contained. A Plankton Shot, the cocktail of life.

5

Anemone

There is a photograph of the young T. S. Eliot, seven or eight years old in the summer of 1896, half-perched on an upright rocking chair in the porch of his family's summer house near Gloucester in Massachusetts. One leg is hooked up under him, the other keeps the chair from rocking, and all his attention is directed down into the pages of a book, his hair curving over his brow towards it. He seems unaware of, or at least indifferent to, his brother Henry taking the picture. It is the world-excluding gaze of the truly absorbed: look in, look carefully, find whatever it is that engages you most deeply.

The Eliots used to spend three months every summer exchanging the heat of Missouri for the cool verandahs of this tall, wind-visited, seaside house and during one of them, the young Eliot experienced something he never forgot, applying that careful, close scrutiny not to the pages of a book but 'peering through sea-water in a rock-pool and finding a sea anemone for the first time'. Looking down into the pool became a model for him of the way he found his poetry, with no conscious choosing but the anemones 'lying dormant in the mind for twenty years', as if memory were a pool full of half-hidden beings, most of them unrecognised, waiting for the swimmer or shore-walker to push a hand beneath the surface and ruffle the weeds. Only then, as

Eliot wrote, would the anemones 're-appear transformed ... charged with great imaginative pressure'.

In *Elsa*, his catboat, he became entranced by that granite coast, by the grandeur of the Atlantic off Cape Ann, and the gardens where 'The salt is on the briar rose, / The fog is in the fir trees.' All of it surfaced in what he would write for the next sixty years, drawing again and again on those waters, so that in a purely Wordsworthian way memory and imagination became indistinguishable to him. At first, he had described his ten-year-old self looking into the pool as having 'a simple experience', but then, in the lecture where he said that, immediately corrected himself: 'not so simple, for an exceptional child, as it looks'. Not a careless glance but a dive into the wonderful.

At the western edge of the pool on Rubha an t-Sasunnaich, where it shallows towards one of the volcanic dykes, the anemones were proliferating all summer. In some parts by September

The intimate co-existence of cloned beadlet anemones in the shallows of the second pool.

there were more than 300 of them in a square yard, all sizes, none quite touching, but each gently sifting from the surrounding water the food they needed.

In other places, I had found the wavering grey-yellow arms of the snakelocks and, in cracks and crevices further down the tide, the green blotched strawberry anemones, their bodies stuck with bits of sand and coralline flakes, the variegated tentacles of a dahlia anemone and some white elegant ones, as bright as candles.

Here in the pool, they were all the usual beadlets, *Actinia equina*, the most common of all, slightly various in their colours but named after the ring of little blue stinging cells or acrorhagi – a Victorian Greekism meaning 'high berries' – arranged as a necklace inside the lip of the columnar body. The acrorhagi are usually invisible when the main tentacles are up but appear as the anemone folds down into itself when conditions are not good – if the tide has dropped away, or the salinity has fallen or the temperature risen.

Otherwise, these simple animals merely wave their tentacles in the passing water like flowers in sunlight. That is why they are called anemones, named only in the late eighteenth century from their resemblance to the flowers of wood and meadow.

Brush your fingers through them, as the Australian poet Gwen Harwood has said, and you will find your 'fingers meet some hungering gentleness'. The little stings the anemones give you with these red tentacles do not hurt, but feel more like a kind of stickiness than an attack.

Some anemones are sexual, and release their sperm and eggs into the surrounding water, relying on some chance union, but these beadlets reproduce asexually, making tiny, genetically identical versions of themselves which emerge into the surrounding world as their fully functioning progeny. If you ruffle through them enough, you will find tiny anemone reproductions spilling out on to your fingers, each baby blob of life looking in a magnifying glass like a raspberry mousse.

They are among the simplest animals, not very different from their long-distant ancestors whose rare soft-body fossils have been found in deposits more than 500 million years old. They have no centralised nervous system, no brain, no organs of excretion – whatever needs to come out as waste is ejected through the same tentacle-surrounded hole by which the food went in. Their muscles and nerves are simpler and less organised than in almost any other animal. They have no skeleton; water pressure alone, held tight within the body cavity by the mouth closing over it, provides their solidity. Foods are dissolved by simple digestive enzymes into the chemical constituents that the anemone can absorb.

They are scavengers, eating the dead and broken parts of animals that float past in the tide. High up near the grass, they ingest plenty of dead midges and mosquitoes. Further down, it is little sandhoppers, parts of prawns, crab megalopses and lots of tiny unattached young mussels: in short, most of the

The all-receiving mouth of the sea anemone.

characters that have populated this book. A large one has been seen to swallow a smelt six inches long. Some Irish scientists have tested the anemones' appetite for something more, popping rather large mussels into the oral cavity to see what happened. The anemones accepted the offering easily enough and the mussels disappeared inside them while the scientists waited. Up to two hours later, the complete and uninterfered-with mussel came back out. The anemone had been unable to get access to the meat. When the scientists cut the muscle by which the bivalve kept itself closed, there was a different outcome. Very nearly nine hours later, the shells were spat out by the anemone, the meat of the mussel having entirely disappeared.

I collected some from the shallows at the edge of the pool. They are easy to peel off, if you lift them gently and carefully from the rocks they are stuck to. They come away almost exactly like Post-its, closing their tentacles with the disturbance but otherwise untroubled. The bodies of these *Actiniae* in the pool are red all the way down, the colour just paling at the foot. Some others that I found at the far end of the headland, and on rocks lower in the tide, had a blue line around the foot of their columnar bodies. Both were beadlet anemones, but of two different morphs, each living in slightly different environments.

In separate lidded boxes filled with seawater, I took them back to the aquarium in the house and left them to acclimatise for an hour or so. By the time I went to look, things had started to happen. One of the Bluefoots had been in a fight and had suffered in it, with pale wounds from its enemy's attack cells, the acrorhagi, stapled down one side of its body. An attacking anemone leaves part of the acrorhagus on the body-column of its adversary, continuing to deliver its toxins even after the fight is over. The flesh around these 'acrorhagus peels' had crumpled and puckered with the damage.

The Bluefoot had now moved to another stone where again it found itself next to a Redfoot. The two of them were meeting each other with their outer tentacles. Redfoot was bigger, its base spread wide and oddly warty, with its tentacles fully displayed, while Bluefoot looked less happy, tentacles retracted, a little inward (see second colour plate section).

Soon, though, Bluefoot made its defensive move and started to lean in towards the Redfoot enemy, which reacted at first by pulling back some of its outer tentacles. It was a temporary withdrawal. Minutes afterwards, Redfoot pulled itself up to its greatest height, reshaping its whole body and contorting its blue attack cells into a tiara of violence towards Bluefoot, leaving its upper red tentacles withdrawn, hooked and clawed. It was a ferocious display of aggression, of selfhood, of one being set against another.

Toxic darts spurted from Redfoot's acrorhagi into Bluefoot's body, sticking into the flesh, standing out from it like arrows in a target and leaving white threads wrapped around the enemy's waist. For the second time Bluefoot gave up the fight, detaching itself from the rock and starting to drift past and away from its aggressor.

This attempt to escape re-summoned all the defensive–aggressive instincts in Redfoot. As Bluefoot rolled over and past it, revealing the pale grey underside of its foot, Redfoot once again came up into its flamboyant, menacing attack form. Bluefoot was now in a hopeless situation, upside down and defenceless next to the fierce, charged presence of its enemy.

As its crumpled body drifted past, Redfoot, still wearing its extraordinary erect war-corona, bent over and down, on to the spot Bluefoot had just vacated, and deposited there a single tiny new anemone, an asexual clone of itself, generated and brooded within its body cavity, placed to occupy the neighbouring area of rock that would now become part of its own clonal territory.

Bluefoot was wafted away by the currents in the aquarium, finding a place at the far end, tucked down behind a large stone. Meanwhile, Redfoot, the crisis over, resumed its composure, with its tiny, soon-to-be-space-occupying clone happily settled beside it. That clone's minuscule tentacles were already sifting the passing water.

These animals were not properly understood for a long time. The acrorhagi were first described in 1829, but were thought throughout the nineteenth century to be primitive eyes, or organs that were especially sensitive to touch or somehow, in an undefined way, connected with defence. Only in the 1950s was it finally recognised that they were the animal's arsenal.

How the anemone knows to attack a stranger and yet feel comfortable tangling tentacles all day long with a clonal relative is still only partly understood. It cannot be the mere presence of another that engenders the violence. Its different attitudes to relatives and non-relatives is so polarised because its progeny is genetically identical to it. These animals are not, in one sense, individuals. Everything that identifies the nature, reality-processing and selfhood of one red-footed *Actinia* is literally and profoundly the same as everything in the child it deposits beside it.

Without doubt, the chemical smell-cum-taste of a neighbour was at work. This so-called 'clonal recognition' depends on genet-ically driven chemical markers in the surface of the anemone's skin. Experiments have shown that although anemones will release the mild toxins in its red tentacles at almost anything – from sponges to fish and my fingers – the acrorhagus violence is only ever directed at other anemones that are not genetically identical. Super-murderous attack is reserved for them, and only when they actually touch the tip of the acrorhagus. Even a distance of half a millimetre brings no response. But should a wrong anemone come into physical contact, the only reaction, within a couple of seconds, is a massive discharge of aggressive poison.

This passionate phenomenon takes one deep into the origins of consciousness. All life, even down to the level of bacteria, responds to the kind of chemical stimuli that is governing the anemone's reaction to a stranger. It is the most shared element of life on earth. The chemical basis of smell and taste, and the neural architecture by which those signals are delivered to the organism, is essentially the same in all insects, crustaceans, molluscs and vertebrates, including ourselves.

When we smell something wrong, or get a strange feeling about another, we may be using some of these deeply buried neural habits by which the anemones are still governed and which had their origins far back in the pre-Cambrian world, more than 540 million years ago, before other senses were invented or needed.

Until that 'Cambrian Information Revolution', all life depended on this chemical form of communication. Only then, and quite suddenly, did 'the Cambrian bloodbath of predator eating predator' begin, a self-generating, mobile and ferociously competitive environment 'that probably supplied the selective force necessary for the evolution of the first brains'. Where a predator could develop nostrils, by which it could detect the source of a smell at a distance, the advantage was soon obvious. Animals that had previously been able to hide in turbulent eddies, where the chemical signals they were giving off would be hidden by the riffles in the water, would suddenly become available to predators that could smell them by processing and understanding what reached them in turbulent currents. Look at a dog sniffing the air and you will see that analysis of turbulence at work. The emergence of eyes, in both predator and prey, ramped up the arms race still further. Driven by these new means of detecting both enemies and food, animals quickly radiated into all the forms from which modern life is descended.

The sea anemones come from before that revolution. They are living ancientness. When you know this history, they seem to be in the dark, quite literally blind, extraordinarily uninformed about their world, knowing only to ingest what seems like food, to accept as neighbours what seem like themselves, to attack what smells like a cousin, at least when skin touches skin. Many species of them hide, tucked away into rock cracks; some like the Strawberry anemone conceal themselves with bits of shell stuck to their bodies. Others are buried deep in the beach, visible at very low tide as strange, translucent, long-limbed stars that at one touch disappear into the sand.

These beadlet anemones are not like that. They are everywhere on the rocks of this shore, neither hidden, nor defended against us, nor equipped with any of the instruments of perception which the revolution in life 540 million years ago seems to have made necessary. And yet, here and elsewhere in the world, they are astonishingly common. What is the secret?

The answer may be in the principle of cloning, a life habit shared by the anemones with other simple intertidal animals, the sponges, sea squirts and sea mats. All of them are able to tolerate their own clones as neighbours, and even to fuse with them. I am

Sand anemone *Cerianthus lloydii* in the low-water shallows at the head of the bay.

told, although I could not perform this experiment myself, that if you cut a fully grown sea anemone in half vertically, each half will within a few weeks grow back to become a whole sea anemone itself. The cut edges naturally push together and rejoin to form a smaller animal. Those cut surfaces know each other as part of one thing and are happy to fuse. All of them are able chemically to distinguish non-clones and to treat them with appropriate violence. The result is clusters of anemones that are clones of each other, from which strangers are excluded, and which can, in effect, be seen as a single being in many bodies. When the sea anemone rejects the non-clone next to it, it is behaving in the way a human body behaves when it rejects a transplant. It knows the interloper is not one of its own; is not, in fact, itself and needs to be expunged.

As a result, the anemone does not need to engage in the post-Cambrian arms race. Rather than compete, it proliferates and in asexual, cloning sea anemones, the individual is effectively eternal. It grows not by getting larger but by developing more and more bodies for itself. Those bodies create still more bodies and the individual anemone exists in every one of them. Its life habit is to say itself again and again. Destroy any single polyp and the individual will persist despite you. In that way, unless a bulldozer or a sinking oil tanker arrives on the shore, the sea anemone escapes mortality. Its self is beyond any particular form of cells that happen to embody it. No particular body needs to become large. An anemone is its colony of genetically identical creatures and its size may be intrinsically unlimited.

The only resource that is limited is space, which is why the identification of a neighbouring non-self by a sea anemone becomes of such ferocious and overriding importance. The one thing the clonal being must guarantee is room for its new-body selves to find a home in the world.

The scenes in the aquarium came from a Redfoot recognising a Bluefoot. What is less dramatic but equally significant is the picture in the shallows of the pool at Rubha an t-Sasunnaich, where a crowd of Redfoots continues to sit alongside each other in what is probably a clonal gathering, not of like-minded individuals but of a single individual, attending to its own welfare in all the different bodies through which its being appears in the world.

Although the Italians occasionally eat snakelocks anemones, in vinaigrette or deep-fried in batter like calamari, all anemones are thought to taste horrible to most fish. Crabs ignore them. Tompot blennies – small fierce rock-pool fish – and the feathery common grey sea slugs both prey on them. Coiled strings of the slug's bright white eggs have been appearing in the deeper parts of the pool – but the shallows probably protect the anemones from them: they are too open to bird predators for the fish and slugs to like it there, or to survive for long. Besides, the sheer numbers and productivity of the anemones is clearly enough to keep the clonal individual alive.

In some American anemones, whose clones cluster more densely than the European beadlets, a radical change has occurred, somewhere between the growth of an anemone society (if one thinks of each individual polyp as a creature) and the development of organs in the anemone body (if one thinks of each clustering of anemones as a single clonal individual).

These elegant, green, pink-tipped *Anthopleura elegantissima* anemones grow on boulders on Pacific beaches or on rocks piled up to make breakwaters. Like the beadlets, each clone is incapable of tolerating non-self anemones within touching distance. The first result is a set of distinct border zones between clones, like the frontiers between warring states, traceable for yards across the boulders, what might be called 'the hate strips' separating one clone from another, and each an inch or two wide.

This social geography – a social distancing between genetically distinct anemones – has created what biologists have called 'a division of labour' within each clone. At the outer edges, where

Two clones of the Pacific anemone *Anthopleura elegantissima* meet at a
narrow frontier that separates them. Warriors of one clone reach across
the border zone to attack their cousins.

there are no rivals, are a set of ordinary, quite small 'free-edge'
anemones, living an untroubled life. Along the border lines with
enemy clones are a set of little 'scout' anenomes. They are also
relatively small and are often damaged when they enter the no
man's land between the lines and come too close to the other
side, acting for their clone as sacrificial battle-fodder. Sometimes,
when badly wounded, a scout will make its way back into the
body of the clone, away from the fighting, where it will recover.
On occasions, a retreating scout is so badly wounded and infected
by acrorhagial peels from the other side that its own relatives
treat it as a foreigner and attack and kill it.

Immediately behind the scouts, in the second, third and
sometimes fourth row, are tall, powerful, heavily armed 'warrior'
anemones, packed with toxic acrorhagi and capable of reaching
out over the top of the scouts to do fearsome damage to the
anemones of the far side. These warriors have been shown to

have a memory of battles past. When confronted with enemy clones they have fought before, their defensive response is quicker and more immediately fierce than with newly met strangers. Intriguingly, the warriors seem almost never to propagate young anemones. That breeding function is reserved to other, lightly armed but big anemones called 'the reproductives' that live in the centre of the clone, protected from any possible attack by the hedges of scouts and warriors that surround them.

The clones, as David Ayre and Rick Grosberg have written, work as 'functionally integrated units'. Attacks are coordinated, the scouts look to expand the territory, damaged warriors can be protected within the body of the clone and chemical information about the state of play on the battlefront can be transferred by them to the reproductives.

Experiments have shown that anemones can be trained up for different roles. Repeated exposure of ordinary 'free-edge' anemones to the tentacles of other non-clone anemones results in them acquiring more and bigger acrorhagi. Warriors that moved back into the centre of the clone can grow bigger and become reproductives. Wounded scouts, withdrawn from the battlefront, can recover and provide a reserve from which future warriors or future reproductives could both be drawn.

All these are evolved dimensions of the anemone 'self'. Each polyp may be genetically identical to every other, but each 'caste' within the clone is different in form. Different local conditions – life on the free outer edge where there are no enemies, the battlefront, the safe centre – summon different body forms from the same genetic source. Even here, in the very simplest of animals, the interplay of inheritance and environment defines the experience of life.

It is difficult to remember that the animals behaving like this have nothing resembling a brain, nor any sense organs beyond an ability to detect the chemical difference between self and non-self. My brief trial in the tank with Redfoot and Bluefoot had been dramatic but was not the natural reality as it evolved with these Americans. Unlike all battles between individual polyps from different clones, clone-to-clone battles typically continue for several days, repeatedly peaking during the flood tide, perhaps because that is when the sea brings in extra nutrients. Individual anemones bear their wounds like stars and continue fighting, even with the darts sticking out of them and acrorhagial peels puckering their bodies. Only when a warrior crosses into enemy territory does it behave like those anemones caught in single combat, soon separating from the rocks and allowing the currents to waft it away defeated.

All this with no brain and no means of seeing or hearing. Even more extraordinarily, it now seems as if individual anemone polyps are able to make decisions which involve assessing the difference between themselves and a rival from another clone. Scientists at Plymouth University have staged meetings between beadlets of different sizes. Just as in red deer, when 'the weaker stag may decide to withdraw after a bout of roaring, after parallel walking or only following a phase of violent antler-wrestling', the smaller beadlet sometimes gave up and retreated after no fighting or when no damage had been done to it.

The anemones were using 'logical decision rules similar to those observed in contests in animals that are often assumed to be more complex in their behaviour'. Somehow, an anemone polyp can ask the strategic questions: is the other one stronger? Am I likely to lose? Will the cost of winning outweigh the benefit? Is discretion the better part of valour? Anemones, it seems, are logical polyps, capable of deference in front of the strong and assertion in front of the weak, and able in the light of those perceptions to conduct limited war.

No one knows how, nor what kind of consciousness is alive in these animals. Perhaps anemones drive on to this far-reaching conclusion: there is no distinction between life and mind. Life is mind and there is no boundary in the continuum of life at which you can draw a line to say 'Here is mind' and 'Here is none'. Life-and-mind is a single condition in which the living share. We are mind. We live in mind. To live is to be mind. Mind is the distinction between what lives and what doesn't, so that thought, that stream of consciousnesses that ebbs and flows in us, is the medium of being.

6

Heraclitus on the shore

I have often thought of my father-in-law in this bay. John Raven died ten years before I met Sarah and so I never knew him but I know, at least, he used to encourage her and her brothers and sisters to look for amethysts on the beach at Rubha an t-Sasunnaich. He said you could find them here among the small grey pebbles, eroded out of the margins of the volcanic dykes. I've often looked but never found one. Perhaps they found them all.

John Raven (1914–1980).

Nevertheless, John Raven remains here, partly at least because Sarah treasures the memory of going out to look for wild flowers with him when she was a girl. He was handsome, tall, increasingly thin, smoking his Benson & Hedges, crouched under an umbrella in the rain, the most careful of detectives, chatting, joking, looking down into the details of the world. An extraordinary man: a classical scholar with a mastery of the whole sweep of Greek philosophy from Thales to the Hellenistic thinkers; a much-loved tutor at Cambridge, carefully setting out for the undergraduates the riches of his subject; a pacifist in the Second World War, who refused to countenance 'murder as a means to an end'; a botanist of world standing, with a lovely straightforward and systematic clarity of mind; kind, funny and considerate to the young; an effortless and remorseless deflater of the pompous; a man, according to his dear friend Bobby Chapman, 'with a sepulchral laugh and a conspiratorial twinkle', who in the 1930s had a brief entrancement with Margot Fonteyn, before she became the star of the dancing world. He was a watercolourist, a gardener, a fisherman and a meticulous searcher after wild flowers here in Scotland and in the mountains of Greece and Crete, whose geography and ecology he knew as well as anyone on earth. And an adored father, often ill, who, even with all these gifts, was increasingly disabled by self-doubt and a drift towards self-destruction.

The most lasting of his books, still available more than sixty years after it was first published, he wrote together with his fellow Cambridge classicist Geoffrey Kirk. *The Presocratic Philosophers* addresses the thoughts of that group of Greek thinkers from the eastern Aegean and the settlements in Sicily and southern Italy who between about 600 BC and 400 BC started to consider existence in new ways, beyond the traditional stories of gods and men. The relationship between sky and earth, Ouranos and Gaia, no longer needed to be seen as a sexual drama played out in the clouds. At the dawn of metaphysical thinking, these first philosophers tried to articulate what being was, what the existence of things might be, what nature was. They were the first to ask the fundamental questions: what is the world? What is it made of? What are its principles? How can we know what it is?

In the radically tidal world of the bay, I found myself reading over and over again what Kirk and Raven had written about Heraclitus, the strange, terse, misanthropic philosopher from the Aegean coast of Asia Minor, who lived in a state of constant strife with his neighbours in Ephesus, where he had been born around 540 BC, berating them for their idiocy, refusing to draw up a law code for a city that did not deserve one.

The received idea of Heraclitus is simple: πάντα ῥεῖ. Everything flows. All is flux. Nothing is fixed and nothing certain. Nothing can be known. There is no identity. Tides run through everything and there is no 'still-stand'. We are afloat in a liquid world.

Both Plato and Aristotle thought this ridiculous. How could anyone say, Plato asked, 'that there is no solidity in anything' – the word Plato used meant 'health' or 'soundness' – 'but that everything is liquid like a leaky pot, or people afflicted with catarrh, dribbling and trickling all day long?' It is the kind of remark I imagine John Raven might have made but the revelatory treatment of Heraclitus in *The Presocratic Philosophers* looks beyond that exaggerated and rubbed-down cliché and starts to reveal Heraclitus, even in his cryptic, fragmentary obscurity, sometimes no more communicative than a crab, as a thinker who questions the world in a way that now seems extraordinarily modern.

All the Presocratics had been interested in change, and in the way change governs what we experience every day. The question was not whether change was part of the world but how identity and meaning persisted despite it. What is the structure underlying change? Is the crab the same crab as it goes through its metamorphoses? To what extent, as I read Kirk and Raven here now, both of them long dead, do they remain present?

Heraclitus asked his neighbours to look beyond the everyday. It was no good thinking that the world consisted of details. There is something that unites everything, which he called the *logos*, the principle of order and knowledge. That 'measure' is present in all change. It is the hidden stability that runs behind and through change. The governing principle of the *logos* is that opposites unite. 'The path up and down is one and the same.' Fish can live only in the sea but salt water is poisonous to men. Exhaustion makes rest good and only hunger makes a full stomach pleasant.

None of these things would have the meaning they do without their opposites, so that when Heraclitus says that opposites are 'the same', he does not mean 'identical' but that they are deeply linked. Opposites are two parts of one substance that undergoes change according to the measure of the *logos*. The tide is a model of existence. High tide and low tide are not separate things. It is the same sea that ebbs and floods so that high tide is inconceivable without low tide. This embracing of a systematic understanding whose wholeness relies on its union of opposites became for Heraclitus the source of wisdom and goodness. 'Man's life is indissociably bound up with his whole surroundings. Wisdom consists in understanding the *Logos*, the common element of arrangement in things, embodying the "measure", which ensures that change does not produce disconnected, chaotic plurality.'

And what of the most famous Heraclitean statement of all: 'You cannot step into the same river twice', since the river is so changeable that each time you dip a foot in, it is a different river. On those grounds, as Cratylus. one of Heraclitus's followers, said to Plato, 'You could not step into the same river even once', because the changes in a river are so constant that at the very moment you step into it, it has become a different river.

It turns out, as I now learn from my father-in-law and his ancient colleague, that Heraclitus never said such a thing. It is Plato's crude and ridiculing version of what Heraclitus had actually said, which is both subtler and more obvious. 'Upon those that step into the same rivers different and different waters flow.'

He was only saying what he had said before. The river remains the same but its waters are always different. The form does not change but its substance is never still. The unity of the river depends on the regularity of its flux. It is a river *because* it changes. If it did not change it would be a lake. The opposites are one and a single river can exist only as a thing of many waters. The same is true of my tidal rock pools: they are what they are only because at each high tide they cease to be what they were at low tide. Their changingness is their identity.

No one in Ephesus could understand that the world was like this, not full of atomised and individualised facts and appearances but all 'in common', all part of one structure. Heraclitus felt he had access to a unique understanding that the world was a system, of which individual nodes, fixed points and 'things', could mean nothing beyond the web of which they were part. Everything consists only in its relationships to everything else. He sounds at times indistinguishable from a modern systems theorist such as Gregory Bateson or the Californian physicist Fritjof Capra who understood 'the physical world as a dynamic web of interrelated events'. 'In a living system,' Capra wrote, 'the components change continually. There is a ceaseless flux of matter through a living organism. Each cell continually synthesizes and dissolves structures, and eliminates waste products. Tissues and organs replace themselves. Matter continuously flows through an organism but its form remains stable.'

In this Heraclitean view, nothing in existence is fundamental. Only in connection does meaning occur. And the observer is necessarily part of that web.

The Heraclitean world is not static or closed but dynamic and open. Everything, within this frame of order, floods through everything, not like a leaking pot or a man with a streaming cold, but like an organism metamorphosing from crab to egg to zoea to megalops to crab to egg again; or a rock pool flicking from a weed-and-crab-rich state to a weedless-and-winkle-rich state. And back again. There is no question of equilibrium or stasis here or even solidity but an understanding of existence, in the words of Norbert Wiener, the MIT mathematician who invented cybernetics in the 1950s, as a set of 'whirlpools in a river of ever-flowing water ... not stuff that abides but patterns that perpetuate themselves'. Life is a *dis*equilibrium, whose only stability is in its passage through time.

Life, from that point of view, is 'the continual embodiment of the system's pattern of organisation', just as a wave form remains stable but the water through which it travels and of which it is made is never and can never be the same.

There is no sense of calm in Heraclitus. His picture is of a world in tension with itself, full of structures that are taut with an internal and hidden antagonism, as if in that tension lay the verve and energy of life itself. 'All things happen by strife and necessity,' one fragment says. The world is not unlike the rock pool, full of claim and concealment, attack and evasion. 'Nature likes to hide,' another says cryptically. What is true is not necessarily apparent. You may perceive a state of balance and calm but it is held like that between forces that are secretly straining against each other. 'They do not understand,' Heraclitus began another famous and difficult fragment, again disparaging his neighbours, and referring to something that might be 'life' or 'existence',

> how, being at variance, it agrees with itself: there is a back-stretched connection, as in the bow and the lyre.

The bodies of the bow and lyre pull against their constraining strings and in that tension combine to create a coherent whole. The essence of life consists of opposite forces in tension.

These strange and powerful statements, so nearly lost – this one preserved by the church father Hippolytus in the third century AD – seem to address the nature of this shore, of life on it, its governing structures and habits, what it *is*. The apparent stability and reality and existence of life is only part of the grand process of things on the cosmic battlefield. All things must eventually change, while, for the time being, some things are evidently real and even good, held in reality by the tensions that frame them.

'The world order' – for which the Greek word is *kosmos* – 'always was and is and shall be an everlasting fire, kindling in measures and going out in measures.' That cosmic fire is the everlasting burning of existence, the medium of change through which all things continuously pass and which, at its heart, has no peace. In one of Heraclitus's most concentrated formulations, this one preserved by Origen, the great Alexandrian theologian, he says simply 'Strife is justice.' If there were no strife, as Kirk and Raven commented 'the victor in every contest of extremes would establish a permanent domination, and the world as such would be destroyed'. If the body of the bow or lyre wins the struggle and the strings break, there can be no bow or lyre. Their strife is wholeness.

The idea that competition creates order is implicit in Darwinian theory. Even at home in Kent, as Darwin described in the 1860 edition of *On the Origin of Species*, the removal of one species at the top of a food web can disrupt all the layers of predator and prey beneath it. Each 'trophic' level – the Greek word means simply 'nutritional', defining organisms by what they consume – is dependent on strife between the levels above it.

I have reason to believe that humble-bees are indispensable to the fertilisation of the heartsease (*Viola tricolor*), for other bees do not visit this flower. From experiments which I have lately tried, I have found that the visits of bees are necessary for the fertilisation of some kinds of clover; but humble-bees alone visit the red clover (*Trifolium pratense*), as other bees cannot reach the nectar. Hence I have very little doubt, that if the whole genus of humble-bees became extinct or very rare in England, the heartsease and red clover would become very rare, or wholly disappear. The number of humble-bees in any district depends in a great degree on the number of field-mice, which destroy their combs and nests; and Mr H. Newman, who has long attended to the habits of humble-bees, believes that 'more than two-thirds of them are thus destroyed all over England'. Now the number of mice is largely dependent, as every one knows, on the number of cats; and Mr Newman says, 'Near villages and small towns I have found the nests of humble-bees more numerous than elsewhere, which I attribute to the number of cats that destroy the mice.'

More cats meant fewer mice meant more bees. More bees meant more pollinators for heartsease and red clover, more of their seeds fertilised and so more plants. Cats made flowers. Remove the cats and the flowers would go. In that way competition creates order, or in Heraclitus's terms, justice.

That dynamic picture, not of static niches but of competitive and tensed relationships between multiple predators, and a mutually exploitative but non-destructive symbiosis of bees and flowers, is essentially Heraclitean but did not take centre stage in biology until the 1960s. For most of the twentieth century, the patterns and structure of the living world were thought of in terms of energy flows, controlled by the quantity and quality of natural resources: the governing fact was assumed to be that there could never be more consumers than the supplies on which they lived.

In 1960 three pioneer ecologists at the University of Michigan called Nelson Hairston, Frederick Smith and Lawrence Slobodkin published a four-page paper asking a different question: 'Why is the world green?' Answer: because the world's herbivores, which would otherwise proliferate to the point where they ate every green thing, are controlled from above by their predators and parasites. That is why there is always far more green food for them than they consume. Only when the predators are gone does the herbivore population balloon and the green world disappear.

The opposite destinies of those alternating trophic levels mirror those in Darwin's garden: cats meant clover and no cats meant no clover. The Michigan insight was to globalise that understanding: if predators thrived, herbivores suffered and the vegetation grew. Resources did not dictate the pattern of life; competition did. Tigers made forests.

Drawing on these insights, a big-boned six-feet-six-inch New Englander called Robert Treat Paine III became the modern giant of intertidal studies. He came from a long patrician line of Boston Brahmins, descendant of the great English revolutionary Tom Paine and of one of the signatories of the Declaration of Independence. More important than all that was an early and deep engagement with the aristocracy of evolutionary biology: at Harvard mentored by the great historian of biological sciences Ernst Mayr; a PhD student at Michigan under Frederick E. Smith, one of the authors of the Green World Hypothesis; and a postdoc at the equally distinguished Scripps Institution on the Pacific coast in San Diego.

It was on the edge of the wharf there, in 1961 when he was in his late twenties, that Paine had an idea, derived from the Green World Hypothesis, for an experimental test. Beneath him at the dock, he watched the huge carnivorous purple sea star *Pisaster ochraceus*, fat-limbed and extraordinarily strong, eating a big Californian mussel *Mytilus californianus*.

The following year, he took a post on the zoology faculty at the University of Washington in Seattle where he remained until

1998. The riches of the north-eastern Pacific shoreline were in touching distance, four hours' drive from the campus, and the bays and islands of that spectacular, fog- and rain-soaked coast became his laboratory. First on the mainland and then on Tatoosh Island, off Cape Flattery (no power or running water), Paine established his 'university of the rocks'. Arrival at Tatoosh involved either trusting to the professor's boat skills in a zodiac on a thrashing shore or 'being hoisted off the deck of a bucking Coast Guard boat in a wooden box dangling a hundred feet in the air then swinging in the wind on to a platform on top of the island'. No one who spent any time there with what one of his students called 'this canopy of a man' could ever forget it.

From his boyhood, Paine had been in love with high latitude rocky shores and for almost four decades he and his train of devoted followers worked there on the complex invertebrate communities of the intertidal, slowly establishing a school of biologists who talked and thought less about niches than the

Bob Paine (1933–2016).

dynamics of systems, 'the complex wiring of species interactions', and the all-importance of the small, manipulative
experiment. Their repeated task was to see what happened
when changes were made to one or two details of the plants or
animals of the intertidal. The experiments may have looked
small and parochial but their findings revolutionised the
science of natural systems in every habitat on earth. All his life,
Paine's mantra remained the same: 'an ultimate understanding
of the underlying causal processes can only be arrived at by
study of local situations'. Reality may be tidal; it is also full of
local variation. He always assumed that everyone and
everything, as a group of his most distinguished followers
wrote when he died in 2016, 'would be a delicate tangle of
interactions and effects'.

From June 1963 until November the following year, Paine
made his first world-changing experiment. He analysed the food
web of a stretch of shoreline on the Washington coast about
twenty-five feet long and six feet high. His diagram of the web,
thick with zoological Latin, revealed a complex community. At
the bottom, the large fleshy seaweeds were eaten by sea urchins,
limpets, winkles and the strange flat, rock-clinging creatures called
chitons. The hard, crust-forming coralline algae were also eaten by
chitons and sea anemones. Those algae-eating creatures were
themselves preyed on by whelks, starfish and sea stars of different
kinds. At the top of the system, sea anemones and the soft-bodied
sea squirts, as well as the mat-forming bryozoans and the tiny
tube-forming worms and sponges, plus the barnacles, goose
barnacles and blue mussels, were preyed on by dog whelks, sea
snails of various sorts and the sea slugs calls nudibranchs. Vast
quantities of many of them and of the big Californian mussel
Mytilus californianus that Paine had watched in San Diego were
consumed by the huge sea star, the carnivorous purple *Pisaster
ochraceus*, which was effortlessly removing twenty to sixty barnacles at one time. As Paine described, that big mussel 'when in

action' also had its own 'brute force competitive capacities: small barnacles are smothered; larger species such as [the barnacle] *Semibalanus cariosus* are overgrown and then abraded to death; the goose-necked barnacle *Pollicipes* is gradually crushed; and so on'.

It was a ferocious and layered world, full of strife. The experiment asked a simple question: what would happen to this multi-level community if the dominant *Pisaster* was removed? From his chosen patch, he prised off all the *Pisasters* with a crowbar and hurled them as far as he could into the sea. If, in the course of the year, they reappeared, he wrenched them off again and threw them back out. A control area next to his plot was 'allowed to pursue its natural course of events'.

Throughout the year he watched the changes. First, once the sea stars had gone, the barnacles floated in from the sea and established themselves on the rocks. By the following summer, the barnacles were being crowded out by rapidly growing Californian mussels and, at least to begin with, by the big goose barnacles. Even they were then squeezed out by the grinding dominance of the mussels. The seaweeds were disappearing

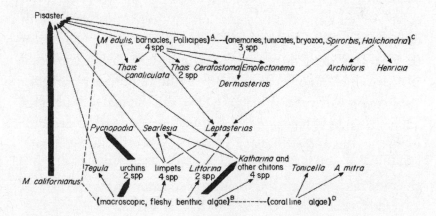

Bob Paine's diagram of the community he found on the Washington shore before removing the purple sea star *Pisaster*.

because the mussels were taking up all the space. The chitons and the bigger limpets had also left, as they had nowhere to go and nothing to eat. Sponges and nudibranchs had gone, along with most of the sea anemones. The bryozoans, the little tube-forming worms and the encrusting coralline seaweeds were all on their way out, driven away by the tyrannical monoculture of mussels that were no longer under pressure from *Pisaster*.

The community had collapsed. Previously, there had been fifteen different species on this patch of shore; now there were eight. Removing *Pisaster* had crashed the diversity of species. In the absence of predation, the mussel had won. The experiment had shown that predation did not, as had generally been assumed, diminish life, but opened the opportunities for a variety of life to flourish. Something which in the Green World Hypothesis had been merely a suggestion had been shown by Paine to be fact. When Robert MacArthur, the great early ecologist and professor at Princeton, read Paine's 1966 paper announcing these findings, he wrote him a letter: 'This changes everything.'

Removal of predators leads to local extinctions. Where predators capable of preventing monopolies are missing, the system becomes less diverse. If 'justice', or order, in the Heraclitean sense, is the balanced coexistence of multiple forms of life, with different demands and different ways of being, Paine had shown that kind of order to be dependent on a condition of mutual strife in which no one power source could dominate all others.

In a ripple of papers emerging over the following years from Tatoosh, he gave the name of 'keystone species' to a top predator in such a system. Remove it and the arch beneath would collapse. The collapse itself often took the form of a rippling sequence of changes that ran down and through the food web, a form of interaction Paine labelled the 'trophic cascade'.

Scientists began to find trophic cascades and their knock-on effects wherever they looked, many created by the impact of human beings on the natural world. Rivers, reefs, lakes, tundras, jungles, mountains and savannahs all demonstrated the reality of the idea, to the extent that by 2011 a leading group of earth and life specialists could announce in *Science* the 'Trophic Downgrading of Planet Earth'. The deep damage done by people to community-organising predators, they wrote, was implicated in the planet's sixth mass extinction, which is 'characterized by the loss of larger-bodied animals in general and of apex consumers in particular'. That loss 'is arguably humankind's most pervasive influence on the natural world'.

The disastrous cascade in Yellowstone – by which the killing of wolves had allowed elk to boom and graze out all the trees – became globally famous but no instance of the catastrophe is more striking than the one developed over several decades by James Estes, Robert Anthony and others in the North Pacific. In 1974 Estes and John Palmisano had already discovered in the Aleutian islands that where sea otters survived, the beds of kelp around the islands and all their associated organisms, including rock greenlings, seals and even bald eagles, were in rude health. Where the otters had been destroyed by fur hunters, there was no kelp, no rock greenling, no seals and no bald eagles. The link in the cascade was the sea urchin. Sea otters preyed on them and kept their numbers down. When the otters were killed, the urchins boomed. Urchins eat kelp and they grazed the kelp forests down to nothing. The fish had nowhere to hide. The seals and eagles had no fish to eat and the system collapsed to a derelict, weedless world of urchins and mussels. It was later found that killer whales were preying on those otters that remained and that bald eagles, with no fish or otter pups to hunt, turned to rock ptarmigan and various gulls for prey. These bird-dinners were nutritionally better than the fish on which they had been relying and the bald eagles did better than before.

It may be that the killer whales had turned to preying on the otters because their traditional prey of the calves of larger whales had been reduced or removed by human whaling. If so, the result is a cascade that runs from (1) an increase in human pressure, (2) a crash of the larger whales, (3) a knock-on effect in the killer whales, (4) a decrease in sea otters, (5) an increase in urchins, (6) a decrease in kelp, (7) a knock-on effect decreasing the rock greenlings and (8) another in changing the predatory targets of the eagles, with a subsidiary cascade (9) on seabirds, whose numbers were reduced and so (10) released predatory pressure on sand eels and other small prey-fish, allowing (11) mackerel to boom, which then also (12) became the prey of bald eagles whose population thrived.

The science has developed subtleties since the pioneering days. It is clear now that bottom-up processes, above all the supply of nutrients, or side-in effects, the battering of storms and the vagaries of weather, the particularities of particular places, will also have their effect. An organism, it has been shown, can act as a keystone some of the time but not at others. A cascade can occur through non-lethal effects, as when winkles leave a pool whose water is tainted with the smell of crab. These dynamic structures themselves shift. In a complex web with multiple pathways, the cascading wave of damage can be dissipated and buffered as it ripples through the system, so that in some cases the shock of removing a top predator can be accommodated within the system without deep change.

Nevertheless, these discoveries have transformed the way we must understand the world. Truly to see a shoreline now is to recognise that its strife is its order, that a balanced community is dependent on power-centres in tension, the frame pulling against the strings of Heraclitus's bow or lyre, and that the injustice and diminution of a dominant monoculture represents the absence of strife. It is a paradigm of nature opposite to the idea that living things hang happily and stably together in a set of mutually accommodated niches. It substitutes tension for stillness, flux for calm. Heraclitus is now the spirit that presides over life between the tides.

It is a mind-changing recognition. Even sailing out one evening in the bay, I am more than ever aware of the mobility of things. The ebb tide is setting to the east, squeezing around the castle headland on which the lighthouse has been built, and slipping downstream of it in volutes of sea that turn in and in. The wind is following the tide, channelled by the hills around the Sound so that whatever its origins, it too drives eastwards towards Lismore and the glens in Appin. The dinghy kicks and lurches in the chop, its bow taken one way and then the other until the wind gathers and the canvas tightens and the sheet hardens in my hand.

This now feels like a model of the stable disequilibrium at the heart of things – and of Heraclitus's and Bob Paine's understanding of them. Nothing is stable and yet everything coheres. Nothing is fixed: the sail itself, the sheet running from it to my right hand, the rudder and its tiller in the other, my own body and its balancing weight on the gunwale, constantly moving in and out of the boat at each change in the wind and knock from the sea. If any one of those forces were allowed to slip or dominate, the wholeness, what Heraclitus calls 'justice' or 'the indicated way', would fall off into incoherence.

I am the governor for a moment, holding in tension the competing pressures. 'The coexistence of many species,' Bob Paine wrote, 'is characteristic of ecologically uncertain relationships.' Diversity is unpredictability; non-singularity is life. That may be obvious – plurality flowers in the absence of the monomaniac – but Paine's great discovery was the same as Heraclitus's: creative acts of uncertainty are dependent on an overarching control in the *logos*. An overall authority, which in human terms might be called the rule of law, is the only thing that can allow diversity to flower.

That is the picture in this boat. If I let go of the tiller, allow the sheet to run out in my hand, or do not balance on the gunwale the forces of wind and tide, one or other of them will take control

and, overpowered or underpowered, the boat will either capsize or come to a stop. It would suffer what biologists call a 'regime shift' and move to a state, either upside down or motionless, where its organisation and structure had gone. The *New Yorker* writer Elizabeth Kolbert has reported what a climatologist told her about the state of the world's atmosphere. It was, he said, like a small boat: 'You can tip and then you'll just go back. You can tip it and just go back. And then you tip it and you get to the other stable state, which is upside down.'

Dinghy, climate or the biosphere: the Heraclitean logic applies.

It is late summer. The flag irises are heavy with bulbous seedheads. No birdsong now. Marsh orchids are flowering in the long grass in front of the house. Young buzzards are learning the wind by the cliff edge, flicked up and flustered when a gust ambushes them, only slowly inching back into steady air. There have been days of rain and the blackberries are juicy but almost tasteless with the wet.

In the pool at Rubha an t-Sasunnaich, where both beadlet and snakelocks anemones are now proliferating, fifty of each of them, I am wondering if anything I have done on this shoreline has brought about any change to its life when a black, green and yellow dragonfly comes beside me almost to the water surface and bending its long tail down towards the pool, deposits its eggs there.

Careful and hesitant like a man placing a piece on a chessboard in a move of which he is not quite sure. It is a golden-ringed dragon-fly, which would not have done that if the pool had not been there.

Then I wonder. Would a dragonfly lay its eggs in a saltwater pool? Was that an indication that the salinity was down? Perhaps the quantities of rain and the low levels of penetration by the neap tides had diluted the saltiness of the water to the point where it was as much a land pool as a sea pool?

The next day: a cloud of tiny fish were in there, two-spotted gobies, each with a black patch on their tail, perhaps to mimic an eye, and bright iridescent blue spots on the sides. These gobies are among the fish whose males defend the eggs after they have been laid, fanning and cooling them in the nest, but which are also the regular practitioners of what is called filial cannibalism: if they are hungry, or the price of defending the eggs against other males is too high, the father eats them and hopes for a more productive outcome next time.

No such scenes here; these gobies were all hanging in the pool in midwater, all at different angles and occupying all levels, but now and then coming to the surface for a fly, rising and sinking away again with real speed, the quickness of that up-and-grab necessary to avoid the bird predators. It was never an entirely clean hit, but a kind of double take, a-nibble-and-then-a-nibble, a splash and then a flash of the body away. I sat for an age watching the rings of the rising fish coming up like raindrops from below.

The third day: I arrived at the pool to find all the rocks around it covered in gull droppings. The big platform in the south-east corner, the boulders on the north shore, the three or four prom-ontory rocks Tom and I had manoeuvred into the edges of the pool, on the southern cliff and by the shallows on the western side – all were painted with the white liquid splashes of gull droppings, looking like the aftermath of a party no one had bothered to clear up. The gobies were gone. There was a

The cloud of two-spotted gobies in the second pool.

half-eaten corpse of one on the floor of the pool, a quarter-of-an-inch long, its little spine poking through the white of its flesh, the skull and tail eaten, and the glitter of its scales crumpled and broken.

The gobies had been caught in here. With relatively little weed in the pool, there had been nowhere for them to hide. The flock of common gulls which hangs around the bay had sat like judges above the water and picked them off. Even here, I realised, I had changed the ecology. On a coast with no pools, there would have been nowhere for the gobies to have been caught by the withdrawal of the water. They could have swept in and out with the tide. I had created a gull restaurant and played my part in the smallest of local trophic cascades: man makes a pool, accidentally traps gobies, provides food for gulls, and the gulls leave leftovers for crabs and other, largely molluscan, detritovores. A mammal-fish-bird-crustacean-invertebrate combination of cascade and knock-on effect from which all benefited in our different ways – all except the fish. With complete inevitability, the pool had become yet another theatre in which Heraclitean strife-and-justice held sway.

PART II

PLANETARY
CONNECTIONS

7

Tide

On calm days, I would watch for hours from different points the movement of the flood into the bay, and, as far as I could, map it, tracing in front of me the lanes of polished water which give away the currents of tide-weight beneath them.

With each tide those lines vary: with the weather, the state of the pressure systems rolling out of the Atlantic to the west, the

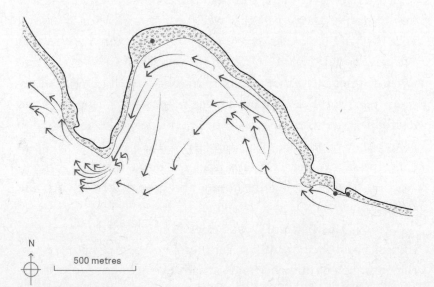

N

500 metres

The Movement of Water into the Bay at Flood Tide

time of year and the thickness of the weed, the time of day, the direction of the wind. It is said to flood here twelve minutes later than at Oban, the reference port, but that varies too, sometimes earlier, sometimes later. No wonder people could think the tide in some way animate, motivated not simply by mechanical action but by some hidden, purposeful being beyond our understanding. Its behaviour is less like the falling of a latch into its socket than the half-predictable, half-uncertain gestures of a living thing. The way it finds its path around this shore is like a dog nosing in the shallows.

It may be gravity in action, but this is gravity doing more than dropping an apple from a tree. Nothing is to be seen in the way this gravity's levers are pulled. All we can feel, as Ronald Blythe said of his time staring at the beach in Aldeburgh in Suffolk, is that we are watching 'the sea on a cosmic leash'. A rising tide, in Hugh Aldersey-Williams's disturbing phrase, is the only time we 'see something falling up'.

Imagine for a moment that you have no preconceptions, that Newton had never lived, and that you watch the tide rising and falling, today, the rest of this week, for months, for year after year. What do you know? Only what Pliny in his *Historia Naturalis*, published in AD 77, knew: that there are two high and two low tides a day; that they tend to follow the highpoint of the moon's arc in the sky by about three hours; that spring tides and neap tides vary with the moon; and that tides at the equinoxes in March and September are larger than those at the solstices in June and December. Not only does the tide come and go twice a day; its coming and going comes and goes twice a month and twice a year.

What is this pattern? What does it say about the nature of things? From the beginning, from long before the written word, the questions of influence and causality were bound up with the pattern of the tides. There were tides in more than the sea; and the moon was part of it: shellfish grew with the moon's increase;

the blood in a man's veins and arteries wavered in proportion to her light. Leaves and vegetables felt her influence. The moon was female and the flow of menstrual blood, called 'the waters' in Gaelic, was governed by her. 'Her power penetrates all things,' Pliny wrote. 'We may certainly conjecture that the moon is not unjustly regarded as the star of our life. She it is that replenishes the earth; when she approaches, she fills all bodies, when she recedes, she empties them.'

That concordance of sea and self is one of the oldest of all human metaphors. Sir James Frazer, attending to the 'rude philosophy of sympathy and resemblance', described in *The Golden Bough* how 'dwellers by the sea' sense in the flood tide 'not merely a symbol, but a cause of exuberance, of prosperity, and of life, while in the ebbing tide they discern a real agent as well as a melancholy emblem of failure, of weakness, and of death'.

The old word for high tide, in use until the eighteenth century, was 'the swell', meaning not as it does today the long rolling waves from old storms but the enlargement of the sea itself with the rising waters. The swell was the time of filling, the impregnation of the sea, the moment of fulfilment. In the West Highlands, eggs, if they were to result in hen birds, were to be set under hens during the ebb, and for dominant cocks during the flood. In Brittany, as Frazer heard, the people thought that clover 'sown when the tide is coming in will grow well, but that if the plant be sown at low water or when the tide is going out, it will never reach maturity, and that the cows which feed on it will burst'.

The best butter was churned when the tide had just paused at low slack water and was beginning, in that most expressive and beautiful of sea expressions, to 'make', as if the tide were self-creating. Milk which foamed as it came from the cow would go on foaming until the hour of high water was past. Water drawn from the well or milk taken from the cow while the tide was rising would boil up in the pot and overflow into the fire.

The ebb also had its potency. According to some, 'the skins of seals, even after they had been parted from their bodies, remained in secret sympathy with the sea, and were observed to ruffle when the tide was on the ebb'.

People have always thought creatures died on the ebb. For some – Frazer had heard it was true in Wales and on the Breton coast – babies were born on the flood and the old expired on the ebb. It is an identification as ancient as Aristotle, repeated by Pliny. Shakespeare had Falstaff die, sick at last with the falsity and wickedness of men, just at the highpoint of the slack, 'even at the turning of the tide', rejoining the natural rhythm of the world as the sea started to drain from the shore. In the Highlands, the haunted cry of the black-throated diver was a knell for the dropping of the waters, sounding in Gaelic like '*Deoch, deoch, deoch, 's an loch a' tràghadh*', 'Drink, drink, drink, the sea is ebbing from the loch'.

Tides have long been a perplexity. Aristotle was said to have drowned himself because he fell into despondency at not understanding how they came and went at Chalcis in the channel between Euboea and the mainland of Greece: sometimes all day in the same direction, sometimes changing direction fourteen times between morning and night. Confusion reigned. Eratosthenes, following Aristotle, thought that different parts of the sea were of different heights and the tide flowed between them as if down a riverbed. But how and when, even his contemporaries asked, did the water flow back?

Medieval monks repeated much of what Pliny – and everyone else who ever looked at the sea – had understood, but there was no progress in grasping the workings of the tides between the first century AD and the scientific revolution 1,600 years later. In the Renaissance, theories were not lacking. Some followed Apollonius, the first-century AD philosopher from Cappadocia, who thought the earth and sea were part of a living creature, 'which, by its Respiration, causeth this ebbing and flowing'.

Others imagined the tides were stirred up by the maelstrom at Saltstraumen, 'a great Whirlpool near Norway, which, for six Hours, absorbs the Water, and afterwards, disgorges it in the same space of Time'. It was suggested that 'the general Motion of the sea', driven westwards in sympathy with the movement of the moon across the sky, was obstructed by the bulk of the Americas, and that European tides were those seas reflected back across the Atlantic. Bernardo Telesio, an early and pioneering natural philosopher from Calabria in the south of Italy, assumed that the sea rose and tended to boil over when heated by the sun. Wanting to preserve itself, as all bodies do, the sea set itself in motion to avoid evaporation, and so generated the flow and ebb of the tides.

Our daily sense of the tide is not very different from all these forgotten and redundant ways of understanding it, which linger on in our minds like the flotsam and jetsam of the tidemark itself. For all the geniuses that have addressed the question over the last 400 years, the actual behaviour of the wave motions and all the vast undulations of the ocean remain formidably difficult to understand, full of local variation, distorted by bay and head-land so that the tide, in detail, remains a lurking mystery. We may know, thanks to Kepler and Newton, that it is to do with gravity but do we know what that is beyond some mathematical constant?

The long story of the tides' motions has been framed around a dialogue of opposites: are they governed by what is hidden, 'the occult', an unexplained power, as the empiricist philosophers of the seventeenth century liked to call it? Or by something that can be perceived in the material and mechanical world? Can we know the tides? Or must we rely for our understanding in the end on some strange and unknowable force?

Two of the great formative minds of the pre-Newtonian scientific revolution were arrayed on either side of that question: Galileo for earthly mechanics, the great German mathematician and astronomer Johannes Kepler for mysterious cosmic powers.

For Kepler, mind and matter were not distinct. The bodies of earth, moon, the other planets and the sun all had within them a sense of purpose and the capacity for affection. What Kepler in the *Astronomia Nova* (1609) called his 'true theory of gravity' involved forces that went beyond the merely mechanical. The mutuality was most apparent in magnets, and for a while Kepler (like Francis Bacon) thought that magnetism may have been the driving force of the solar system as a whole. But this sense of attractiveness was also a universal principle, applicable to all things. Earth and moon were like each other and because of that affinity had come together in the heavens as one system. 'At certain moments in the search,' the philosopher of science Ernan McMullin has written, 'when plausible physical explanations proved difficult to come by, Kepler had tentatively resorted to explanation in terms of a planetary mind capable of steering its home planet.'

The planets had something Kepler called 'perceptive cognition', 'a directing mind', and ocean tides, the most fluid and mobile elements on earth, were a manifestation of that thinking and feeling planet, of a connection between the earth and its great satellite. For Kepler, long celebrated as the great rational, mathematical genius, the first to establish through the painstaking analysis of Tycho Brahe's many careful observations of the night sky, that the planets orbited the sun on elliptical paths, nevertheless thought that the liquid sea had an affection for the moon. 'If the earth ceased to attract (to itself) the waters of the sea,' he wrote, 'they would rise and pour themselves over the body of the moon.'

Kepler's mysterious, animate world has a rich and melancholy beauty: things are separate but they yearn to be together. Objects, stones on the beach, rocks in the sea, the waters themselves are full of longing, and the universe is filled with mutual but unachieved desire. So powerful was this attraction that Kepler knew he had to provide a reason that earth and moon were not locked in each other's arms. The phenomenon that needed explaining was not the closeness of the two planets but the distance that remained between them. What was keeping the planets apart? Why had the earth's seas not been able to embrace the moon?

His solution was to imagine that the sun was spreading out beyond itself an immense, immaterial, swirling and rotating force field, a 'whirlpool', as Kepler called it, whose arms urged the planets onward in their paths. Two great forces were in tension: the gravitational love between earth and moon pulling them together; the solar vortex keeping them apart. Every tide, drawn by the mysterious force called 'gravity', threw its arms out towards the moon which was ever separate from it, held at a distance in the grip of the solar whirlpool.

I have stood on the beach and tried to think myself back into Kepler's world, to see the long ebb, the emergence of dark offshore rocks from the coloured skin of water, as a sign that something on earth is longing to be out there with the moon, that 'gravity' is a kind of desire, and that the sea is leaving this bay for another because it wants to.

There is a story that allows one to move back into Kepler's mental world. One day, the great mathematician and astronomer, after many hours dwelling on the universe and its workings, was called to dinner by his wife Barbara, who put a salad on the table in front of him. 'Do you think,' he said to her, 'that if, from the day of creation, tin plates, lettuce leaves, grains of salt, drops of oil and vinegar, and pieces of hard-boiled egg were floating in space in all directions and without order, chance could assemble them to-day to make a salad?'

'Certainly not such a good a one,' Mrs Kepler said, 'nor so well seasoned.'

Barbara Kepler's salad takes its place alongside such other things present here now as Ariel's song, Leo Pardi's arena for his

Talitrus saltator, Mandelbrot's wriggled rope, Heraclitus's lyre-cum-bow, as something emblematic of the questions raised by the tides. The Keplers differ in their approach to life. Johannes, who has been cogitating all morning, thinks that the salad can only be the outcome of a profound order in the organisation of existence. Chance alone could never have brought it into being. Barbara, who has after all cut and washed the lettuce, cooked and peeled the eggs, disagrees. This particular salad, on this tin plate, with its sprinkling of salt and oil and vinegar, can only be dependent on what she has done that morning. This salad here now, this Thursday in this chipped bowl on this checked table-cloth in this house in Prague in 1604, is what is, whatever might be happening out in the further reaches of the cosmos.

It is the deepest of divisions. On one side is Johannes's belief in an ordered and harmonious universe, aligned with the emergent beauties of Ariel's song and with the assumptions behind any sacrifice to the gods. All three share the assumption, common to religion, philosophy and science, that there is a structure to the world. Barbara Kepler's pride in her salad comes from the opposite position, shared, say, with the patterns of protean flight or the structural anarchy of a breaking wave, the ungraspability of truth. Barbara, *Talitrus* and the wave do not reflect any over-arching system. If there is one, it is not apparent in this world. If it exists at all, it is unreachable and the ultimate nature of reality is concealed behind an endlessly contingent surface. The breaking surge on the seashore, the tang of Barbara's seasoning, the indifference of wild birds – the quiddity of those things from moment to moment matters to them more than any month-long or year-long unrolling of the tides. And so the depiction of the tide as a form of longing, a mysterious affinity between things at a distance from each other, is an aspect of the need for order, of the assumption that coherence is the ultimate reality, however obscure it might be. Kepler is the philosopher, the descendant of Heraclitus, forever seeking the unknowable *logos*; Barbara one of the citizens of Ephesus, knowing her salad, its deliciousness, her care.

Kepler's contemporary and rival in Italy, Galileo, had no truck with his mysterious cosmic forces. Galileo was also looking for order, but the order was to be worldly. In about 1595, when he was teaching at the University of Padua, he went often to see friends in Venice. In times of drought, the wells in the *campi* ran dry and fresh water was imported in barges from the mainland at Lizafusina near the mouth of the Brenta, which was Galileo's embarkation point to cross the brackish lagoon. 'Let us consider a large vessel full of water,' he wrote,

> such as, for example, a large boat like those carrying fresh
> water from one place to another over salt water. First we see
> that as long as the boat stands still, the water contained in it
> stays equally calm. Then let the boat start moving, not slowly
> and gradually, but suddenly with great speed; we see the
> water being left behind, rising towards the stern and
> subsiding towards the bow, because unlike the solid parts,
> the water is not firmly attached to the vessel.

In the same way, if the barge stopped suddenly, running into a sandbank in the lagoon, the fresh water in it was 'pushed up towards the bow then bounced back toward the stern, doing this several times with ever decreasing agitation until it returned to a level state'.

No occult forces were involved. The water merely slopped from one end of the barge to the other because it was liquid and the barge was not. That image remained with him and in 1616, Galileo wrote to his patron Alessandro Orsini, recently made cardinal in Rome, to describe how the coming and going of the sea was not, as the whole of humanity had previously thought, 'a process of expansion and contraction of seawater' but 'of true local motion in the sea, a displacement, so to speak, now towards one end and now towards the opposite end of a sea basin'.

All naive and local observations of the tide had guessed that the rising of the water was the slow and vast upwelling of the sea, like a great boil, in sympathy with the shrinking and swelling of the moon, a bulge of connection between the moist, inconstant planet in the heavens and the moist, inconstant elements on earth. Galileo was the first person to reject that idea. For him, from the start, the tide was a huge wave, or more precisely, a set of huge waves lurching to and fro within the ocean basins of the world.

John Wallis, an Oxford polymath and one of the founding fellows of the Royal Society, wrote to his friend Robert Boyle in April 1666 about Galileo's basin theory:

> If a broad Vessel of Water, for some time evenly carried
> forward with the water in it, chance to meet with a stop, or
> to slack its motion, the Water will dash forward and rise
> higher at the fore part of the Vessel: And, contrarywise, if the
> Vessel be suddenly put forward faster than before; the Water
> will dash backwards, and rise at the hinder part of the Vessel.
> So that an Acceleration or Retardation of the Vessel, which
> carries it, will cause a rising of the Water in one part, and a
> falling in another.

Galileo's sea, as Wallis described it, was 'a loose Body, carried about with the Earth, but not so united with it, as necessarily to receive the same degree of Impetus with it, as its fixed parts do'. The rocks might turn on their way but the planet's rotation would cause 'a dashing of the Water, or rising at one part, with a Falling at another', the movement that 'we call the Flux and Reflux of the sea'.

Galileo's tidal theory relied on the idea that any point on the earth daily experienced this stop–start motion. He took from

174

Copernicus that the earth turned daily on its axis and every year orbited the sun. Every day, for this bay as for any point on earth, there is a moment in which we are rotating in the same direction as the planet is orbiting, and so, from the point of view of an observer in the universe, moving relatively fast through space; and another moment, twelve hours later, when this point on earth is turning in a direction opposite to the direction in which the earth is orbiting the sun, and, seen from a fixed point in space, the bay is moving relatively slowly.

Any point on earth accelerates and decelerates every day; the water in the seas cannot keep up with the movements of the rocky earth and so the tidal wave develops, running to and fro, just like water in the barge making its unsteady way across the Venetian lagoon. For Galileo, not only was this an outcome of

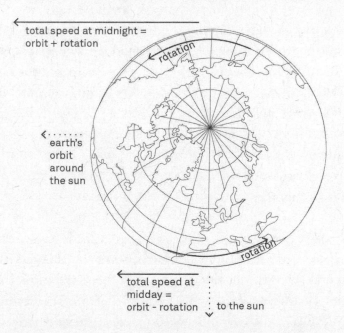

Galileo's tidal theory: every day, every point on earth goes through a
phase when the earth is rotating in the same direction as it is orbiting
the sun; and another phase, twelve hours later, when it is rotating in a
direction opposite to the way it is orbiting the sun.

Copernicus's great insight; it was proof that the insight was true. The tides revealed the reality of a rotating, orbiting earth.

Dr Wallis loved this idea: 'From the first time that I ever read it,' he told his co-fellow of the Royal Society, Edward Boyle, 'it seemed to me so very rational that I could never be of other opinion.'

To attempt a sympathetic understanding of Galileo's theory now takes as much of a leap as imagining Kepler's desire-filled sea. I have tried it. Look out at the bay. The geese are parading up and down offshore, the house martins are flick-steering in among the trees, but it is not them to which I am attending. It is the movement of this planet in space. The headlands in front of me are slowing down in their daily rotation, but the sea has retained its momentum from before and is still moving faster than the rocks around them. And so, astonishingly, the tide is pouring into the bay from the south-east, filling it on a scale and with a strength that only the planet could manage. But then the movement reaches its end, there is a pause and the rocks begin to accelerate again, the sea starts to be left behind, and drains out towards Duart and the Firth of Lorne.

It cannot be true, for two insurmountable reasons: it predicts only one high tide a day; and from the point of view of anyone on earth, one part of the planet is never rotating faster than any other. Everything – of course! – turns at the same speed and the seas never experience the acceleration or deceleration on which the theory depends.

Galileo's barge is no good as a picture of how things are. What could make sense of the tide? How could the sea be moved when nothing seemed to be touching it? What invisible levers were there to shift the waters? The next to attempt an explanation was the great French philosopher René Descartes, as intent as Galileo on providing a purely material solution to the problem. He set the earth and the whole of creation in the flux of a real but unde-tectable fluid whose globules whirled unceasingly through the cosmos from day to night and year to year. The solar system contained fourteen vortices in this fluid, the sun's the most powerful, but all the planets, including the satellites of Jupiter and Saturn, with their own.

Since everything was connected, globule to globule, there was no such thing as action at a distance. The planets themselves and the tides on earth were merely pushed along by the giant, globule-thick vortices, as if gravity were a kind of cosmic weather, with pressure systems sweeping through the atmosphere of space. When the moon was full, the substance of this heavenly or ethereal fluid pressed on the earth, squeezing the sea into low tides,

Descartes's pattern of globule-thick vortices in the solar system intended to explain the movement of the planets.

and allowing them to bulge out into high tides at the intervening quadrants.

Descartes's answer seemed at least possible, but not for long. From early 1664, Isaac Newton, a twenty-one-year-old under-graduate at Cambridge, started to keep a series of little 'pocket-books', one for theology, one for maths and one for chemistry. That year and the following, in the middle of a fourth notebook, Newton began to write out his *Quaestiones Quaedam Philosophicae*. Ranging through the nature of matter, place, time and motion, the cosmic order, the qualities of fluidity and soft-ness, of violent movement, of hidden powers, of light, colour, vision and sensation in general, he began to question the struc-ture of physical being itself.

Under the heading 'Of Water & salt', Newton interrogated the tides. Descartes had suggested that when the moon came near the earth, the particles in his lunar vortices squeezed both sea and atmosphere and pushed the earth out of its usual path. Newton, troubled by 'ye chinkes betwix ye Globuli', saw that the theory could be tested easily enough. Check, first, if the air pres-sure in a barometer varied with the tides (it did not). Then, check 'Whether ye Earth moved out of its Vortexes center bye Moones pression cause not a monethly Parallax in Mars' (which it would if the moon pushed the earth out of its usual orbit; it did not).

In two brief blows, and in private, the Cartesian theory of vortices had been demolished. But what could replace it? Already in discussion in London was the idea that something like Kepler's magic and affectionate 'gravity' might be controlling the move-ments of the planets. It was an ancient and accepted principle, stemming from Aristotle, that anything would continue in a straight line if not diverted by another force. What then ensured the planets continued to orbit the sun? The ancients had placed them in crystal spheres, but observations from Ptolemy onwards had revealed the inadequacy of that idea. Slowly the picture had been assembled: Copernicus replacing the earth with the sun at the centre of the system; Tycho Brahe's meticulous observations of the positions of the planets; Galileo's turning of the telescope on to the heavens and the revelation that Jupiter had satellites which orbited it just as Copernicus had suggested the great planets orbited the sun; Kepler's recognition that the planets followed elliptical not circular paths. But the mechanism remained unknown. This was the question asked in the mid-1660s, among many others by the great and cantankerous micrographer Robert Hooke:

> I have often wondered why the planets should move about the sun according to Copernicus' supposition, being not included in any solid orbs (which the ancients possibly for this reason might embrace) nor tied to it, as their center, by any visible strings; and neither depart from it beyond such a degree, nor yet move in a straight line as all bodies that have but one single impulse ought to do.

Isaac's Newton's great insight was to understand that the moon was falling towards the earth. If you stood on a high mountain and fired a cannonball, it would soon be pulled down in an arc towards the ground. The harder you fired it, the further it would go. If that cannonball was fired from the mountain with ever greater force, it would in the end fall towards earth in a curved trajectory which was long enough to mean it would never touch the ground but forever circle the planet to which it was drawn. The stone, like the moon, would be in orbit.

The mysterious force that holds the moon to the earth and the earth to the sun is the very force that brings a stone, or an apple, to the ground. It is the force that deflects the planets from travelling in a straight line. And it is the force that draws the sea towards the moon and sun.

After long delays, and with the encouragement of Edmond Halley, secretary to the Royal Society, who saw the book through

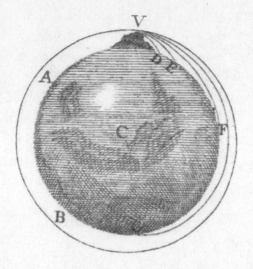

If a cannon is fired with ever-increasing force from the top of a
mountain, the cannonball will travel ever further around the earth.
Eventually it falls no faster towards the earth than a satellite in orbit.
The same force of gravity ordains the path of a falling object as the
orbit of the moon.

the press, Newton's *Principia Mathematica* was finally published
in July 1687. Halley presented a copy on fine paper to the king,
James II, an experienced sea captain who had commanded fleets
in wars against the Dutch. To James, Halley explained how
Newton had made clear 'all the surprising phaenomena of the
flux and reflux of the sea'.

The sole principle, Halley told the king, was 'no other than
that of gravity, whereby on earth all bodies have a tendency
towards its centre; and there is the like gravitation towards the
centre of the sun, moon, and all the planets'.

That was the reason the earth and all the planets were round.
A universal clustering of matter would create spherical objects.
And if there were no moon or sun, the sea would arrange itself
in what Halley called 'a perfect stagnation, always at the same
height, without ever ebbing or flowing'.

If we were alone in space, the planet would be encased in a shallow, still shell of sea. But the gravity of sun and moon disturbed that '*Aequilibrium*' and 'it plainly follows, that the sea, which otherwise would be spherical, by the pressure of the moon must form itself into a spheroidal or oval figure, whose longest diameter is where the moon is vertical, and shortest where she is in the horizon'.

This, in the simplest and earliest non-mathematical explanation, is the beauty of the Newtonian picture that unites heaven and earth. The rocky earth rests in space within a very slightly ovoid sea, a solid yolk within an elongated, watery egg. The moon's gravity both pulls the sea towards it on the side of the earth that is nearer to it; and pulls the solid earth towards it more than it pulls the sea on the side that is further away. Every twenty-four hours, that rocky earth makes a full revolution within its ill-fitting sea-envelope so that each point on the coast comes in turn to luxuriate in deep sea and be exposed in the shallows, a rhythmic coming and going of the tide as if this were some teasing, planetary game of I-love-you, I love-you-not.

The presence of the moon makes the water-bulge but the turning of the earth makes the tides. In the Newtonian picture, it is not the water that moves when the tide rises or falls but the rocks of the planet rotating within the skin of sea. The spin of the earth drives these headlands and islands through the water sphere that encases them, a sea that remains effectively almost still in space. Watch water draining out over the lip of a tidal pool, or making its way in between the boulders at the head of a beach on a rising tide and you are watching the earth turn. Find yourself in a tide race full of turbulence and overfalls and you are feeling not the potency of the sea but the giant flywheel of the earth itself, its huge angular momentum driving these rocks through waters that are held in place by a satellite 250,000 miles away.

Out in the Sound, marking the channel for bulk carriers north of the Grey Islands, there is a cardinal buoy anchored to the

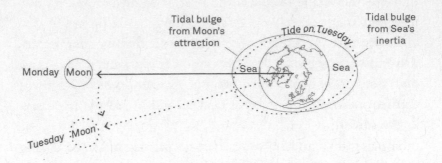

Newton's tidal theory: the gravity of the moon draws the nearest parts of the sea towards it. The solid earth is also drawn to it, less than the sea on that side, but also more than the sea on the far side. The earth spins within that watery ovoid, hence two high tides and two low tides a day. The moon also orbits the earth and so Tuesday's high tides (dotted lines) are fifty minutes later than Monday's (solid lines).

seabed, with two upward-pointing arrows as its crest, all kinds of solar equipment on its body and a big yellow steel hull in the sea; about a mile to the west is another, warning against Yule Rocks, with only four feet of water over them at low-water Springs, this one a red steel can, flashing at night its steady once-every-fifteen-seconds red.

Up close, the buoys are bewitching objects. When a big tide is running, the flood sets north-west at two knots or more, the ebb south-eastwards scarcely less. Both buoys tip in the current, tugging and jolting at the chains that hold them to the floor of the Sound. Both look for all the world as if they are making their way through the sea, which rubs up into a bow wave around their tubby, tug-like bodies.

That is the Newtonian reality: according to the vision in *Principia Mathematica* it is the floor of the Sound that is turning within the sea, pulling these chained vessels along with it like a pair of reluctant hounds. They must stay in the same place in relationship to the earth but, seen by an aerial observer out in the universe, they make a long and troublesome journey every twenty-four hours, following the earth to which they are bound.

To see the tide running is to see quite literally the physical drive of the earth. Not that the moon is without its part. Two high tides do not fit exactly within the twenty-four hours of the earth's rotation because the moon also moves around the earth, in the same direction as the earth spins, so that every day the moon rises fifty minutes later than on the day before, dragging the tidal bulge around with it. Each high tide is twenty-five minutes later than its predecessor and so we live in the planets' embrace, pulled out towards worlds that are not our own.

The Newtonian picture of a rock yolk in an ocean egg was essentially static and throughout the eighteenth and nineteenth centuries subtler understandings were gained of the tide as a dynamic system. Through careful calibration of records across

Isaac Newton

many oceans, it emerged that each ocean in each hemisphere had its own almost independent tidal regime. Each ocean was its own Galilean pond. Here in the North Atlantic, as the earth turns towards the rising moon in the east, the waters off the coast of Senegal are drawn to it. As the moon begins its transit of the Atlantic, sliding steadily west towards America, the bulge of water it makes does not follow immediately beneath it along the lines of the earth's latitudes, but, like any movement in ocean or atmosphere, turns to the right – the Coriolis effect – and begins to flow north up around the rim of the ocean basin, performing a giant oceanic circle.

If the high tide is flooding into the bay at, say, nine in the morning, that tide began its life off the coast of Senegal at midnight. It pushed north and the peak of the wave reached the Canaries by four in the morning, Lisbon an hour later, was in the Bay of Biscay at six and off Land's End as dawn broke at seven in the morning. Only an hour after that, it was rounding the north-west point of Donegal in Ireland, while two of its subsidiary tongues pushed slowly and laboriously, thickening as they went, into the Irish Sea and eastwards just as slowly up the English Channel towards Dover.

The tide that came up the outside of Ireland travels fast, reaching the west end of Mull by 8.30 in the morning and flooding here into the bay half an hour later, a mere nine hours after it has left Dakar, 3,000 miles away. This long, low wave sweeps on up to the north of Scotland, rounding Cape Wrath at ten, through Orkney by one in the afternoon, then slowing down the east coast, Edinburgh at four, pushing into the Thames Estuary at two the following morning.

Meanwhile, the faster-running deep ocean tide, which out in the Atlantic away from coastal shallows is no more than nine or ten inches high, has swept up to Iceland (at eleven in the morning, only an hour after it has filled the bay here in Argyll), around the southern tip of Greenland at 2 p.m. (Senegal time) and

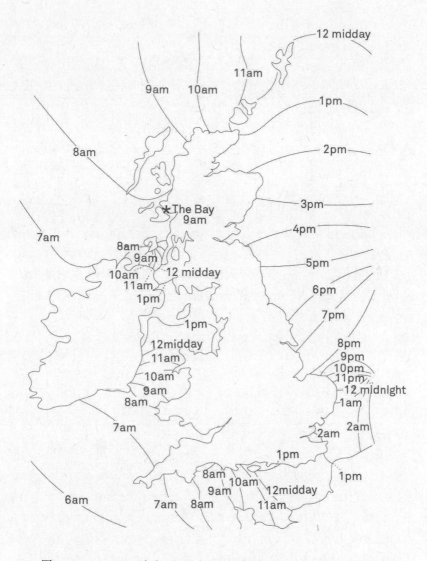

The progress around the British Isles of the peak of a high tide that arrives at the bay at 9 a.m.

Newfoundland an hour later before making its way down the Atlantic seaboard of North America and back across to West Africa to begin again.

We may think of the tide as a rise and fall of the water but the real movement is this long, fast, shallow, rotatory wave, swirling brandy-like around the ocean basins, a different wave for each ocean in each hemisphere.

One more element: the drag of the tide in these shallow seas is slowing the earth. The planet is not indifferent to the brake applied to it twice a day so that the earth's day is steadily growing longer, by about 2 to 2.5 milliseconds every century. Five hundred million years ago the earth was rotating faster, each day was shorter and so in the year there were more of them, perhaps about 415. Since then the tides have been rubbing away at the rocks and the earth has been dragged towards stillness by the moon and sun. Every morning I look out of the house at the tide rising in the bay, I am witnessing, unfelt by me, a world being dragged to a stop, the spin of time seeping out towards the final entropy. All will be quiet in the end, the sea at an everlasting still-stand and the oceans a pool of 'perfect stagnation, always at the same height, without ever ebbing or flowing'.

8

Rock

If the tides are our twice-daily connection to the universe, the rocks are our ever-present library of time. The geology in this bay marks three vast, life-destroying catastrophes, more global and pervasive the further back in time you go; and record one moment in which life recovered, radiating into new forms as it came back from the worst of those disasters. As I dug the pools here, it was, like any digging, a journey into the forgotten, through the skins of which this place is made, into the litter of the past. Rocks go long. To cut into them is not a digging but an unpeeling, slowly revealing the story of what it has been to live and die.

Those three moments of destruction were each the product of a different element, worlds transformed, and life destroyed, in turn, by poison gas, molten rock and ice.

First, the most recent: the ice. Intermittently, 3,000 feet deep over the last 2.7 million years, glaciers streamed across this whole landscape, dragging from east to west, removing every single living thing, gouging hollows in the Sound, perhaps on the line of a pre-existing river valley, so that the seabed there is now a series of basins and ridges, some parts 200 feet deep, others more than 400 at low water, the corrugations and interruptions over which the tide bumps and churns.

All of that ended about 10,000 years ago, as the world started to warm. The ice wasted away, and vegetable life began to reclaim

The erratic of Moine schists dumped on the beach by a glacier
about 10,000 years ago.

the place: first a grass tundra, then a heather and juniper prairie
and finally hazel and birch woodland into which the great browsing herds wandered up from the south. No more than 1,500
years after the ice had gone, you would never have known it had
been here. This life that is here now is evidence of a self-mending
world.

Almost the only memory of those traumas on this beach is
half-buried in the sand: a bruised and battered lump of something almost infinitely older, a boulder of Moine schists, some of
the most ancient rock in Scotland, maybe a billion years old,
brought here by the ice sheet from five miles or so further east,

its body chipped and part-rounded by its journey under the glacier, surviving here in the way other ice-leavings have disappeared simply because of its hardness. Photographs make it look like a miniature asteroid or a misshapen planet. What does it mean to us? Only something to watch out for when bringing a boat into the beach at half-tide, a rock to which thin green weed and sprigs of channelled wrack cling.

There is one other strange residue of the ice. When all the fresh water was tied up in the glaciers, the sea level was something like 300 feet lower than today. As the ice melted, the sea rose but at the same time the vast weight of the ice was lifted from the land and the land itself, afloat on the semi-liquid rocks of the earth's mantle, began to bounce up, relieved of its burden in what is called 'the post-glacial rebound'.

All over the west coast of Scotland, the rebounded shores can be found as raised beaches, some, in Colonsay, 135 feet above the

The black basalt sands.

present sea. At first, the bounce was fast, an inch a year, a foot a decade, a man's height in a man's lifetime, the whole of this coast bobbing up like the limb of a glacier than has calved and fallen into the sea. The relationship of rising sea and rising land remains unclear, but the post-glacial rebound is still happening, if more slowly, perhaps at one to three millimetres a year. It is probably just keeping ahead of the rising sea level. It may be that in the thirty years I have known this bay, it has risen ninety millimetres, three or four inches, the land itself creeping upwards out of the flood, so that the shore I now know at the lowest of low tides is a sliver wider, the paring of a single fingernail, 'dwindled and thinned to the fringe', as Gerard Manley Hopkins described the crescent of a new moon, rising in all its slowness around the rim of the bay.

Next in this catalogue of disasters came the volcano that erupted in Mull between 58–60 million years ago. Fountain after fountain of the basalt poured from the vents – the Atlantic was opening and a plume of core heat was breaking into the surface layers – so that the volcanic rocks coated everything beneath them to the depth of 3,000 feet, a dark match to the ice that millions of years later would overlie them. The upper reaches of the cliffs above the bay are made of those successive flows, as is the whole mountain of Glas Bheinn behind them, and the hills on the far side of the Sound in Mull, where flow after flow steps up the mountainsides, stacked like flagstones in a yard.

The eruptions poured out over a paradisiacal world. In some parts of Mull, layers of life have been preserved between successive lava flows and ash storms. In these crushed and concealed horizons, red volcanic soils thickened on the rocks and in them a beautiful warm-country flora emerged, whose leaves and fruits, even some insect wings and bodies, can be found compressed as if in the pages of a plant-collector's journal. The finest, at Ardtun in Mull, are thought to have fallen into the still waters of a lake or quiet river, ferns, magnolias, oaks and planes. In other places, several whole pine trees were overwhelmed with the liquid lavas, enclosing them, in a scene that is almost impossible to visualise, a rock engulfment to a height of twenty or thirty feet, where they stand today surrounded by the twisted forms of the solidified lavas.

I have looked among the basalts of the bay for these precious signs of life 58 million years ago but there is none. The dark and heavy rock is as lifeless now as when it came up out of the volcano. It preserves the mineral blankness of its origins as much as any fossil preserves its form of life, made in an instant, without a history. Sometimes, at the top of a flow, where the lava was frothy and full of gas, and its consistency mousse-like, the holes in the mousse (or 'amygdales' as geologists call them, from the Greek for 'almonds') filled with quartzite liquids and this mousse-stone survives on the beach as little satellite bodies, the dark brown stone speckled with white, as pretty as chocolate chip but in truth only another glimpse into sterility.

The third episode here at which life was removed from this world is the oldest and by far the most unsettling. At Rubha an t-Sasunnaich, where I made my second pool, the hard grey lime-stones are the most sobering of all remnants, a ruin of life, a monument to emptiness. They mark one of the great crises in existence, a moment at which it is not too much to say that life almost died. They come from just after the episode known to geologists as the End Triassic Extinction, the ETE, 201 million years ago. There are sermons in stones and these ones are terrifying. This place was somewhere in the latitude of the Mediterranean, warm and life-filled. Here was not here but was nevertheless undeniably here; its substance then is here now. And so in here-not-here, slowly, far beyond the consciousness of any organism, unrolling over about 600,000 years, disaster happened.

All the continents of the world had been gathered together in a single supercontinent, Pangea, the whole earth, surrounded by a single ocean, on some edge of which this bay was then to be found. Giant convective cycles within the mantle set to work and Pangea began to break. Over a good proportion of the earth, about 4 million square miles, across what is now Brazil and Nigeria, Newfoundland and southern Europe, an area called the Central Atlantic Magmatic Province (CAMP), more than half a million cubic miles of liquid basalt came up and out of the mantle and on to the surface of the earth.

This was the breaking of Pangea but it was not the basalt as much as the gases that came with it that caused the catastrophe. Carbon dioxide and methane came blowing out of the rifting planet, into the atmosphere and absorbed by the ocean. Geologists have calculated that CAMP emitted something over 20 million tons of CO_2 a year, for about half a million years, a total of some 10,000 billion tons in addition to 5,000 billion tons of methane. These figures may mean little, but there is a comparison to bring one up short: our modern industrial life emits 10 billion tons of CO_2 every year, 500 times the annual amount coming into the atmosphere at the end of the Triassic.

This is what happened then: carbon dioxide in the atmosphere rose to between ten and 200 times its present levels. A ferocious global greenhouse developed and the earth started to burn. Sea temperatures rose. Warm water can hold less dissolved salt and so the salinity in which creatures had evolved dropped below the levels at which they could survive. Everywhere, life systems started to fail. There was less oxygen in these warm and stratified waters and animals suffocated. The high levels of CO_2 began to acidify the sea. Corals and creatures whose life structures depended on the making of hard, protective calcified shells and armatures, including many calcareous phytoplankton, found it at first difficult and then impossible to keep going. Experiments recreating these conditions in which carbon dioxide blankets the earth have led to the shell-making animals developing strange and malformed versions of themselves. The volcanic rifting and its associated gases continued to pour from the CAMP. On land, much of all previous life was removed. Niche after niche was emptied. About 80% of all species and nearly all life died. Genera after genera went extinct, particularly at sea. Heavy and suffocating blooms of green phytoplankton sucked yet more oxygen out of the water. The floor of the world's oceans was coated in thick layers of black, oxygenless muds. Nothing could breathe; almost nothing could live. For 8 million years afterwards, there were no coral reefs on earth.

The rocks Rubha an t-Sasunnaich were made as that moment ebbed, just as the sea began to become less acid but before life could recolonise it. The stone here is still utterly lifeless; the entire headland is a fossil of lifelessness, limestones accumulating in an ocean where next to nothing lived, a heartbeat away from the ending of the whole of life. Something of that is communicated by the stone. Unlike, say, a fossil-rich limestone in Portland or even the chalk, the sheer blankness of these rocks, gradually now being dissolved again in a newly acid sea, still looks and feels like the remains of a derelict, post-anoxic planet, an earth-layer in which hundreds of millions of lives had struggled and failed, dying in the chemical hostility of a poisoned planet.

If the balance had been only slightly different, if the volume of outgassing had been slightly higher or had gone on for longer, nothing would have survived. But it did and we are here, you reading, me writing. Life squeaked through.

This sea here today in front of me is performing as a sink for half the CO_2 that is expelled by the burning of fossil fuels. The absorbed gas is acidifying the water now as it did 200 million years ago, making life difficult for the shell-builders, all the periwinkles and whelks, the crabs and hermit crabs, the prawns and squat lobsters, even for the bony fish which will have trouble building their skeletons in an acid sea and for the birds that must concentrate the calcium for their bones and eggs. An acid sea is hostile to the life forms we have loved to find in it. Ever-continuing greenhouse gas emissions will deliver only a kind of

The lifeless limestones at Rubha an t-Sasunnaich, laid down just after
the catastrophe at the end of the Triassic, 200 million years ago.

ubiquitous and dominant green mush, at least for the next few
million years.

Life did recover, and the head of the bay, outside the house, is
full of evidence for that resilience. The rocks there are the residues of the reoccupied levels, the matrix of the recovery after the
ETE crisis was over, when the basalt had ceased to flow, the gases
were no longer polluting the atmosphere and the earth had
begun its long and slow rebalancing. Over millions of years, the
oceans de-acidified and life started again. It was the beginning of
one of the great ages, the Jurassic, life remaking itself in a global
act of persistence, a return to possibility.

In the 200 million years that have elapsed since then, the level
beds in which the mud and limey clays of the new post-Pangea
seas were originally laid down have been played with by earth
movements and tipped about thirty or forty degrees up from the
horizontal. The sea has then cut roughly across them, like a blunt
saw through a sheet of marine ply, so that what was once stacked
neatly one bed above the other, is now revealed as a low but
jagged series of peaks and troughs across the intertidal.

I dug my first pool into one of those troughs. I soon understood that the rocks were making their own signals to me. The
layers in them were pulsed, a regular and rhythmic sequence that
repeated again and again the same three layers one above the
other: a hard grey-blue limestone; a soft lime-rich clay; and some
dark, finely laminated black shales. The limestone broke off in
chunks if I hit it with a sledgehammer or a pickaxe; I could slice
away at the clay which had a consistency somewhere between
cheddar and brie; in it were some rounded lumps of iron-rich
sandstone, the size of goose eggs, which I could rootle out with
one of my wrecking bars like nuts from a cake; and finally the
shale shivered off in showers of millimetre flakes when I attacked
it with a jemmy.

Slowly I deepened the pool through these layers. Something
had happened here which had this rhythm built into it. The
geologists are not agreed. It seems clear at least that there was a
repeated shallowing and then re-deepening of the sea, a steady
flux and reflux across time. The dark black shales are not unlike
the worldwide seas of the ETE, the fossilised muds on the dark,
fine-grained and anoxic floor of a relatively deep sea in which no
life could persist, much like the floor of the Black Sea now. From
slightly shallower seas is the grey clay with the egg nodules in it.
Those nodules, the scientists agree, are concretions of the iron-
rich elements when pressurised by the rock layers above. The last
is the hard limestone, which is solid with the fossils of a richly
curved and sculpted early oyster called *Gryphaea arcuata* – the
hooked griffin in Linnaean Latin, the Devil's toenail for the
pre-scientific. This stone was laid down in a warm, clear and
shallow sea, not unlike the Bahamas now.

In all, a single repetition of the rock sequence records the passing of about 38,000 years of the early Jurassic sea. Half of it is
the limestone, about a fifth the clay and the rest the dark shales.
Again and again, for millions of years, the pattern repeated, the
sea came and went, deepened and shallowed, not arbitrarily but

metronomically, pulsing and fluxing as a tide, one of the slowest of all the earth's many songs.

In the 1920s the Serbian mathematician and astronomer Milutin Milankovitch established that the movements of the earth were governed by a series of interlocking and repeated cycles. The planet was not fixed on some cosmic armature but was afloat in its gravity field. One cycle, 90,000 years long, reflects the coming and going of the earth's orbit around the sun, pulled this way and that by the gravities of Jupiter and Saturn, so that the ellipse of its year stretches and contracts over time. Another cycle, perhaps a long-lasting effect of a collision with another body at the time the earth and moon were formed, marks a wobble, 20,000 years long, in which, like a slowing top, the rotational axis of the earth itself rotates.

The third, and the one that has shaped this beach, is subtle – a slight shifting back and forth by a few degrees every 40,000 years or so in the earth's axis of rotation. Over that period, the earth

The pulsed layers of rocks at the head of the bay from the early Jurassic. The large fossils are Devil's Toenails, *Gryphaea arcuata*. Winkles and limpets populate the surface.

tilts to and fro, towards and then away from the sun. When at maximum tilt, the seasons are more extreme: more sun in the summer, less in the winter. As the earth comes upright, the seasons rebalance and become more like each other. At the moment we are half-tipped, halfway through one of these cycles and so the seasons are neither extreme nor particularly mild.

The early Jurassic wobbled to and fro as we do. At maximum tip and maximum seasonality, the summers had no difficulty melting the winter snows. At minimum tip, the summers were cool, the winter snows did not melt and both ice caps and glaciers grew. Minimum tip was, in other words, an ice age, maximum tip an age of near-Siberian shifts each year from heat to cold. And so this is the picture here 200 million years ago. We were in the subtropics, far south of any ice sheet. The climate flowed around us. When summers were cool, volumes of water were locked up in the ice sheets and the sea level was low. The bay at those moments was in the warm shallows of somewhere like the Caribbean. *Gryphaea* sat in the surface of the pale oozy mud on the sea floor filtering their plankton food from the turquoise waters above them. As summers warmed with the turning of the Milankovitch cycle, sea level rose, the sea here deepened and it became a place first of clay ooze and then of ever deeper dark and anoxic muds. Ammonites and other animals fell to the bottom and were preserved there. Within time, the tilt began to turn, the summers cooled, the ice grew, the sea level dropped and we were once again in the warm life-loving shallows. These rocks record that rhythmic earth.

I took some pieces of the rock back to the house where there is a bench against the bay-facing wall. A spring morning. I sat there with a small hammer and the lumps of Jurassic sea floor and began to tap and chisel at the laminations. My copy of *Mesozoic Fossils*, a cup of coffee, cold sunshine.

First: the hard limestone in which the *Gryphaeas* cluster in such thick bands. But they are difficult to dig out of the stone.

A pair of Devil's Toenails yin-and-yanged into each other's arms and
then polished by the sea.

A *Gryphaea* orientated as it would have been in life, its rounded body
settled into the mud, its opening closed with a lid.

Its concreted grip is fierce and I had little success. In places, though, the oysters have already fallen out of their matrix and lie smoothed and ready-polished on the beach. One I picked up and treasure is a pair of the little griffons, clamped in each other's arms, yinned and yanged into each other's hollows. Another had its lid in place, where the muscle of the animal had clamped it 200 million years ago.

Where the sea creatures further out from the shore dropped into the dark muds at the bottom of the sea and were preserved there, they are easier to disinter. In one of the sandstone nodules were the fleeting remains of an ammonite, too blurred to identify its species, a splay of curved indents, nothing more. The finely laminated shales were the best. Soon their flaky pastry began to fall apart in my fingers. Out of it came the little fossilised creatures that had died and fallen into the mud. First, part of a tiny shell, as if of a slightly asymmetric queen scallop, but impossible to align with anything in the handbook.

Then, best of all, a pair of tiny cockles smaller than my little fingernail, about the size of a hazelnut picked out of its shell.

The trace of a Jurassic ammonite left in a sandstone nodule.

A pair of tiny Jurassic cockles as small as my little fingernails,
Calcirhynchia calcaria.

They were *Calcirhynchia calcaria*, finely cast, with the joint between upper and lower shell dipping down in the centre, as if with a pouting lip.

These things that look like life, and carry all the signatures once made by life, are not now life, and for one reason: they are over. They have no future but merely indicate the place where life once was, lacking the one identifying mark of the living: an openness to time, a vulnerability to risk, a readiness to enter again and again the furnace of existence. They have become, almost literally, monuments to themselves. Everything they once were has already been burned away.

The sympathetic and reproachful ghost of the great Victorian naturalist Philip Henry Gosse (1810–88) hangs over this story of life, fossils and the pools. Gosse was the fundamentalist king of the Victorian shore. Almost alone, he had invented the view of it as a place in which to see God's world in miniature. He loved the intertidal, knew it as well as anyone, promulgated its beauties, made a career out of it, encouraged thousands to love it as he did, and finally failed to understand the essence of what he saw.

He was the son of a semi-successful miniaturist from Poole in Dorset and spent his youth in Canada and America, gradually learning to examine and understand the natural world. The near-death of his sister in his late twenties pushed him towards a fervent and literalist Christianity, which again and again found in nature signs of God's beneficence, and of his having made a happy world.

An enormous workload of papers, lectures, books and pamphlets led to nervous exhaustion and in 1851, when only forty, he retired with his beloved wife Emily and their son Edmund to the Devon coast, where he began his researches into marine biology. He found a way of keeping sea animals and plants alive in unchanged seawater, by balancing oxygenating coralline seaweeds with oxygen-consuming creatures, and his ecstatic, Elysian adventures on the shore resulted in book after book, richly illustrated from his own watercolours, describing his discoveries among the life of the pools.

He recognised that the beauties of God's nature were 'never more great than when minutely great', and the sense of wonder is palpable two centuries later. He loved the sight of a winkle 'marching soberly along beneath his massive mansion, leisurely circumambulating the pretty tide pool which he has chosen for his present residence'.

Watching a barnacle wafting food into its mouth reminded him 'of the Gospel net, mentioned by our Lord, which is "cast into the sea, and gathers of every kind; which, when it is full, they draw to shore, and sit down, and gather the good into vessels, but cast the bad away"' (Matthew 13: 47–8).

He and his son Edmund spent whole summers exploring

submarine gardens of a beauty that seemed often to be fabulous … their sides and floor paved with living blossoms, ivory-white, rosy-red, orange, and amethyst … the great prawns gliding like transparent launches, *anthea* waving in the twilight its thick white waxen tentacles, and the fronds of the dulse faintly streaming on the water like huge red banners in some reverted atmosphere.

Emily developed cancer and in 1857 died an agonising death. Gosse was left alone with Edmund, for whom he had promised Emily on her deathbed the strictest and most rigorous of Christian upbringings. The desire for the consolations of changelessness, for the denial of catastrophe in the pattern of life, became overwhelming. That Platonic longing – for a perfect and eternal world of stillness beyond this one, a pool in which truth, beauty and goodness could have their everlasting being, and

P. H. Gosse.

where change was unknown – led him to write *Omphalos: An Attempt to Untie the Geological Knot*. It was the most elaborate and maddest effort ever made to deny mutability in living things and to see in the facts of nature the mind of an eternal God who in the six days of Creation made every animal and plant as they now were and ever would be.

Omphalos, he wrote, would offer 'a stable resting place' for those who were troubled by the apparently irreconcilable differences between the account in Genesis of God's creation and the evidence of the rocks. By the 1850s, the tectonic plates were stirring around traditional Christians. The 'stone-book' seemed to say the Bible was wrong. Rocks from the Silurian seas lay 50,000 feet thick; some coral reefs were 2,500 feet deep. Fossils of enormous frogs the size of a hippopotamus had been found. Creatures in the fossil record had appeared, lived, bred and died for thousands on thousands of successive generations.

> Sometimes the whole existing fauna seems to have come to a sudden violent end; at others, the species die out one by one. New creatures supply the place of the old. Species change; the very genera change, and change again. Forms of beings, strange beings, beings of uncouth shape, of mighty ferocity and power, of gigantic dimensions, come in, run their specific race, propagate their kinds – and at length die out and disappear; to be replaced by other species, each approaching nearer and nearer to familiar forms.

The idea of a single moment of creation was fatally challenged. These other animals, from the vast depths of time, 'had shells, crusts, plates, bones, horns, teeth, exactly corresponding in structure and function to those of recent animals', but body parts that seemed to have little to do with them. Millions of forest trees had grown and died, now crushed into the coal strata. Succulent plants lay in beds hundreds of feet thick, pressed together like paper-pulp. None of them was like anything found in the modern world.

It was, as Gosse said, 'a mighty array of evidence'. How to reconcile its vision of the vast, rolling cycles of change with anything in Genesis? 'He who made the world is One Jehovah, who cannot be inconsistent with Himself. But [people] cannot shut their eyes to the startling fact, that the records which seem legibly written on His created works do flatly contradict the statements which seem to be most plainly expressed in His word.'

Some hoped it could all be explained by Noah's flood. Others suggested the early world might have developed very quickly and that all the layers of the rocks could have been laid down by God in a week. Just because the world develops slowly nowadays did not mean to say it did so in the past. Maybe the six days of Creation were just a manner of speaking. Perhaps each day was many millions of years long. Or there may have been many worlds before this one and this was the one made in six days some 6,000 years ago. For one idea, Gosse reserved particular scorn. An author had 'hatched a scheme, by which the immediate ancestor of Adam was a Chimpanzee, and his remote ancestor a Maggot!'

Gosse's own solution was ingenious. At the moment of creation God did not make individual adult animals. No animal exists only in its adult state. Every plant and animal is dependent on a life cycle that has embedded in it the process of generation, from adult to egg, to embryo, to child to adult. And so God did not make animals; he made life cycles. Creation was 'the sudden bursting into a circle', an irruption into the processes of life, each species of which from the first would continue to generate the potential that God had put into it. Every plant and creature was made with its whole past and future implicit in it. This is the idea that lies behind the title of the book: *omphalos* is the Greek for navel. Even though God had made Adam whole and adult, he would have given him a navel because the cycle of life, his own generation and birth, required it.

Gosse's conception was explicitly miraculous. The first butterfly had already been a caterpillar. All creatures were created with the evidence in them of their having lived before they were created – an impossibility, but an aspect of the divine miracle.

He asked his readers to imagine the morning of creation on a rocky shore.

> In this weed-fringed tide-pool there is a fine specimen of the Shore-crab (*Carcinus mœnas*). It is a male just arrived at the perfection of adult age; its carapace smooth and wholly dark-green in hue, its under parts rufous orange.
>
> To all appearance this Crab is several years old … But four distinct metamorphoses were passed before the commencement of this form … And before this, there was the egg, which was laid by the mother Crab.
>
> All these evidences of age, clear and unanswerable though they are, are yet fallacious, because the Crab has been created but this morning.

This was the crux: not only were the creatures made with their past and future already implicit in them; the earth itself and all its life was made, in this one week of Creation, with its past pre-enclosed in its rocks. God made the fossil record as he made the world. It was a solution to 'the painful dilemma'. Just as the first trees had rings in their timber, the first shells had growth lines and the first man had a navel, the earth itself had all the cycles of its own immense past embedded in it. 'It may be objected,' Gosse wrote, 'that, to assume the world to have been created with fossil skeletons in its crust – skeletons of animals that never really existed – is to charge the Creator with forming objects whose sole purpose was to deceive us.' His answer was straightforward and unanswerable: 'The law of creation supersedes the law of nature.' God made the world with the past that was natural to it.

His contemporaries thought it absurd. Those who believed in God did not like to think of him as a deceiver. Those who valued the findings of science could not accept this distorting of the evidence. Almost at a stroke, the hero of an entire generation of shore-lovers had his reputation destroyed. As Darwinian ideas rapidly took hold and it was increasingly understood that flux, chance and change were the governors of life on earth, Gosse became a fossil, an entirely coherent but entirely previous form of existence that had suffered its catastrophe and from which the world had moved on.

PART III

PEOPLE

9

Sacrifice

If I had been here 10,000 years ago, after the glaciers melted, I could have done what I do today, raking the sand on the ebb for cockles; searching the lowest of the tide for the telltale dimples of the razor clams; picking mussels at the mouth of the big burn where it falls from between the alders on to the foreshore; collecting a plateful of sand eels caught just out of their burrows by the dropping sea.

I would have whooped with delight, as we still do now from time to time, when crowds and crowds of herring fry land on the boulders at the edge of the beach, driven ashore by the mackerel,

Sand eels off the beach, lunch a few minutes later.

the prey fish fizzing and jumping all over the surface of the water, hazing the skin of it, and coming to lie dead and glittering in the drying pools among the wrack, a sudden, crazed silver bullion, a protein feast from nothing in the ochre of the weed.

These were the riches to be had on this edible shore, but for a full one hundred generations, no one came. For spring after spring, summer after summer, for more than 3,000 years, no one was here. People were living in England, as far north as York, hunter-gathering in the marshes and oakwoods of a pristine country, but no nearer. They fished down there in lakes and rivers, hunted and killed deer and aurochsen, feeding largely off that huge reservoir of herbivore protein and feeling no need to come further north or west up into the moors and mountains.

Herring fry come ashore in their thousands when chased
there by the mackerel.

In the northern temperate zones of America and Eurasia, for a hunter-gathering life in an untouched country every person needs about 15,000 acres. In England, by about 5500 BC, with the growth in the population and diminishing quantities of wild meat, that limit had been reached and the long drive to recolonise the country could begin again. The world was warming – fewer storms, gentler winters – and people at last began to make their way up towards the maritime riches of the west coast of Scotland.

On one headland and island after another, up and down the Atlantic shore, these Mesolithic people (so called from the Middle Stone Age, between the Palaeolithic and the Neolithic, named after their neat, slight tools made of slivers of flint) left behind them the earliest human monuments in Europe: huge piles of used seashell, gathered above the shores from which they had picked them. There was one just north of Morvern in Loch Sunart on the tiny uninhabited island of Risga, a bony place, now almost inaccessible in summer and blanketed in bracken, but where in 1920–1 a large collection was discovered of stone mattocks, antler harpoons and limpet-hammers – fist-sized stone truncheons for smacking limpets off the rocks – all abandoned next to a vast quantity of mollusc shells, fish bones, lobster and crab shell and the bones of seabirds, seals, otters and porpoises.

The techniques of the 1920s archaeologists were clumsy by modern standards and most of the detailed information has been lost. I have looked for the remains of the midden on Risga, landing there one sultry summer day, but there is nothing to be seen, at least on the surface.

Other more recent investigations have examined these limpet middens more carefully, sieving every last fragment from the dust, and finding all the shore animals on which the people here preyed 7,000 years ago: limpets and keyhole limpets; cockles, periwinkles and smooth winkles; oysters, mussels, scallops, queen scallops, cowries – often perforated and used as beads and in necklaces – the ridges and twirls of *Nassarius* shells and topshells. Some of the bigger shells, from razor clams and the scallops, are often reshaped as scrapers. The claws and legs of edible, velvet, swimming and shore crabs; plus the vertebrae and skull parts of bream, wrasse, gilthead, hake, pollack, cod and tope, a small

---

Eat the shore: ingredients on the Mesolithic menu

Mammals

whale	porpoise	seal
otter		

Birds

shag or cormorant	razorbill	guillemot
little auk	great auk	thrush and chat
duck		

Fish

tope	dogfish	ray
herring	eel	rockling
saithe	pollack	cod
haddock	whiting	horse mackerel
sea bream	corkwing wrasse	ballan wrasse
cuckoo wrasse	butterfish	sand eel
mackerel	plaice	flatfish

Crustacea

crab	lobster	prawn

Molluscs

limpet	cockle	periwinkle
dogwhelk	topshell	mussel
scallop	carpet shell	razor shell

Plants

hemp nettle	yellow water lily	nettle
fat hen	sorrel/dock	bog bean
chickweed	knotweed	

shark, are often mixed in this astonishing *fruits de mer* with products of the land: apple pips, plum stones and the shells from hazelnuts, along with the occasional bones of a hare or a goat. Often with them, most poignantly, are the skeletons and skulls of the great auks still then thriving on the European littoral.

This Mesolithic intimacy with the intertidal was total. Analyses of the bone collagen of the people who made the middens have revealed in bone after bone that virtually all the protein on which these coastal-dwellers lived came from the sea: birds, fish, seals, the occasional cast-up whale or dolphin. Unlike their immediate ancestors, deer or wild cattle were nearly absent from their diet. To the sea-vertebrates, they now added the resources of the shore and its pools.

Nothing of their equipment survives in Scotland, but elsewhere, in wet or drowned landscapes, Mesolithic log boats, along with wooden fish traps, baskets, string, nets, floats, weights, fish hooks and the ability to tie good, quick and useful knots, have all been found. These were the sea people, the sea almost literally in every pore of their bodies, the sea margin more important to them than anyone before or since in the long European story.

One set of middens on the pale, grassy, tidal island of Oronsay, the far side of Mull, has revealed that these piles of shells were more than mere rubbish tips. Because fish are cold-blooded, they grow fast in the warm-water months of the year, more slowly in the winter. If you look carefully at their bones, you can read the annual pattern of rapid translucent summer growth and thicker winter growth patterned through them like the rings in a timber tree. The last and outer ring in any fish will record the time it was caught. Analysis of the ear bones of the young saithe picked out of the Oronsay mounds has shown that, as the year progressed, the people moved from one corner of the little island to the next, each shell mound, made next to a hearth and a simple shelter, little more than a windbreak, containing the fish in turn from spring, summer, autumn and early winter. Only the winter itself, when the young saithe move offshore, inaccessible to the baited hooks and hand nets of the Mesolithic people, was without a catch. Instead, the winter was the time, above all at low tide, when they harvested the limpets from the rocks. For about 300 years, just over 5,000 years ago, each mound in turn received the same seasonal addition of shell and fishbone.

One cold and windy afternoon I walked across the machair of Oronsay with Sarah and the children, wandering from one of these grassy knolls to the next – some still thirty feet high – thinking of the people 5,000 years ago, next to this same eye-blue sea, with the same white beaches and the skyline of the Paps in Jura to the south. Each party of shell-gatherers would have come to the old familiar summer place, or spring place, or autumn place, and begun to add to what they and their parents and grandparents had gathered there before. They can only have viewed their slowly grassing middens, as we do our summer and winter haunts, as marks of time, a way of calibrating the world, each yearly arrival a re-summoning of the seasons we have had there before. For all of us these places are memory pools, with the past embedded in them, full of the pleasures of renewal, the consolations of continuity and the sense of loss in time.

The archaeologists, led by Paul Mellars from Cambridge, found one other intriguing phenomenon in the mounds: they were full of human hand and foot bones, at least seventy of them. Most were scattered almost at random through the mass of limpet shell and from all sorts of people: women, children, young and old men. There are no cut marks or other evidence of cannibalism. Many of the bones showed that the hands of which they had once been a part were heavily muscled, working tools, the instruments of survival. One of them, almost complete, was laid next to and aligned with the flipper of a grey seal, of which many come ashore here in the autumn to pup. Finger to finger in the midst of the mound, the two species very nearly touched.

A quiet mystery floods in behind that 'signature of a purposive cultural act', as the archaeologists austerely describe it. What can it mean? Had the hand belonged to a great seal-hunter? Were all these hand bones somehow a memorial to the engagement in the realities of the world that a well-led life involves? Did the seal-touching hand belong to a man who had his hand in, who had a hand in everything this small island community needed, who handed it on to his successors, in whose hands they had felt safe and good? And whose hands were no good now? Who had moved over towards the half-hidden sea world in which those close and sentient sea companions, whenever one looks up, are found afloat and bristling, aware of us, looking to us, just offshore? There is no answer to any of that. But it does bring to mind a man I know in the Hebrides, a fisherman, whose hands are the biggest and strongest I have ever known. When he greets you, your hands disappear inside the grip of his, which are scarred, knobbled and muscled with decades of work on the decks of herring drifters and scallop boats. Quantities of Donald MacSween's existence are folded into his magnificent hands and it may be that the Oronsay seal-hunter was a man like him.

Soon after 4000 BC, this whole habit of life came to a sudden end in what modern archaeology and genetic science have revealed to be the most radical revolution in the history of the temperate world. It may be that the sheer richness of life in the rock pools had allowed the population to grow and for pressures to come on their survival. The very fact that the limpets in the Oronsay middens are almost entirely the flatter form that grow on the lower shore, and are to be reached only at low-water spring tides, may mean that the mound-builders had cleared the more accessible limpets at the upper end of the tide and were squeezing the resource. Overfishing was already a factor at the end of the Mesolithic.

For whatever reason, the new arrivals around 4000 BC swept all before them. The bone analysis that showed coastal Mesolithic people to have been entirely dependent on seafood has revealed their successors in the Neolithic to have ignored it just as completely. With no gradual transition, the products of the land were substituted for food from the sea and shore. The reason is not far to find. The archaeologist Geoffrey Bailey worked out that to provide enough protein for one man for a day would, if he ate nothing else, take 400 limpets, 700 oysters or 1,400 cockles. The protein punch of a single cow was equivalent to 31,000 limpets, 52,000 oysters and 157,000 cockles. Farming – the Neolithic revolution that brought domesticated animals, the use of pottery, land clearance, the growing of cereals, the building of farms and villages – was to be the future.

New genetic evidence has shown that this 'Neolithic package' did not come unaccompanied but was brought to these Atlantic shores by a new race of people, carrying with them the genes of their ancestors in the Near East and south-eastern Europe, that genetic inheritance fused with other strains from the steppes of Central Asia, the source of the languages we speak and the stories that have always been told here. They brought the animals with them: the closest relations of the early sheep that survived on St Kilda are from Palestine and Syria; even the deer on the Outer Hebrides have no genetic connection with deer on the mainland of Scotland or even Norway. Astonishingly, it looks as if they too were brought by boat in the Neolithic centuries from the mainland of Europe. The genetic origins of the dogs they brought with them were probably in Nepal or Mongolia.

Very rapidly, the people stopped eating the products of the shore. Milk and cheese took their place but it is not as if the food on the beach and the rocks disappeared. It was always there for the taking even if people did not make use of it. Many archaeologists have concluded that a taboo was at work. Here on the western and northern shores of Scotland, as in many other world cultures, the eating of fish came to be seen as degraded and even unclean. Reliance on farmed products had become the norm.

That most radical shift in the human relationship to the natural did not come without hazards. All over the Neolithic world a familiar pattern was repeated: forests were cut down, land was cleared, crops planted and stock animals bred. The new system provided a far stronger source of food than the Mesolithic reliance on nature. Children survived and the populations grew, providing still more labour to clear the ground.

From about 3000 BC, the climate worsened: colder, wetter, stormier. Inevitably, the Near Eastern cereal crops brought in by the Neolithic people started to fail. With increasing regularity, famine struck and death swept through the villages. It was a time, as the Ohio anthropologist Sean Downey and his colleagues have written, of 'rapid demographic growth, followed by periods of devastating societal instability'. What were they to do? A brilliant analysis of the bodies of some Neolithic farmers in Orkney has shown that although shore-protein does not appear in the bone collagen, which averages out food consumed over a lifetime, the fine layers of dentine laid down on a tooth, examined at thicknesses representing less than a single year, do reflect the food that was eaten while they were being made. These Neolithic teeth have revealed that from time to time the dominant land-signature drops away and at moments of crisis people turned again towards the shore for famine food.

Lady's Rock with the Duart peninsula on Mull behind it.

Resorting to the shore for sustenance in an emergency remained the pattern throughout history. Seafood on the west coast of Scotland was eaten out of compulsion not pleasure, and that alliance of crisis and the shore became the background to the most powerful of all the stories from these waters. It comes not from the infinite depths of the past but from a quite identifiable moment, perhaps 4,000 or 5,000 years ago, when life here was threatened and in need of the most terrifying remedies.

Of all the stories that turn on the turning of the tide, none is more gripping than the myth of Lady's Rock which drifts in from the late fifteenth and early sixteenth centuries but carries with it echoes of far earlier lives and other meanings.

I have sailed down to Lady's Rock in my small sixteen-foot wooden lugger, launching from our beach at the head of the bay and, with a sunny day and a following tide and wind, taking no more than an hour or so to cover the seven miles to where the rock and its beacon stand mid-channel between Mull and Lismore. The rock itself is a disturbing and alluring thing. At the highest tides, seas break over it even on a still day and when the rock clears above low water, its surface is as smooth as a turtleback, draped in weed, overwashed by the swells that come up and around the beacon tower. Before there was a light here, storms would have wrecked vessel after vessel on its low and lurking presence. Of the many, most have gone unrecorded but the *Rhind*, of Wick, a schooner, can stand for them, totally destroyed here on 8 December 1851 during a heavy gale. 'It is feared,' the clerk to Lloyd's List noted that week, 'that some other vessels have gone to pieces, as portions of wreck have been driven on shore on the Islands of Kerrera and Lesmore.'

Even at the lowest of tides, Lady's Rock never quite feels like an island. Common gulls and blackbacks sit on its dark surface but it remains, when visible, part of the hidden world. As the tide fills into the Lynn of Morvern to the north and up into the Sound of Mull, the cramming of those big and heavy streams

The sea of knives raised at Lady's Rock by the meeting of the tides.
Lismore lighthouse behind.

through this narrow gateway between Mull and Lismore kicks the sea up into steep-walled peaks and overfalls. The water either side of here is in places 600 feet deep, but the channel through which the tide must push between Mull and Lady's Rock is less than half that and between Lady's Rock and Lismore at its shallowest is only eighty feet deep. It is a constricted passage and around the rock the sea breaks for no apparent reason, driven by its own constrained and hidden dynamics.

The tidal stream, which in the Sound runs at two knots or so, accelerates here and with a following wind can run at four or five knots over the submerged rocks, often boiling up into weirdly unsettling slicks as the water meets and bubbles over those underwater projections and that surface mounds into low domes, spreading out from the centre, with in-sucking spirals at the margins. All around them the stiff-spiked and troubled seas are frightening in an open boat, when the confused, steep-walled waves can stand beside you, each peak level with the gunwale.

I have never known it comfortable there, and it is always one of those anxious stretches you are happy to get through whatever the weather. In a contrary wind, it can turn positively dangerous, with large boat-swallowing holes opening up in the meeting of the tides. The Admiralty charts still carry a warning for small

The unsettling slicks and domes of upwelling water as the ebb tide
meets the rising seafloor around Lady's Rock.

vessels here as a place to avoid in fierce weather. In a story told
by Norman Macleod, minister of Morvern in the nineteenth
century, this part of the tideway 'was called "the dirks", from the
figure of the waves which rose on every side, tossing their sharp
heads in the sky'.

It is the sea of knives. 'Whoe'er has raised the sail / By Mull's
dark coast has heard this evening's tale', Walter Scott wrote in
1810, as his prologue to a play he had put on in Edinburgh,
written by his friend Joanna Baillie, and with the principals acted
by Mr and Mrs Siddons.

> The plaided boatman, resting on his oar,
> Points to the fatal rock amid the roar
> Of whitening waves.

This is the place around which the story has gathered. There is,
first, what feels like an applied historical frame. A mile and a half
to the west of the rock is the tall grey bulk of Duart Castle, high

220

on a crag overlooking the entrance to the Sound. It was built in parts and in stages in the fourteenth, fifteenth and sixteenth centuries, and restored with a romantic silhouette in the early 1900s. For at least 500 years it has been the headquarters of Clan Maclean. At some time, perhaps in the late 1490s, but all documents are uncertain, a marriage was arranged between the heir to the chief of the Macleans in Duart and the increasingly powerful Campbells, earls of Argyll who were at various times both their rivals and their allies.

Argyll's daughter, called in different versions either Catherine, Janet or Elizabeth, was given in marriage to Lachlan Maclean, chief of his clan, the laird of Duart. Stories of this Lachlan – his name, shared by many Macleans, means Norseman in Gaelic – are told even now on Mull as a man with at least six wives or mistresses, the 'only bad chief of Clan Maclean'. Two carved slabs on the ground outside the south-east corner of Pennygown chapel, near Salen on Mull, are pointed out as the graves of this chief and one of his wives. Both, it is said, were witches, burning

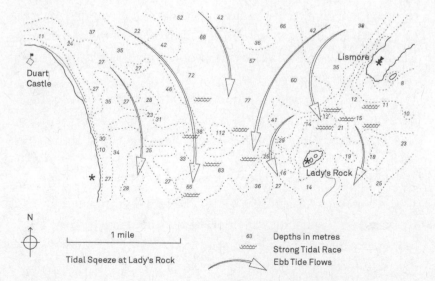

The tidal squeeze at Lady's Rock.

live cats when their squalling summoned the Devil. Such wickedness could not be buried in hallowed ground and the two of them remain outside the church.

Argyll's daughter was brought to Duart from her father's castle at Inveraray on Loch Fyne. The story now riffles into different versions. In some she had a lover at home who came with her disguised as a monk. He was to aid her plan to steal the land of the Macleans and give it to her brother, heir to the earl of Argyll. In another, when she came to Maclean's bed, she found beside him the sword he always slept with. She objected to sharing a bed with a sword and he fell first into a rage and then to plotting against her. In some versions of the story, the union between this Maclean and the Campbell girl was barren. In others, she bore him a son, but the Maclean clan as a whole, in particular the chief's own foster brothers, were hostile to her. They came to him and said they would desert him and the clan would be broken if they could not put his wife and son to death, 'so that the blood of the Campbells might not succeed to the inheritance of Maclean'. One version says she tried to poison him. In another, the chief had 'entertained a violent passion for a young daughter of a vassal chieftain, Maclean of Treshnish [on the far side of Mull], and the only hope he had of obtaining her was by getting rid of his present lady'.

The chief resisted his clansmen, fearing the power and vengeance of Argyll; but at length gave way, fearful for his own life. The only condition he imposed was that no blood should be shed.

> The better to accomplish his end, and to lull suspicion, on the eve of his infamous attempt, he for some time bestowed more than his usual attentions on his unsuspecting victim, and proposed that on a certain evening they should make an excursion on the water in the neighbourhood of Duart Castle; to this his confiding lady consented, and on the

The woman on the rock.

proposed evening he had one of his galleys in readiness, manned by a few tools whom he had admitted into his secret. They embarked and proceeded towards a solitary rock, distant about two miles eastward of Duart Castle, and only visible at half-tide, where he left her, in the anticipation that the tide, now rapidly rising, would soon sweep her away for ever from his sight.

She was to die in the sea but as she was about to drown on her rock, she saw a boat in the channel. The water was as high as her breast, 'so that the boatmen at first mistook her for a large bird'. In some versions the boat was full of her own Campbells, one of them her foster father who had looked after her as a girl, and recognised her cry. In other versions, the origins of the people in the boat are scattered across this loch-and-land interlace of the West Highlands: either from Lismore; or Loch Don in Mull; from Knapdale further south on the mainland; or from Taynish on Loch Sween. In several of the versions, she shelters for a while in a corn mill (which is later given to her rescuers) before she comes at last to the castle of her father at Inveraray.

Argyll hid his daughter, waiting for news from Mull. Maclean sent a solemn account of her death, and soon came himself to Inveraray with his clan, all in mourning. In one version, the would-be murderer brought with him a coffin filled with turf, and with great solemnity either had it interred at Inveraray or set in a chamber there to await its burial. Argyll received him with all honour. A feast was served in the hall; everyone took his place, while a seat was left empty on the right hand of Argyll. As they ate, the door opened, and Catherine Maclean entered, superbly dressed, to take her place beside them. 'Maclean stood for a moment aghast, when, the servants and retainers making a lane for him to pass through the hall to the gate of the castle, the earl's son, the Lord of Lorne, followed him, and slew him as he fled.'

In another version, 'the crafty and suspicious chief had taken such precaution in arming himself and his followers as to render it dangerous to attempt the summary punishment he so justly merited' and the Campbells allowed him to escape. Only many years later was he murdered in his bed in Edinburgh by his wife's brother, Campbell of Calder, who did not trouble to remove his knife from its scabbard but pushed it whole and sheathed into the sleeping man's heart.

What to make of this tale? It haunts the whole stretch of the Sound from Duart up to our own bay. I never see the tall beacon on the rock, or its light flashing solemnly at night, without it coming to mind. But what is it? A vivid and brutal incident from a lawless time in the history of the West Highlands? An exciting drama of the tidal landscape, to which a string of late eighteenth- and early nineteenth-century writers were drawn for its Gothic ingredients? Or something deeper and older than that?

Push beyond the late-medieval surface, first, into Maclean of Duart himself. His nickname, Cattanach, means the Wild One, the Shaggy or Hairy One. Hairiness is long associated, in the wide spread of Indo-European myth, with a kind of transgressive potency. It marks a man out in the economy of these stories as bestial, shamanistic, even demonic, a signal that the tale is dealing with more than the human.

Then the woman: Elizabeth or Janet or Catherine Campbell. She is an outsider, who brings threat in her wake. The Maclean clansmen do not trust her, nor does Cattanach himself who greets her in his bed with a sword. For a sword to be lying between lovers or potential lovers is a symbol of chastity in many Irish and Scandinavian stories. Tristan and Isolde, in the Breton and Welsh myths on which Wagner drew, are found by King Mark of Cornwall to be sleeping with a sword between them as a sign and symbol of their purity. Here, though, the sword is more potent than that, the presence of violence and hostility deep in the place where there should be sexual union.

Catherine Campbell seems to have poison about her, ready either to poison the pure Maclean blood with the admixture of her own Campbell blood; or more directly to poison Cattanach himself. Whichever way she turns she is toxic, either in the barrenness of her marriage to Maclean; or in conceiving a child. She also is a witch, with powers of evil beyond ordinary choosing, and it is against those powers that Cattanach's sword lies in the bed.

And so, it seems, Catherine Campbell must be given to the sea. The community of clansmen demand it. No blood must be spilled. The sea itself must have her whole. Her body must go into it, up to her middle, to breast and neck, so that she loses the appearance of humanity and becomes like a wild bird, returning, as a witch often will, to her animal form. She must be executed by drowning as an offering to the tide.

The oldest rites of the Indo-European peoples, from Scandinavia to the Indus, stretching back into the pre-literate centuries before 2000 BC, finds religion connected to a tripartite cluster of sacrifice, feasting and the telling of tales. Those three elements are all in play here. But there is something more precise too. Among the ancient Gauls and in pagan Germanic tribes, there was a three-part system of punishment by which an offence against a priest or governing authority was subject to hanging; against the warrior code, to burning or execution by the sword. The fertility gods, who presided over earth and generation, the growing of food and the survival of humanity, were to be satisfied only with death by drowning.

Echoes of this story are found first of all in the widespread Andromeda myth, one of the great templates of sacrifice and rescue to have migrated across centuries and worlds. In the myth, a queen boasts that her daughter is more beautiful than the sea nymphs who live with Poseidon. They insist that the sea god avenge this unforgivable human hubris. He agrees and punishes the queen by devastating the land with disastrous floods, sending a terrible sea monster to devour every human and beast in his path. The people tell the king that the land can be saved only by the sacrifice of the king's daughter, Andromeda.

The king is uncertain and delays but eventually gives in to the demands of the people. Andromeda is taken to a rock by the sea's edge where she will drown to appease the rage of Poseidon. The young Perseus then appears, armed and in flight. He cuts off the sea monster's head with a magical curved sword. Andromeda is set free and he sweeps her off to marry her.

Andromeda is the bride of death, led out to the seashore at night, and left there to keep the devastation of the human world at bay. She is to be killed to ensure the survival of others. This legend is told by Hesiod, Homer, Euripides, Pliny and Ovid and in every one the vital spirit at the heart of the tale is arrogance, the daring of mortals to assume they can be equal to the gods, neglecting the primacy of the great and dominating forces in the world.

A lord, a rock, the sea, woman, death and rescue – the connection to that famous myth is clear enough, but the Lady's Rock story holds on to some darker and more essential elements that have been sanitised away from the classical story.

'Sacrificial killing is the basic experience of the sacred,' the great mythographer, anthropologist and Greek scholar Walter Burkert wrote. It is one of humanity's most powerful and paradoxical acts of connection with the natural world, dependent on a recognition of the reciprocal nature of existence. We must live in the frame of mutuality. To give is to expect to receive. To receive is to expect to give in return. 'Sacrifice is an act of killing that simultaneously guarantees the perpetuation of life and food,' a 'two-sided act' compressing into one highly charged moment 'the encounter with death and the will to live'. To sacrifice is to recognise flux and return, to acknowledge the tidal nature of reality.

These are deep waters but ones which were long fundamental to the pre-modern world. Sacrifice is everywhere: in ancient China, in the proto-Indo-Europeans of Central Asia, in pre-Columbian America, in Egypt, with the Phoenicians, the Babylonians, Persians, Greeks, Etruscans, Romans and, symbolised and spiritualised, in the central rituals of Christianity. The killing is always followed by feasting, a reassertion of the social fabric after a hole has been cut in it with the knife, the reward in some sense for which the sacrifice has been made.

Life is guaranteed by these deaths and so the value of the life that is desired is measured by the value of the creature that is killed for it. The most precious lives, the best that can be found, must be the chosen victims. The sacrifice of young women is found all over the world from Asia to Polynesia. In America the Hurons and Algonquins sacrificed a virgin before fishing; in Mexico young women were killed before the harvest. In many places, animals were substituted in the sacrifice. In Stone Age Germany, young does in springtime after being killed and weighed down with rocks were pushed into the depths of pools where archaeologists have found their remains surrounded by the weighting stones. In Genesis, Abraham is required by God to kill his son Isaac. Isaac's place is taken at the last moment by a ram. Iphigenia in Greek mythology is magically replaced by a deer before her father kills her as a sacrifice to allow the Greek fleet to sail to Troy. In Greece more generally, a goat was substituted if the sacrifice was to Artemis, the goddess of hunting; if to Demeter, the mother of fertility, by a pig. These stories hinge on the interchangeability of the young innocent animal with the young innocent person, symptomatic of a moral retraction from the horror of killing people.

It may seem as if these human practices are buried too deep in the past still to be playing in stories that are now located no more than ten or twelve generations ago, but intriguing elements of them were to be found in tales told on the west coast of Scotland in the seventeenth and eighteenth centuries, and repeated to folklorists by old men and women who remembered them in Victorian Britain.

In about 1865, the Reverend Malcolm MacPhail, a schoolmaster in Lewis in the Outer Hebrides, recorded a story from the Atlantic shores of the island, in which

> a goat or sheep was brought to the seashore where the fishermen were in the habit of landing their fish. Then the oldest fisherman in the district, revered alike for his age and seamanship, was appointed *Pontifex maximus* to conduct and preside at the public sacrifice. The temporary priest now led the victim to the place appointed for the sacrificial rite, and this was so near the edge of the sea that any of the blood spilt would fall into the water. The aged sea-man, conscious of the solemnity and dignity of his position, reverently uncovered his hoary head, and on bended knees slew the victim by cutting off its head. With scrupulous care the blood was caught in a boat's bailer. When the blood had ceased to flow he waded into the sea and there poured it out to him whom he considered the ruler of the deep and its numerous inhabitants. He then turned to the carcass of the victim and divided it into as many portions as there were paupers in the district, sending a piece to each, for it was touched by no one else.

This ceremony, called 'the Beheading', had last been performed, MacPhail thought, in about 1805. Every ingredient of the ancient rite is here: the young victim; no blood to be spilled; the sacrificial animal brought to the sea edge; the prayer for plenty; and a version of the feast that followed the killing, the distribution of meat to those in hunger.

MacPhail recorded another equivalent ritual from Lewis, first described by Martin Martin at the very beginning of the eighteenth century, which retained other aspects of the ancient rite. In springtime, the women of the township collected some grains which they dried and ground and used to brew some ale.

> As soon as it was ready, it was conveyed in libatory vases (craggans) to the seashore, where, wading knee deep, they poured it into the sea, at the same time ejaculating: *Shoni, Shoni! thugain failteas bruca am bliadhna agus bheir sinne barrachd lionna dhutsa an ath-bhliadhna*, i.e., 'Soni, Soni! send us plenty of seaware [seaweed to be used as manure] this year and we will give thee more ale next year.'

Who or what Soni was remains uncertain. The name may be a reference to John the Baptist, or perhaps a descendant of Són, the mythical vessel in which the mead of poetry was kept, 'obtained from the dwarves by marooning them on a tidal rock until they handed it over'. Or the name simply of a Celtic sea god.

A letter written by the minister of Ness at the northern tip of Lewis in 1700 describes 'some heathenish & superstitious rites used in the Isle', adding a more salacious element. At the ceremonies, the people of Lewis who gathered for the sacrifice to the sea 'kindled great fyres all the neght over, & spent the whole neght in pyping singing prophane songs, danceing & whoreing too, that seldom I heard of these meetings (when I was a child) but I heard also of such & such persons falling in fornication or adultry at such occasiones, & this made a sport of'.

Sacrifice, the sea margin, sexuality, fertility, communality, violence and transgression: these are also the under-conditions of the Lady's Rock story. They persisted in Lewis, even if driven to secrecy and disapproved of by the church, in a way that had vanished earlier from the lands around the Sound of Mull and the Firth of Lorne. Even so, Alexander Carmichael, the great mid-nineteenth-century folklorist from Lismore, met someone who had witnessed it in Iona at the western end of Mull. Deep in the night on the Wednesday before Easter, Carmichael wrote,

> people in maritime districts made offerings of mead, ale, or gruel to the god of the sea. As the day merged from Wednesday to Thursday a man walked to the waist into the sea and poured out whatever offering had been prepared, chanting:

> *A Dhe na mara,*
> *Cuir todhar's an tarruinn*
> *Chon tachair an talaimh,*
> *Chon bailcidh dhuinn biaidh.*

> O God of the sea,
> Put weed in the drawing wave
> To enrich the ground,
> To shower on us food.

> Those behind the offerer took up the chant and wafted it along the seashore on the midnight air, the darkness of night and the rolling of the waves making the scene weird and impressive.

How to relate this casting of the grain into the sea, the stuff of survival, with the blood sacrifice, the act of the knife? Walter Burkert reconstructed the core moment of an inherited sacrificial ritual. The virgin, 'an untouched girl', led the way to the place of sacrifice, carrying a basket filled with barley grains, 'the most ancient agricultural product'. Just before the moment of killing, the attendants reached into the basket, took handfuls of grain and 'flung them away on to the sacrificial animal, the altar or a sacrificial pit in the earth'.

231

Hidden beneath the grain in the basket was the knife which now lay uncovered. Soon came the death blow. The women raised a piercing scream, whether in fear or triumph or both. The blood flowing out was treated with special care. It was not to spill on to the ground but was reserved for the altar or pit (on land) or, as here, for the sea itself which must be seen to fill with the blood.

Is that what in the deep past would have been witnessed here on the rock awash between Duart and Lismore, in times that are recorded in no other way than in the distorted story of Catherine Maclean and her husband? It seems to be a story that reaches into the beginnings of our relationship to the natural world, a myth from a much deeper level of human experience and consciousness than the sixteenth century, a way of addressing the realities of life and survival in a place where the tides of well-being and trouble have always swept across the human landscape, a story that dramatises in remembered ritual the structure of a human ecology in a world tense with hunger, danger and the need to avert them.

It also can be seen to represent the most modern and urgent myth of all: the assumption that we do not need to take into account the demands of the world around us, that we are equal in our wilfulness to its power, that we are better than the sea nymphs. The world around us will take its vengeance whether we like it or not. And so we must make our sacrifices to it, giving the most beautiful and treasured and life-giving things we have to the iron forces of existence. That is the instruction behind this tale: obeisance in front of the world's inflexible demand.

What of the strange non-funeral banquet at Inveraray? It is clearly a version of the post-sacrifice feast, but guilt-ridden rather than triumphant, aware more of the wickedness of the act than of its efficacy for those who had killed and surrendered the woman.

Even in older myth, these two elements are in fierce tension. How can the provision of food be worth the death of a young woman? Surely such a sacrifice is a crime? Is the demand that fierce, that the best of us must die for it? Those questions lie behind the Isaac story, the Iphigenia story and all the stories in which the human being is saved and the animal sacrificed in its place. But the Lady's Rock story straddles these categories. As far as the Macleans are concerned she is dead, she must be dead for the good of the clan and they fill her coffin with turf from their own ground. Her killing is a gift to the gods. For the Campbells, she has survived and deserves to survive. Her killing is barbaric and a crime.

And so she comes like a ghost or an avenging angel to the feast, the embodiment of guilt for the Macleans; justification for all the killing the Campbells will now enact, slaughtering and reducing the Macleans for centuries to come. Maclean guilt over her death will allow the Campbells to do what they want for as long as they must.

'War can be vengeance for the maiden's death,' Walter Burkert wrote of a pervasive pattern in Greek myth. And for those communities that used the woman's death as an excuse for subsequent killing, she often 'returned, symbolically and ritually restored, as the focus for a company of youths'. Here, then, is Catherine Campbell at the Inveraray feast, transmuted into a kind of presiding goddess of innocence and power, back from the dead, perfect and inspiring, leading the Campbells to their future career of invasion, destruction and dominance.

It may be curious that such an ancient tale and set of memories should be locked quite so firmly to the story of a Maclean chieftain at the beginning of the sixteenth century. But there is precedence in the Highlands for that kind of drift, the migrating of a story from the distant and mythic past to a historical moment.

In recent and local memory, recorded as late as the 1960s, the ruins of several buildings at Bunrannoch to the east of Pitlochry were known to be the remains of a village that was burned down in 1746 as a reprisal by government forces against the people there who had risen in rebellion with the Jacobites. Rannoch was famous as a wild place, its habits said to be outside the confines of a civilised society, the people described by their (hostile) minister in 1795 as previously living 'in an uncivilised barbarous state, under no check, or restraint of laws', in huts that 'could only be entered on hands and knees, with no beds, with people lying on the ground with a single blanket and subsisting on very little, bleeding their cattle to gain sustenance'.

In a remarkable piece of detective work by Gavin MacGregor, the Glasgow University archaeologist, this story has turned out to be untrue, or at least to be a conflation of truth and untruth, of distant past and more recent memory. Early maps showed that there was no settlement at Bunrannoch in 1746. There were no houses to house rebels or suffer vengeful atrocity. Dr MacGregor had the ruins of two of the buildings examined and the excavators found that they had indeed been burned, with charcoal from some hazel sticks within the walls and carbonised oats in a pit in one of the floors. He had these fragments carbon-dated: they had been burned at some time between AD 660 and AD 940.

The houses at Bunrannoch had been destroyed a thousand years earlier than the stories of Hanoverian vengeance. The memory of the terrifying destruction had been retained throughout the Middle Ages and only in the nineteenth and twentieth centuries been conflated with other atrocities performed by the Campbell forces in 1746. 'The tradition,' MacGregor wrote, 'remembered a number of "truths".' Places and actions are precisely recalled but the time at which they occurred is as elastic as a vision. Like the killing at Lady's Rock, the burning of Bunrannoch floats somewhere only in the stream of the remembered past.

I have sailed back home alone at night through these blood-soaked waters with a warm wind blowing in from the south-east. On the cliffs the golden eagles were nesting as they have done these last few thousand years and the sea trout beneath me were quietly making their way towards the waters of their burns.

The ghosts of Catherine Campbell and her many predecessors were not far away. The tide turned in my direction and the summer sea was mildness itself, a surface rippled with waves so small they were like the ribbed skin of an estuary sand. Only in the distant west, over the hills in Mull, was there any paleness in the sky. The lights winked around me, a silent concerted night harmony: the big lighthouse on Lismore, white, once every ten seconds; the light on the Grey Islands, white, once every three seconds; the beacon on Lady's Rock, also white, once every six seconds. In a mathematical dance, they came together every half-minute before diverging again. The sectored light on Ardtornish Point was steady ahead – white for the channel, green and red for the shoals and rocks on either side – and the lights in the windows of our own house at the head of the bay showed apricot yellow in the blue of the dark, the glow of home.

I was listening to the surface of the sea running and bumping against the hull, looking at the three-part stripe of the wake behind me. I fixed the tiller to the transom and went forward, leaning over the bow, putting my head down there where the water surged and broke around the stempost. This is what they talked about in the sagas, the sea absorbing you, taking you up, making you its own, quietly telling you and anyone like you that this was its kingdom and here, without challenge, its government.

10

Survival

Have human beings in this bay responded to the same biological imperatives as the animals? Is it possible to see human history here as a branch of natural history? As another dimension of ecology?

The spirit hanging behind those questions is the bleak figure of the Reverend Thomas Malthus, the late-eighteenth-century clergyman, curate at a small country chapel at Oakwood in Surrey, a few miles from his parents' house in Albury. He arrived there, freshly graduated from maths at Cambridge in 1789, a rich, tall twenty-three-year-old who spent his time 'socializing, walking, riding, and shooting'.

The people in Oakwood were poor and small – the average difference in height between rich and poor in late-eighteenth-century England was nearly nine inches – living in dirt-floored hovels. Malthus described them:

> The sons and daughters of peasants will not be found such rosy cherubs in real life as they are described to be in romances. It cannot fail to be remarked by those who live much in the country that the sons of labourers are very apt to be stunted in their growth, and are a long while arriving at maturity. Boys that you would guess to be fourteen or fifteen are, upon inquiry, frequently found to be eighteen or nineteen.

Malthus reflected on the causes of these small bodies, and in his *Essay on the Principle of Population*, published anonymously in 1798, came to the conclusion that the poor were small because they were underfed; they were underfed because there were too many of them; and there were so many of them because the drive to procreate was unstoppable. Lust will always outstrip food supply and humanity will forever be held between the pincers of hunger and desire, victims of what the French *Annales* historian Emmanuel Le Roy Ladurie called the 'Malthusian scissors', the ever-closing blades in which human populations are caught between growing numbers and the inability of the environment to feed them.

Malthus had been reading the Marquis de Condorcet, the French rationalist philosopher, whose *Essay on the Progress of the Human Mind* had been published just after his death in 1795: 'When the increase of the number of men surpasses their means of subsistence,' Condorcet had written, 'the necessary result must be either a continual diminution of happiness and population … or at least a kind of oscillation between good and evil.'

Condorcet had suggested that this miserable swinging between enough food and too many people would occur only at some time in the future. Malthus understood, from baptising and burying too many of the shrunken Oakwood poor, that the time of suffering was already with us. He knew that

> the period when the number of men surpass their means of subsistence has long since arrived, and that this necessary oscillation, this constantly subsisting cause of periodical misery, has existed ever since we have had any histories of mankind, does exist at present, and will for ever continue to exist, unless some decided change takes place in the physical constitution of our nature.

It is a grim, post-Enlightenment view. The rationalists' dreams of perfectibility and happiness were over. Human misery was the face of necessity. Populations would rise to the level of subsistence, and then be cut down by epidemic and famine, leaving more room and more food for the survivors. After famine, there would be a time of relative plenty but the prospect of poverty would always remain. As the population expanded again, the productive capacity of the land, despite the extra labour expended on it, would not be able to keep up, the law of diminishing returns would kick in and food production per head decline. The poor would starve again. Alongside its apocalyptic companions of war and disease, famine acted as what Malthus called a 'check' on the lives of men, women and children.

The fate of human populations in this Malthusian picture can only follow a sawtooth graph in which the natural increase is intermittently but regularly scythed away and cut back to the carrying capacity of the land. Famine, sickness, battle, and in many societies infanticide, abortion and emigration, were the inevitable responses to the repeated and unending pregnancies and the clamouring mouths of the children that emerged from them.

This nightmare was the dark twin of Rousseau's picture of the simple life: a human existence before culture, a radical exposure to nature, no barriers between people and the biological facts of existence, a subjection to the disciplines and opportunities of the natural world. For Rousseau, the inhabitants of modern society had lost touch with that beautiful world of nature and connectedness; Malthus, looking at the poor around him, saw that they had never escaped its control or vigilance.

There is something horrible in the acceptance of these conclusions. To decide that there was nothing to be done; that charity (Malthus argued against the Poor Laws or any taxes or rates intended to support the able poor) was throwing good money after bad; that subsidies only delayed the moment when the food ran out – by when all efforts at kindness had only created a larger population to die: to think like this is a surrender to nature, to assume that humanity can do nothing to lift itself away from the kind of existence experienced by most natural populations.

That assumption of a Malthusian necessity was a way of thinking indulged in by the early-nineteenth-century advocates of the Clearances, including those who lived in this bay. Nevertheless, the facts are there. As the Australian biologist Tom White has straightforwardly set them out:

> The number of organisms in any habitat is determined by the amount of nutrients available for the primary producers. The greater this is, the greater the biomass in subsequent levels of the food chain; each depends upon the one below.
>
> All are driven by their genes to maximise the number of young produced, and so are constantly 'pressing hard' against the changing limits set by their environment.

This is the Malthusian basement. Did it apply to people here? Was pre-modern life here shaped by the Malthusian miseries?

Without question, at one level, it was. Along with the rest of early modern Europe, life in the pre-modern Scottish Highlands was afflicted and even dominated by frequent but unpredictable mortality crises. Many of these episodes were linked to famine, others to smallpox or the plague. Lack of food caused death rates to increase, especially in young children, largely because in children the competition between the maintenance of physical health and the growth of their bodies is at its fiercest. The stress of malnutrition shuts down the immune response to infection and it is from infectious diseases that children in a famine usually die. This connection of hunger and disease remains today the leading cause of child death worldwide.

In evolutionary terms, this response to stress is among the most ancient of all animal responses, going far beyond mammals,

birds, amphibians and fish, deep into the territory of the invertebrates. Shelley Adamo, a specialist in psycho-neuro-immunology
at Dalhousie University in Halifax, Nova Scotia, has found
that 'stress hormones modify immune function in all molluscs,
insects, and crustaceans'. In these animals, as in the vertebrates,
stress usually suppresses the immune system.

It may be that evolution has selected the suppression of the
immune response in children, allowing them to die during
famine, so that adults of breeding age can monopolise the food
that remains. Many animal populations that are confronted with
hunger abandon their offspring – called 'brood neglect' among
ornithologists – since there is a clear advantage in prioritising the
survival of adults that can breed again the next year.

Sheer difficulty has shaped life here. Morvern, like all the
ragged fringe of the West Highlands and islands, is difficult to
survive in, difficult to get to and difficult to communicate within.
The land which might have grown crops for people and fodder
for animals in a more sheltered and less wet environment was
either too high, too acid, too thin, too exposed or too wet. The
annual rainfall in the bay is about eight feet, a swimming pool's
worth across the entire landscape. The growing season is short.
'In a climate so wet,' the minister of Morvern wrote in 1798, 'it
is not to be supposed that sowing can commence early: We
commonly begin about the middle of March.' Harvest was
always threatened by wet or the early arrival of winter. 'The
whole of the parish, especially the west side, or that part which
looks towards the Sound of Mull, is so much exposed, that the
raising of crops is always a precarious business, and, in some
seasons, a certain loss.' Even now, silage for cattle can be made
only in September, three months or more after the south of
England.

The West Highlands as a whole could expect a crop failure
once every three years. For every grain of black oats sown, the
most that could be expected at harvest was four or five in return,

of which one had to be kept as seed corn for the following year. Barley did better if sown on ground manured with sheep dung (a sevenfold return). If sown on ground manured with seaweed, that could double again. But to manure many acres by hand was ruinous and exhausting work. Most of the arable area never received any manure but was used for a season or two until its naturally occurring nutrients were exhausted and then left for a decade or more to recover.

No generation would pass without a famine. They appear as soon as anybody thought to record them: in 1680, 1688, the 1690s, 1740, 1751, 1756, these according to Eric Richards, the Australian historian of the Highlands, 'only the most publicised'. Even after the great changes of the eighteenth century, and the acceptance of the potato as a staple, famine returned. The winter, spring, summer and autumn of 1782–3 were particularly pain-ful: rain and cold throughout 1782, a bitter December, January and February, a late spring and then excessive rain at harvest, followed again by an early and severe winter. Potatoes and cereals were both destroyed. Hundreds of people were found dead lying by the roads, 'in caverns and amongst thickets where they had taken shelter'. Starvation, near-starvation and 'the prevalence of destitution' returned to the West Highlands in 1806–7, 1811, 1816–17, 1837–8, the mid-1840s and the six terrible years of 1847–53.

It would have been no different in all the unrecorded centuries and these are the foundational realities, the Malthusian assaults on people's lives. As soon as visitors from the south came to see what life was like in the Highlands, the poverty horrified them. Among the earliest was Edmund Burt, an English government administrator, appointed to oversee the estates confiscated after the Jacobite rebellion in 1715. He wrote a series of letters in the late 1720s to a friend in London. At a winter fair, Burt told him, if you could conceive rightly of it, you must imagine you see two or three hundred half-naked, half-starved creatures of both sexes, without so much as a smile or any cheerfulness among them stalking about with goods, up to their ankles in dirt; and at night numbers of them lying together in stables, or other outhouse hovels that are hardly any defence against the weather.

The Highland gentry were well fed but the poor were haggard. 'You would hardly think, by their faces, they were of the same species.' Burt concluded, accurately enough, that the poor had been starved when in the womb and had never recovered. 'Here is a melancholy Appearance of Objects in the Streets; – in one Part the poor Women, Maid-servants, and Children, in the coldest Weather, in the Dirt or in Snow, either walking or standing to talk with one another, without Stockings or Shoes.'

When travelling out into the country – Burt became the manager of the lead mines at Strontian just north of Morvern – he found a landscape of poverty as distressing as the sight of the people themselves. In the townships, dwellings and barns and stables were 'all irregularly placed, some one way, some another, and at any distance look like so many heaps of dirt'. Robert Southey later called these houses 'man-sties'. Burt saw children 'come out from the huts early in the morning stark naked, and squat themselves down (if I may decently use the comparison) like dogs on a dunghill'. Inside the huts, he found people chronically 'liable to fluxes, fevers, agues, coughs, rheumatisms and other distempers'. In the windowless dark, 'they sit brooding in the smoke over the fire till their legs and thighs are scorched … the long continuance in the smoke makes them almost as black as chimney sweeps'.

Thomas Pennant on Islay in 1774 found 'a set of people worn down to poverty; their habitation scenes of misery'. They were 'left to Providence's care', he wrote. 'They prowl like other

An oystercatcher.

Two beadlet sea anemones from different clones – one with a blue foot (on the right), one with a red foot – are brought together in the aquarium. Their tentacles start to tangle.

Redfoot rises into a war posture, exposing its dangerous blue beadlets, or acrorhagi, with which to attack the bluefoot.

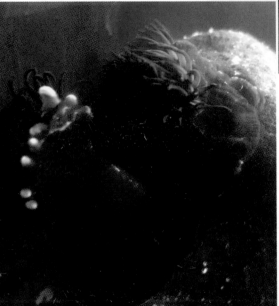

Redfoot has attacked, leaving Bluefoot wounded with toxic darts stuck into its body (see detail below). Bluefoot has abandoned the struggle and separated itself from the rock, and is wafted away in the currents of the aquarium.

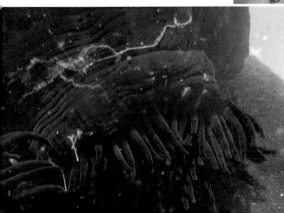

As Bluefoot drifts past, now upside down, revealing the pale base of its body, Redfoot rises once again into its attack posture.

Bluefoot has floated off and Redfoot, having won the contest, is now bending over towards the place Bluefoot has left.

As Redfoot stands up again, it becomes clear that it has deposited a small clone of itself on the rock from which it has driven Bluefoot away.

By the time Bluefoot has left the arena, Redfoot now calmly occupies the site, with its clone established beside it, the battle won, territory extended.

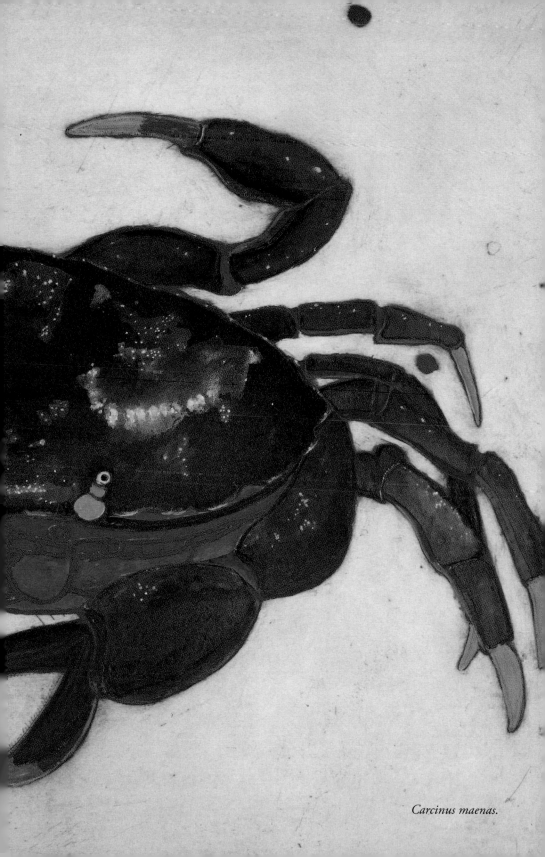

Carcinus maenas.

Pool 3 takes shape in the pre-lockdown winter as an 800-foot-long bulk carrier heads for the Glensanda superquarry; the first strip of water is held in the pool; and in the summer of 2020 it begins to welcome its inhabitants.

Visitors to Pool 3: a sea star, a sea urchin and a cluster of top shells.

animals along the shore to pick up limpets and other shellfish. Numbers unknown, in all parts of the western Highlands, fall beneath the pressure, some of hunger, more of the putrid fever, the epidemic of the coasts, originating from unwholesome food, the dire effects of necessity.'

The spring, when the grain derived from the harvest the year before had run out, was known as 'the starving season'. The shellfish could add a little to the diet and the proverbial wisdom of the Gaelic world was full of reflections drawn from that bitter harvest. There may have been plenty of them – '*Is lom an leac air nach dèanar (nach fhaighear) maorach*' ('It's a bare stone where no shellfish are to be found') – but it was a small consolation that '*As t-Earrach nuair a bhios a' chaora caol bidh am maorach reamhar*' ('In spring when the sheep is lean, shellfish are fat'). You must take your chances: '*Rinn e maorach fhad 's a bha'n tràigh ann*' ('You must gather shellfish when the tide is out'). And only attention would allow you to survive: '*Cha dèan cas luath maorach*' ('A hasty foot won't get you shellfish'). In these ways, the austerity of the environment, the paucity of its gifts and the scratching of a living from a hostile world all played their part in shaping the mentality of a people.

The scale was pitiable. The half-starved horses were little bigger than asses. Their carts were the size of wheelbarrows. The goats' kids would sell in the 1720s for no more than sixpence or eightpence apiece, the price of three or four hours work by a labourer. The spoons they used were made of horn or wood, their platters of wood. One boy, when asked in the nineteenth century by the minister of Morvern what he ate for breakfast, answered 'Potatoes.' And for dinner? 'Potatoes.' For supper? 'Potatoes.' Do you have nothing else? The boy thought for a moment. 'Yes: a spoon.'

Everywhere Burt looked, he saw people squeezing the resources on which they relied. 'I do not remember to have seen the least spot,' he told his London friend, 'that would bear corn uncultivated, not even upon the sides of the hills, where it could be no otherwise broke up than with a spade.' The desperate shortage was of fertility:

> Not far from Fort William, I have seen women with a little horse dung brought upon their backs, in creels or baskets, from that garrison; and on their knees, spreading it with their hands upon the land, and even breaking the balls, that every part of the little spot might have its due proportion.

Here at least, the seaweed could add a little, to enhance the carrying capacity of the land. The seaware when it was harvested in May was draped over stone field walls and left there to dry. All along the Atlantic seaboard, the gathering was women's work, heavy and wet as they brought it up from the foreshore in creels on their backs. Tim Robinson heard the story of a farmer in Aran on the west coast of Ireland looking for a wife: 'Whatever his other ideals of beauty, modesty and gentleness', the farmer would never consider a girl who could not carry a good burden. '*Is é moladh na mná óige, a droim bheith fliuch*' ('"Praise of the young woman that her back be wet" – wet, that is, with the brine from a basket of weed').

The dried seaware was taken to the growing grounds above the beach, and applied heavily before the oats or barley or, increasingly after 1760, potatoes were sown in the enriched soil. The average needed for each crop was about 160 creels an acre, perhaps two and a half tons when the weed was wet. In a place where the natural fertility was so low, the seaweed was a good fertiliser, with as much nitrogen and twice the potash of farmyard dung, even if its effects did not last as long. Across the centuries of subsistence agriculture here, about an acre of cultivated ground was needed for each person. A family of five would in an ideal world have 800 creels of this seaware or about twelve tons wet weight carried up and on to its arable grounds. It was goodness to be derived from the sea, but only with unending labour and physical exertion. Exhausted hunger lurked in the margins of this life.

Only one or two generations beyond living memory, there was famine here. Donald Morrison, then in Mull, interviewed in 1974, remembered as if it were his own experience the 'terrible time' in the 1840s, when his father was alive in Morvern, and, as Donald said with an indraw of breath, 'the people were eating the shellfish then'.

The old, carefully chiselled and close-set stone pier giving on to the narrows at the mouth of the loch was built as relief work in that horrendous decade for thirty-one Morvern families who were starving after the potato crop had failed. The men, women and children who built the pier received food (oatmeal and wheatmeal) instead of money for their work, part of the Victorian understanding that charity in return for nothing rotted the moral substance of its recipients. The usual allowance for a man was one shilling's worth of meal a day. Women were given five pounds of meal a week and children more or less according to their age. Without it they would have died.

Norman Macleod, minister of this parish, described the dignity and spiritual grandeur of those coming in dire hunger to receive charity:

> The old people suffered deeply ere they accepted any help. I have known families who closed their windows to keep out the light, that their children might sleep on as if it were night, and not rise to find a home without food. I remember being present at the first distribution of meal in a distant part of the Highlands ... Their clothes were rags, but every rag was washed, and patched together as best might be ... Yet, during all these sad destitution times, there was not a policeman or soldier in those districts. No food riot ever took place, no robbery was attempted, no sheep was ever

stolen from the hills; and all this though hundreds had only shell-fish, or 'dulse', gathered on the sea-shore to live upon.

Human existence here was on the boundaries of the viable and that poverty generated community. As archaeology and the earliest maps reveal, human settlement was crammed into every niche where life was possible. The large-scale maps of the Military Survey of Scotland made after the Jacobite rebellion of 1745–6, a series known to its contemporaries as the 'Great Map' and now named after its chief surveyor William Roy, are speckled with the tiny settlements of the people. Little clusters of red buildings pimple the level, sheltered places, the names usually misspelt by the non-Gaelic-speaking surveyors. Each gathering of houses is surrounded by its sketched-in arable fields, with the hills and rocks and rivers of the difficult country above them washed in as though for a watercolour view. (Paul Sandby, later famous for his views of Windsor Castle, was the artist employed by the Survey.)

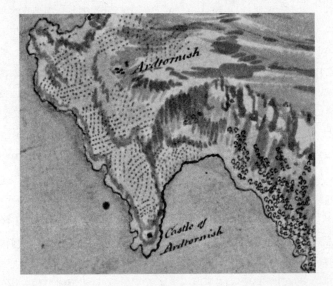

The bay and its surrounding lands on the Roy Military Survey of Scotland made in 1747–51. The settlement called 'Ardtornish' here has been completely erased.

It is the most poignant map of Scotland: a hostile military authority delineating with such confidence and elegance a world of poverty, suffering and subjection. Nearly all of the small places the Roy map shows are ruined and abandoned now. The main settlement here, high above the bay on a saddle of land between the Sound of Mull and Loch Aline, is painted in and named 'Ardtornish' by the military surveyors, surrounded by the stipple of its arable fields, but is now entirely gone. The modern maps still mark above it the *achadh na craoibh sgitheich*, 'the field of the hawthorn tree', but the site of the township itself is a forgotten place, where any remains of buildings are unseen in a flood of bracken and gorse.

The village was tucked into a hollow, invisible from the sea in all directions and hidden from the wind. You would have felt safe there. The old tracks, to the loch on one side and to the bay on the Sound on the other, are still there, used by James Shanks, the shepherd, on his all-terrain vehicle, and their surfaces are worn down to the underlying plates of basalt. The grass beside them is thick with the little yellow stars of tormentil, rowan trees flower in springtime next to the old village and a lovely small burn, its water the colour of the back of a dark trout, runs through the settlement and down to Miodar Bay on Loch Aline. There was another settlement below this one, called Nether Ardtornish, perhaps on the site of the Victorian house where the Shankses now live, overlooking the fields on which the sheep and cattle now graze.

People were folded into the place. The place itself was a map of their lives and their connections, held not directly from the chief of the clan but from his chief tenant or tacksman, and arranged in a ring structure: at the centre houses and barns, with kailyards or vegetable gardens beside them; beyond that the regularly cultivated infield; then the rarely cultivated outfield; then the rough hill grazing, in which all members of the township had common rights. Up there too were the shielings where the

A clachan of part-stone, part-wattle dwellings on the shores of Loch
Duich, Wester Ross in about 1880, of a kind to be found all over
the pre-modern Highlands.

women and children took the animals for the summer weeks and
made cheeses.

Until the mid-eighteenth century, when the Duke of Argyll,
whose land this was, insisted they should be made of stone, their
houses were built of wood from the surrounding country, from
the materials that still grow here: the inner walls made of woven
hazel hurdles 'wattled like a Basket', connected to heavy crucks or
'couples' on a drystone foundation. The slight, sea- and wind-
twisted Morvern oaks provided the curving timbers. Turf walls
were laid around the outside, each turf laid grass to grass, earth to
earth, and the walls bound together by the growing grass roots.

The houses were models of energy-conscious coherence. The
peat smoke from the central hearth filled the house's roof and
worked as a fungicide to preserve the timbers. Meat and fish
could be cured up there and the never-absent fire created what
the ethnographer Alexander Fenton has described as 'a smoky
shimmer of heat', the essence of homeliness for generations of
Highlanders, within which, on long evenings, people would

gather for storytelling and gossip. The thatch was replaced every ten years and the entire roof, enriched by its years of soot, could profitably be spread on the fields.

The third element in this system, connected to poverty and communality, was a ferocious reliance on hierarchy. The internal discipline of the clan and group violence directed towards others ('clan warfare') was an integral part of this life. It was not an egalitarian world but highly stratified, with six or seven levels in

The bay from the outcrop on the cliff traditionally identified as the clan chief's place of judgement and execution.

The execution cliff from below. The flat land immediately to the left provided the outdoor courtroom.

it: chief; tacksmen; joint tenants; cottars; landless labourers; the weak and indigent. In pre-modern centuries, punishment was in the hands of the clan chief and, as the Morvern minister in 1843 reported, 'in the face of the rock, overhanging the bay of Ardtornish, is pointed out the precipice over which the transgressors of feudal laws were thrown'. On the small piece of flat land above the cliff, it was said to a traveller in 1800, the clan chief held his court and if the prisoner was found guilty, the place of execution was to hand.

The clan was an insurance system, a straightforward response to shortage and the likelihood that the land, every few years, would fail to feed the people. The chief exacted rent, held reserves, or organised the stealing of them from others, and in that way looked after the people who depended on him. His own castle was accompanied by a 'girnal house' in which goods and food could be stored, with a drying kiln for the grain beside it. In times of plenty, the chief accumulated food. In times of dearth, he distributed it.

The castle on the headland that closes the bay to the west is a ruin now, a rather rough grey stone box on the summit of a

Ardtornish Castle standing above the Sound of Mull, with Mull itself beyond.

mound that overlooks the point. In the Middle Ages, it was not especially defended. What remains is only the basement, with grassed-over rubble filling most of it. When in use, a stair within the walls led to a single upper chamber that probably had large and magnificent windows looking out on to the Sound. This belonged to the Macdonalds Lords of the Isles and they used it as a place for gathering and feasting, surveying the apron of sea around it, with a good anchorage in the bay in its lee, away from the westerlies, and yet visible as a tall silhouette for ten miles in each direction up and down the Sound. No one sailing the length of this waterway could fail to recognise its lordliness and near-regal position on its headland.

The Macdonalds were no insignificant parochial chieflets. They could command forces in their thousands, numerically, at least, far more than any bodies of armed men raised by English royal dukes for the invasions of France in 1415 and 1475. In the summer of 1461, they conducted wild sea-reiving raids on Arran and Bute to the south, and across the north of Scotland to Orkney descending that June

in great numbers with their fleets and ships in warlike manner to the said earldom of Orkney and burned [the] lands, villages, houses and buildings to the ground, and most cruelly suppressed [the] people of both sexes and of all ages with the sword and cruelly carried away with them their goods, animals, household stocks, jewels, money and everything they could for their own use, leaving little or nothing except the burnt soil of the ground empty and useless.

This enormous and violent energy of clansmen on a raid can be seen in a Malthusian light. The clan was itself an instrument of survival, an essentially warlike structure of chief, tacksmen and subtenants. The women did most of the farming, the men the fighting and cattle raiding. The clan's lifeblood was in raiding. Stealing food in the form of cattle and destroying the lives of rivals by burning their crops was an integral part of the system. Feuding, loyalty, punishment for disloyalty, feasting, the summoning to war, the use of violence as a habitual and even theatrical tool of community cohesion – all were part of an ecology whose essential condition was the poverty of the land.

'All men naturally hate each other,' Blaise Pascal said, and here, as in other societies threatened by hunger, the possibility of hatred was always in the air. A clan, united by real or fictional blood ties, was a means of controlling that potential for mutual destruction and channelling the aggression away from neighbours towards more distant others. Clan raiding prevented neighbourhood anarchy; war with others created local community. Only with loyalty to the chief – a loyalty itself imposed by the threat of violent punishment – could those local rivalries, driven by competition for resources, be defused.

What is lost in the historical documents that describe this three-part structure of poverty, communality and outward-directed violence is the other and most precious dimension of this world, a sense among the people who lived here that their lives were founded on a rich and subtle amalgam that fused elements of their own families, their songs, the place in which they lived, their right to be here, the sea and land on which they depended for their well-being, the presence of the past and their telling of the stories that came down to them from it.

Gaelic has no term equivalent to 'landscape', that purely visual, painter-cum-surveyor's word used to describe a place. Instead, there is something richer, folded into the one complex idea of *dùthchas*. It can mean a hereditary claim; anything that is a birthright, an ancestral estate, a patrimony. *Dùthchas* can be the tradition or custom by which something is made legitimate. *Dùthchas* is how it has always been done. But it can also mean a person's native place or country, their ancestral home, full of their traditional connections. A man who leaves for the south has forsaken his *dùthchas*. He is no longer at home. And if he returns to his *dùthchas*, he has gone back to where he belongs, and metaphorically become himself again. He is in his old haunts, once again as he always was.

Dùthchas describes a world of natural affinities and connectedness, where people are surrounded by things of their own kind. It represents a psychic home, where, through heredity, everyone shares innate qualities and a natural bent. *Dùthchas* is an aptitude and inclination. It is how you naturally are. You can be musical by *dùthchas*, or a good seaman, or it can be used of a cow that is 'of a good milking strain'. According to a proverb, *dùthchas* is stronger than any upbringing. *Dùthchas* is the gathering of your instincts but it is also your native place, your habitat and how you think. It is both homeland and innermost being, your right to what is yours. It is what you inevitably are. If in the hierarchical structure of a clan there are echoes of prawn life, in *dùthchas* there are suggestions of a kind of clonal arrangement like the anemones'.

Dùthchas is what the English words 'tradition' and 'place' and 'heritage' all try to say. The dependence of pre-modern human life here on the products of the land and the need to resist the exigencies of the environment mean that self, family, world, survival, memory and song are moulded to each other more intimately than could be imagined in a modern, commercial and urbanised world.

Community, the woven thing, is one of the foundations of life on earth. Seabirds live like this, many of them exploring the widths of the Atlantic Ocean each winter, but profoundly tied to where they were born, most of them returning for many decades to breed in the place they undoubtedly know as home, more often than not nesting near where their parents had raised them, surrounded by their cousins, siblings, uncles and grandchildren,

The spirit of *dùthchas*.

deeply familiar with every nick and wrinkle of their homeland. It may be that *dùthchas* is also a natural phenomenon, undescribed because we cannot learn or know the languages in which it is known.

It is not easy to recover the actual, living reality of that fusion of memory, daily life, places and story, but there is no doubt it was alive here. 'The combination of extreme privation and a rich culture is by no means unusual in peasant societies,' Eric Richards the historian of the Highlands has said, but not until the coming of the tape recorder was it possible for outsiders to catch the ways in which *dùthchas* played out in people's minds.

Sorley Maclean, the greatest of all modern Gaelic poets, who in 1938 experienced one of the fulcrum years of his life as a teacher in Tobermory across the Sound, made a series of tape recordings in Edinburgh in 1982, in which he provided an extraordinary window into this world, spinning out a picture of his life in which genealogy, inheritance, song, place, culture, pride, love, energy and vivid being were sewn into the one treasured fabric of existence. 'He was prepared to go a certain distance towards the horizon but not prepared to leave the landscapes and seascapes where the navigation markers of his spirit were located,' his admirer Seamus Heaney said in Edinburgh in 2002. Heaney spoke of Maclean's 'highly cultivated genealogical awareness' and of his speech which came to Heaney with

the force of revelation: the mesmeric, heightened tone; the weathered voice coming in close from a far place; the surrender to the otherness of the poem; above all a sense of bardic dignity (and calling) that was without self-parade and was instead the effect of a proud self-abnegation, as much a submission to heritage as a laying claim to it.

A sense of bardic dignity, the weathered voice coming in close from a far place: those are the sounds of *dùthchas* as it was heard here for generation after generation, within the walls of the houses where now there are only moss and cranesbills, absence and silence.

Well, I am Somhairle mac Chaluim 'ic Chaluim 'ic Iain 'ic Tharmaid 'ic Iain 'ic Tharmaid [Sorley son of Malcolm, son of Malcolm, son of Iain, son of Norman, son of Iain, son of Norman] That's as far back as we can go with certainty …

Now the Macleans: my father was a very fine singer and he was a very fine piper. My brother Seonaidh used to say that he could recognise his father's playing anywhere. And my uncle Alasdair was a piper too and my father was a very good singer. And my grandmother, my father's mother. She was Mairi Matheson … [and] she was a very fine singer. In my early memories she used to sing splendid old songs. Oh what didn't she sing! Wherever she went to live she learned new songs. She had a splendid memory. She was confined to bed for the past four years of her life but that didn't stop her singing. And they say she was very good-looking herself. It seems that her nickname was Siucar Iain 'ic Sheumais [Iain 'ic Sheumais's sugar].

She was full of old songs. I can't forget them somehow. My father's sister Peigi we had to go out fishing with her and it's all songs. She was full of old songs. I used to threaten to go on strike unless she sang songs. My father's sister Floraidh was good at the songs too. Peigi had things that her mother didn't have. I think it may have been from her father they got it, for he was a sort of bard, my grandfather Calum Maclean.

My grandfather was Somhairle Iain 'ic Somhairle Phiobaire. He was a piper in Spain and he got his hands damaged … the frost got him and his fingers stiffened and he came out of the army. He was at [the Battle of] Corunna [in January 1809] and it was in the retreat to Corunna that that happened to him.

The thing was I couldn't sing as most of my people could, so I got tremendously keen about a lot of the old Gaelic songs. And so though I could get the pitch right, it used to drive spears through me almost, the rhythm the movement and the time, when I heard something I thought was wrong.

I grew up at that time when symbolism was such a thing in European poetry and I was affected a lot by … Hugh MacDiarmid and Yeats, and my symbols almost automatically became the landscape of my physical environment. But of course that was always affected, blended with what I knew of the history of my people.

Hear that voice and you can hear the voices of those who once lived in this bay and are now gone. What is the answer to the question? Is human history here a branch of natural history? Is our own story merely another dimension of its ecology? In part it is: we suffer and struggle like the other animals, fight and dominate, threaten and display, make alliances, establish our hierarchies and exploit the weak like all the others. But we are different in this: we are the storytelling, past-remembering, culture-making animals. It is that which distinguishes us and which means that Malthus can never have the last word.

In 1940, in despair at his disappointments in love, his fear that courage had failed him in not going to fight the Fascists in Spain, and grief over the destruction of the Gaelic world he had witnessed in Mull, Sorley Maclean felt his

life running to the seas
through heather, bracken and bad grass,
on its fanked eerie course,
like the mean and shallow stream

257

that was taking its meagre way through a green patch
to the sea in the Kyle.

In part, he felt as much a victim of circumstances as any creature.
But there was more; he knew he could hope for resilience. Every
ebb implied a flood.

Again and again a spring tide came
to put beauty on the river foot,
to fill its destination with richness,
and sea-trout and white-bellied salmon came
to taste the water of the high hills
with flood-tide in Inver Eyre.

Mo bheatha ruith chun nan cuantan
tro fhraoch is fhraineach is droch fhiarach
air a cùrsa fangte, tiamhaidh,
mar an sruthan staoin suarach
bha gabhail slighe chrìon tro chluaineag
gu cuan anns a' chaol.
Ach uair is uair thigeadh reothairt
a chur dreach air bun na h-aibhne,
a lìonadh a ceann-uidhe le saidhbhreas;
is thigeadh gealag is bradan tàrr-gheal
a bhlaiseadh uisge nan àrd-bheann
ri làn an Inbhir Aoighre.

11

Belief

The oystercatchers make their nest at the edge of the beach, above the tideline of the highest tide, just where the shingle fringes into the grass. It is in the bank of pebbles in front of the house and every time I come back from the boat the birds are troubled. The sitting oystercatcher never leaves with hurry or alarm, just a slow, measured walk away as though wandering

The sitting oystercatcher never leaves in a hurry.

Just above the reach of the tide.

casually across the upper part of the beach. For such a heraldic and noisy creature, the discretion is extraordinary. Alarm at a nest would, I suppose, demonstrate something to be alarmed about.

The nest itself, which I have marked with sticks so that no visitor stands on the eggs, shares that cryptic genius. It is a shallow depression dished into the stones, with an odd, cousin relationship to my dug pool. The pale khaki eggs are speckled, so that the effect is of the beach itself flecked with its own shadows. Neither nest nor eggs have any smell. The dogs can walk and nose within inches of them and not realise they are there. And yet the birds have decorated their scoop with pieces of broken cockle and one or two old, bleached periwinkles. In other places, oystercatchers quite consistently choose what they like for their decoration, some nothing but limpets, others striped land snails, but here the theme is a rudimentary scatter of white things. I wonder why. To distract from the eggs themselves? To conceal the eggs with the brightness of their surroundings? To make the important unseen?

I am at the nest for a moment, the birds are anxiously away from it, and they begin to talk. In Gaelic, the oystercatcher is *bridein*, the bird of St Bridget, or of Brigid the pre-Christian goddess of poetry and song whose cult was fused with hers. And so now Brigid's song begins. *Bi glic, bi glic*, be wise, be wise, the oystercatchers are meant to say when a stranger comes near their haunts. But I wonder if that suggestion of sagacity is an old joke. At first maybe they are like that, saying merely *quick, quick*, with the comma audible between the notes. Or as if this were a kind of hello, an interrogative *quick? quick?* But soon enough the wisdom goes, the gaps shrink, the pace picks up *quick quick*, the liquid runs faster from the throat, and soon the cry rises to the point where there are no gaps at all, no understanding is in evidence and all the birds are crying, feverishly, *quickquick-quickquickquickquickquickquickquickquick*, ending at last with a long and assertive *quiiiiiiiiiiiiiiick* which says 'This is my place, this is *my* place. *WHY ARE YOU HERE?*'

The ever-desperate, high-pitched oystercatcher is also called the *trìlleachan*, a name which has the same elements as the word 'thrill' in it, connected in the depths of Indo-European language structures to 'piercing' and the ancient root of the word 'through'. Unkindly, then, the oystercatcher might be thought of as the mind-penetrating screecher.

There are eleven different oystercatcher species spread across the world and they all 'pipe' like this. The song itself, if that is not too complimentary a term, is innate, a shared and inherited habit, neither learned nor different in different places. Young oystercatchers raised alone and in private know how to screech as well as any other. The birdsong ecologists Edward Miller and Allan Baker have shown, by tracing the evolutionary relation-ships among oystercatchers and other near-related shorebirds, the stilts and avocets, that many of the sounds they make are of deep antiquity. They are not the oldest of living sounds still to be heard – grasshoppers and crickets began chirring 230 million years ago, filling the air of the Permian moss forests – but piping similar to the modern oystercatcher, as Miller and Baker have said, 'contributed to the biological sound-scape more than 65 million years ago. These sounds would have been audible to most dinosaurs.' *Bi glic, bi glic* is as old as the basalt boulders on which the birds stand.

Few cultures have been so attentive to the sounds of the natural world as the one that lived on this bay. Alexander Carmichael, the great Victorian folklorist and collector from Lismore, listened to one of his informants, Janet Campbell, a nurse from Lochskiport in South Uist. She sang

> many beautiful songs and lullabies of the nursery, and many
> instructive sayings and fables of the animal world. These she
> sang and told in the most pleasing and natural manner, to
> the delight of her listeners. Birds and beasts, reptiles and
> insects, whales and fishes talked and acted through her in the
> most amusing manner, and in the most idiomatic Gaelic.

In what voices did Janet Campbell sing? Was she a cricket? Or a slow-worm? Or a periwinkle? Or a prawn? Or a lesser rorqual? Or a porpoise? Or a shoal of herring? Or a dab or plaice? Or a frog maybe? Did she imagine the voices of animals that could not actually be heard? All lost to time, but there is no doubt that the boundary-crossing habit of mind was alive here through the millennia. The natural world, seen by us now as something sufficient in itself, was, for all the centuries this bay was fully inhabited, intimately continuous with human lives. Vocal affinities spread far beyond the oystercatchers and all the evidence suggests that for the Gaelic world the boundary was permeable between natural and cultural, animal and human.

Listen, for example, to the west coast Gaelic song of the court-
ing frog, sung with passion to his hesitant frog-amour. Even if
you can't hear the Gaelic, you can at least see it on the page, the
burp-glottal *glug glug glug* of the lovesick amphibian:

> *A chaomhag, a chaomhag*
> *An cuimhneach leat*
> *An gealladh beag*
> *A thug thu aig*
> *An tobar dhomh*
> *A ghaoil, a ghaoil.*

> My dear, my dear
> Just remember
> The little promise
> You gave me
> Beside the well
> My love, my love.

Animals in traditional societies, as Claude Lévi-Strauss famously
wrote, are chosen by people as totems 'not because they are
"good to eat" but because they are "good to think"'. In the
pre-modern world, animals were understood as co-actors in the
drama of existence. Usually, Lévi-Strauss's phrase '*bonnes à
penser*' is translated as 'good to think *with*', another way of using
the animal as a tool in the human manipulation of the world, a
set of metaphors and a vocabulary by which our minds can
acquire and arrange our surroundings. More fruitfully, and
more sympathetically, '*bonnes à penser*' might be seen as more
directly equivalent to '*bonnes à manger*'. Just as an animal can be
delicious and 'good' in the mouth, it can be delicious and good
in the mind. They don't need to be part of our surroundings.
They can exist for themselves and that sheer co-presence of
animals in our mental life is a source of well-being. When the

singers of the Gaelic world become frogs or bees or whales, their vision acquires a contour beyond the demands of survival, competition or fear. There is more to this existence, in other words, than Malthus could ever dream of. Animals are good to think.

Of course, animals can play out the powerful and difficult parts of human relations in a way that allows the scarcely sayable to be said. If a simpleton forgets the necessary realities, wanders gormlessly away from home and a thief sneaks in, it does not take much to see those events as the story of an oystercatcher who is interested in many things and walks away without thought from his nest. When he comes back, he finds the eggs gone and 'in great distress' cries out (peeping and squealing):

Cò dh'òl na h-uighean? Cò dh'òl na h-uighean?
Cha chuala mi riamh a leithid! Cha chuala mi riamh a leithid!

Who drank the eggs? Who drank the eggs?
I never heard the like! I never heard the like!

A hoodie crow listened to the shrieking, his head turning now on this side and now on that, giving his bill some busy-looking wipes on the moss at his feet, looks up 'with much affected inno-cence' and calls out in deep and sympathetic tones, '*Cha chuala na sinne sinn fhèin sin, ged is sinn as sine san àite*' ('No, we have never heard of such a thing ourselves, though we have been here quite a bit longer than you').

The metaphor does not collapse; the story remains a tale of the oystercatcher and the crow, just as much as of a naive youth and a lying, dark-coated reprobate. It may be a morality tale – using the birds to think with – but they are also clearly 'good to think'. There is a mental tastiness about them and the experience of the world broadens with the reality of other creatures made vivid within it.

A mile or so west of the bay, according to the minister of Morvern in 1845, 'an old respectable person' rented both the inn at Lochaline and the small foot-ferry by which passengers paid to be rowed across the mouth of the narrows there, a short water-journey that saved a detour of five miles around the head of the loch. To entertain his guests, the innkeeper trained a magpie to talk. All went well, the bird amused the customers and trade blossomed. The innkeeper would regularly ferry customers over from the other side. One day he heard the familiar call from the far shore – 'Ferry please, ferry please' – and so as usual, patiently and laboriously, he went down to his boat and rowed over to the landing on the other side, where 'he found his docile pupil perched upon a rock, chuckling with hearty mirth at the success of her imitations'.

As the distance the ferryman had to row was about 300 (usually windy, often tide-rippled) yards, this story cannot be true. Nor are its elements difficult to decipher. The voice of a magpie sounds like mocking laughter and 'an old respectable person' is by definition someone to be mocked – nature will

always taunt the stupidity of human self-importance. The magpie was the only bird that did not go into the ark with Noah, and preferred to sit outside on the roof. He is the voice of otherness, suspected everywhere of wickedness and deceit. Witches in both Mull and Morvern had become magpies in the past. Like other corvids, they are clever birds, can certainly learn to parrot human speech and so the story admires them for that cleverness, at least in part. It also dramatises the uncanny, making the strange ridiculous and so emasculating and accommodating it. The two stories are the same: the innkeeper is as stupid and vain as the oystercatcher, the magpie as canny and wicked as the crow. All these animals are both good to think and good to think with. There was no illusion in Gaelic consciousness that human beings were alone in the world.

The shoreline itself was said to be a place of sanctuary. 'The black shore', the *dubh-chladach*, was the name for the intertidal zone, below the roll of seaweed thrown up by the tide (*ròlag ròid*) and above the sea itself. According to Highland belief, this half-place was an asylum from all kinds of supernatural beings that filled the night – fairies, ghosts or evil spirits. *Cha tig olc sam bith on fhairge*, it was said. 'Evil comes not from the sea.'

But little here was ever given its true name. 'Evil comes not from the sea' was merely a signal of the sea's implacability. According to his biographer the abbot Adomnán, St Columba when he wanted to wreak vengeance on his enemies 'prayed in the sea up to his knees / Till robber and blasphemer were drowned'.

The sea and its shore were part of a haunted landscape full of fears and projected anxieties. Our natural scepticism will put a barrier between us and the universe of fairy belief, which was general in the Highlands and islands of Scotland until the early nineteenth century, and with residues of it lasting for 150 years more, but the world of fairies can provide one avenue into the mind of the past, which it would be vain to shut off.

They were known as the still folk, the 'silently moving' people, invisible and quiet, oddly like the presence of a virus in the air, except on those rare occasions when the gifted or haunted would see them as they were: as strange women and elf-like men, most of them only four feet tall, the women like little girls, often dressed in green. They were often called '*fiosaichin*', meaning, neutrally, 'those that know'; or, in an effort to keep their power at bay, the 'good people', a sign that they were essentially bad.

They could be anywhere, unseen, present with us now, as if they were our memories, often near to hand because they liked the haunts of men. They would hurt you and yours. You could know they had been with you or in your house only when something had gone or changed, or a person or animal had died or was diseased. They were the slinking, sneaking ones, with no more substance to them than an eddy in a cloud of dust as the wind blew across a yard. To call anyone by the name of the fairies was purely derogatory.

This part of the world was full of them and just as human ecology was open to the world of the animals at one end, there was scarcely a boundary between people and fairies. Strontian, just north of Morvern on Loch Sunart, was Sròn an t-Sithin, the promontory or 'nose' of the fairy mound. Beinn Iadain, the tall and elegant hill in the centre of Morvern, carpeted in summer with rare, lime-loving alpines, was one of their strongholds.

How to find any access to this all-significant but remote mental world? It becomes more intelligible and more connected to the reality of life here if its stories are read backwards. These Gaelic fairies are not the sweet little tinkerbells of *Peter Pan* but frightening creatures, somehow related to the ghosts of the dead, perhaps to an earlier, forgotten set of gods, but coexisting in our world as present as ourselves, a third dimension of life alongside the human and the natural.

Often their stories end in damage or disappearance – a man unexpectedly dying; a boy injured when his mother is away; a child or old woman turning strange and disturbed, disconnected from those around them; old or troubled people who had become lost or seemed to have lost their selves. These are the phenomena we know every day as depression or dementia or kidnap or injury or murder. If you begin with those outcomes and substitute for the causes we turn to – the defects of age, genetic impairment, or the reality of domestic or sexual abuse and neglect – another set of explanations that rely on the sense that the dead may not be dead, and that there are spirits alive in the world, the fairy stories become understandable.

They are an explanation of the damage and grief implicit in a hard and demanding life. As such, they perform a service to well-being. People suffer and go mad; are hurt and lost; are undernourished and shrink from deprivations; are deformed, toothless, horribly thin, endlessly hungry, or unable to suckle their demanding, unthriving child. And none of this is the fault of any human being, but the work of the silent, slippery ones.

In their thieving, they take away the substance of animals, crops and people but not their outward form. If it looks, for example, as if a stand of oats has been emptied of its goodness; or a cow quite inexplicably sickens and weakens; or a child is born odd or fails to do well: what the people are left with is not what they knew but a fairy changeling, something that resembles the original but which has none of the original goodness in it. Women in childbirth were especially vulnerable because fairy mothers found it difficult to suckle their own children. Instead of the mother, it was said, they would leave a lump of wood; instead of the child 'an old mannikin'. The mother and child, it would be said, after the trauma of childbirth and its aftermath, would have been 'taken out of themselves', and were now away with the fairies.

Explanation is a form of comfort, and at least with the fairies – strange as they are – it was possible to imagine something of the structure of reality. They were not a source of delight or magic but the accommodation of grief, oddity and, as the great Gaelic scholar Ronald Black has written, of crime. Fairies provided 'a code for the forms of behaviour society does not want to face'. Crimes which socially and psychologically it would have been difficult to confront in a world without police or social services 'are spoken of through a symbolic language' which makes them acceptable, or at least allows life to continue past them. Dr Black quotes the Irish writer Angela Bourke:

> This is not to say that such explanations would normally be accepted or taken literally. Fairy legend charts the territory of no man's land. It comes with an air of the preposterous, the nod and wink, that allows one thing to be said, while another is meant. It permits face-saving lies to be told, and disturbing narratives to be safely detoured into fiction.

The double meaning is allowed to persist, its doubleness retained, not collapsed into guilt or rage or retribution or even grief – all of which might be psychologically or socially intolerable.

The shore played its part. In 1862, Arthur Mitchell, Deputy Commissioner for Lunacy in Scotland, reported from Mealista on the west coast of Lewis that he had seen 'an emaciated, shrivelled, helpless idiot, a dwarf with that puzzling expression of face – a compound of senility and babyhood'. It was a distant part of the world where a man called Wild Murdoch had been suffering from episodes of mania. Murdoch's friends 'used to tie a rope around his body, make it fast to the stern of the boat, and then pull out to sea, taking the wretched man in tow'. It would not have been safe, they said, to have him in the boat. He was so buoyant he didn't drown but the idiot dwarf was not so lucky.

> He is believed to be a changeling of the fairies, who are supposed to steal away the human child, and leave for it one of their own young-old children to be nursed. The only

remedy for this of which I heard, is to place the changeling on the beach by the water side, when the tide is out, and pay no attention to its screams.

The fairies, rather than suffer their own to be drowned by the rising waters, spirit it away, and restore the child they had stolen. The sign that this has been done is the cessation of the child's crying.

It was a widespread practice. John Sands, a travel writer visiting Tiree in 1881, heard from the minister, the great folklorist J. G. Campbell, 'that five years ago a woman left her child, which she supposed to be a changeling, upon the shore that it might be taken away by the fairies and her own infant restored'.

No account is given of the true outcome of these exchanges, but the phrases are telling: 'pay no attention to its screams'; the 'cessation of the child's crying'; 'taken away': all are transparent code for the murder of mentally damaged children whose continuing presence was neither helpful nor endurable. In families with no birth control, where women regularly bore eight children or more, the idea that the mother might have 'her own infant restored' is indistinguishable from 'fall pregnant again'. Her own infant would return as another child. It is likely enough that, over the centuries, this shore witnessed such scenes.

Unbaptised children were buried in the shores of the Sound of Mull. People who killed themselves were usually buried even further down, at the lowest of the tides. Arthur Mitchell found that if a suicide's relatives tried to avoid this terrible fate, and secretly buried the body in a graveyard, the neighbours would dig it up, take it to the beach on the ebb and bury it there.

In the winter of 1822, he heard, a poor old woman, 'in a fit of melancholia', cut her throat.

She was buried at low-water mark, but the sea disturbed her grave, and her body floated and was washed ashore. It was found there, and not being at first recognised, the people proceeded to carry it to a neighbouring house. When on their way, the gash in the throat was observed, the body recognised, and instantly dropped. For two days it lay at the roadside on the snow, till a person of influence in the neighbourhood had it buried a second time, and more securely, in the same fashion as at first.

What is the lowest of low-water marks but the one place in the ground which is least like a place on earth? It is the place of placelessness. The taboo on suicide is so powerful that the body of the self-murderer, like the changeling, cannot be allowed a secure resting place in the known and human world. The act of suicide, like the theft of the person's being by the fairies, has removed these people from the known or the tolerable. They must be given to the sea, to be absorbed by it, to mark their final and terminal exclusion from humanity.

In story after story, the weed marking the sea edge is the realm of trouble. In February 1623, on Oronsay – the tidal island lying off Colonsay, out to the west of here, besieged by Atlantic storms – the prior of the ancient monastery lay dying. He called for his kinsman, the last chief of the Colonsay Macphees, to visit him. In the distant past this had been Macdonald territory and Coll Ciotach Macdonnell, known as Colkitto, a pirate and seaborne gangster operating for years in these western seas, was attempting to reclaim his ancient lands.

Colkitto landed on Oronsay, his men armed with bows, dirks, two-handed swords, muskets and pistols. The tide was up and as the Macphee chief arrived to see his cousin, the Macdonalds killed two of his men. The chief himself escaped, running to the southern tip of Oronsay. At the shore there, he flung himself into the sea and swam from skerry to skerry across the reefs about 800 yards to the low rocky island of Eilean nan Ròn, the island of the seals, and there spent the last brutal winter's night of his life.

The next day, Colkitto came out to the little island with his men. They knew Macphee was there but could see nothing of him. After a long search they found him: he had buried himself under the bolt of seaweed lying at the top of the Atlantic-facing beaches – there is nothing but ocean between here and Newfoundland 2,000 miles to the west. They tied him to a stone and killed him before, famously, digging the musket balls out of his flesh because lead was short. Colkitto then took possession of Macphee's lands.

On an open skerry without trees, the bank of seaweed was the only place in which the sodden, frozen and terrified man could have found hiding. But there is surely more to this. The Gaelic term for his night-time's covering is *ròlag ròid*, meaning 'the roll of seaweed'. The word at the heart of that phrase, *ròd*, can never be used for weed still growing in the sea. It comes into play only when the weed is cast ashore, where it can also mean 'foam', or more exactly the 'foaming sea that beats against the land'.

In this emblematic universe, the *ròd* is the tangible form of the sea itself. It remains dynamic, not a pile of rotten weed but the element of wildness cast up on to the land. Just as the suicide's grave is at the lowest point to which the ebb drops, the *ròd* is at the highest point to which the sea comes. Those who hide in it are in effect hiding in the sea, or at least that part of the sea which has frothed and foamed up beyond the edge of the tide. All the potency of a transitional zone gathers in it, a place of safety and a place of threat, and on the mythic level at which these stories operate, Macphee had attempted to hide himself in a realm beyond reach.

The *ròd* retained its power to frighten. In the early nineteenth century, on the coast at Drumarbin near Fort William, 'a great shore-searcher after storms' was often found wandering 'ghost-like in the grey dawn by the margin of the sea, diligently picking up every conceivable article of flotsam and jetsam that came in his way'.

Everything he found he kept, even if he suspected the gear belonged to his neighbours. A man who thought his goods had been taken decided one morning to give him a fright. The neighbour

> lay down at length on the shingle, and covered his head and body down to his ankles with the drift-ware that had been cast up by the storm. All he left exposed was his feet and its pair of good substantial new shoes. Meanwhile the 'wrecker' was advancing along the beach, carefully searching about, and stooping from time to time, oystercatcher or curlew-wise, in order to pick up such waifs and strays as he fancied worth the while.

When he reached the man lying under the seaweed, he slowly removed the shoes but then

> a smothered sepulchral voice from under the sea-ware struck his ear: '*Gabh mo chomhairl' 's fàg na brògan sin!*' 'Take my advice, and leave these shoes alone!' At the same time he saw the mass of drift-weed heaving and moving. Dropping the shoes as if they had suddenly become each a mass of red-hot iron in his hand, he started off with a yell that frightened the sea-birds all the way to Camus-na-Gall.

He ran for his life back home, never went shore-wandering again and soon after sickened and died. The story itself hangs in the margins of the mortal: the shore-searcher is grey and ghostlike; the neighbour pretends to be a corpse; and the greedy man dies from the fright he has been given. It is a comic version of persistent terror and has a cousin in a third story, from the coast at Kingairloch, in Loch Linnhe around the corner from the bay.

Between here and there are the rough grounds of Garbh Shlios, the steep and difficult ravined country with which Morvern drops to its eastern shore, still now unoccupied for many miles, with no easy path through it, and the setting for some of the most ancient and inaccessible tales of giants fighting with enormous satanic bulls in battles that lasted all day.

Near Kingairloch a boat was upset and the two men in it were thrown into the water. One hung on and was saved. The other, who was a strong swimmer, set out for the land. He had forgotten to cut off his shoes and as he came near the shore and to the mass of weed that was turning in the surf there, his feet were

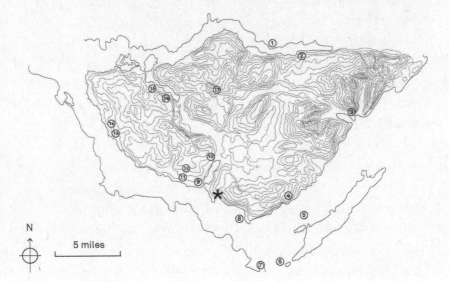

N

5 miles

Morvern Otherworld

✻ Ardtornish Bay

① Strontian
Named after fairy hill

② Liddesdale
Fairy helps with ploughing

③ Kingairloch
Fairy haunts the seaweed

④ Garbh Shlios
Haunt of the Glaistig

⑤ To Lismore
The Glaistig rows across the loch

⑥ Lady's Rock
Ritual Sacrifice

⑦ Duart Castle

⑧ HMS Dartmouth
The witches' wreck

⑨ Lochaline
Magpie plays a trick

⑩ Kinlochaline
Fairy woman changeling

⑪ Achabeg
Fairy kidnap

⑫ Sithein na Rapaich
Fairy hill of storms

⑬ Rhemore
Cailleach drops her stones

⑭ Bonavoulin
Donald swims in the sound with whales

⑮ Barr
Fairy kills a bride

⑯ Rahoy
Fairy woman and baby changelings

⑰ Beinn ladain
Fairies haunt travellers on fairy mountain; fairy attacks bridegroom

entangled in it and he drowned. When, some time later, his brother came past the place where the body had been picked up, a figure joined him on the road, looking something like a billy goat, murmuring to him in a voice he could scarcely hear or understand, warning those who did not take due care in life that they should mend their ways. The *ròd* would clutch at any man in shoes.

Morvern is full of such fairy tales. Occasionally the little people did good. At Liddesdale a fairy helped a lonely man with his ploughing and reaping. To some, they brought bowls of meal or filled the meal chest so that whenever the woman of the house looked into it the chest would be full, only, one day, for it to be unexpectedly bare. More often, they brought strangeness and unhappiness to people's lives. On Beinn Iadain, a fairy attacked a bridegroom who was walking over to the woman he was about to marry at Barr at the foot of the mountain on Loch Teacuis. She died before he got there. At Rahoy and at Kinlochaline, fairies substituted changelings for babies and nursing mothers. Above Knock at Lochaline, at the mouth of the safe harbour of the loch itself, they lived in the hill called Sithean na Rapaiche, the Fairy Hill of Storms; or, in another reading, the fairy house of noise and cursing. At Achabeg, a man was kidnapped by them overnight and could remember nothing the next morning of what he had done or where he had been. In many places, little fairy women came to the houses dressed in green, often sitting down to eat, and often taking more than their share, a consistently terrifying presence and never to be followed out of the house when they left. Fairies took away cows in the night to milk them, leaving them dry or with milk that had no substance in it, so the people could make no butter and have no cream.

The fairies' own habitations were usually out in the wild, in the margins of the high ground and in the rough inaccessible woods and gullies of Garbh Shlios on Loch Linnhe. There a *glaistig* – not a fairy but a little thin woman whose soul had been taken by them, strong, grey-skinned, with thick yellow hair and dressed in green – watched over the cattle in the wild corners. Like so many of these fairy stories, the *glaistig*, whose name means the grey one, the wraithlike one, can be understood as a version of a social truth – a simple woman, excluded from the mainstream, pushed quite literally to the edge of the inhabited world and considered odd and dangerous. She was often heard but rarely seen, her voice caught in the wind, her home a yew tree, the only other occupant of the hills a rough man called Yellow Dougal of the Cave. He was a thief by profession and wanted one day to row across Loch Linnhe to Lismore. The *glaistig* came and took an oar in his curragh. He had never known anyone, man or woman, to have pulled so hard. When at last they arrived on the Lismore beach, he looked round to see who it was that had rowed with such power; there was no one in the curragh with him. When she died, the *glaistig* was buried alongside the unbaptised children in the boundaries of the sea, where the tides in the Sound washed over her body.

The sea floods in and out of these tales, always the setting for strangeness, for a magic not unlike Ariel's, flirting with the terrible, finding the marvellous. There is the story, first, of Donald Livingstone of Bonavoullin on the Sound of Mull. He was a man who could charm cows, even from his own house, without seeing them, but the great moment in his life was in September 1746 when he was swimming home from Mull across the Sound with the news that all Morvern had been waiting for: Bonnie Prince Charlie had at last escaped to France. Hairy Donald, as he was known, had been a hero at Culloden, and now he flung himself into the water.

In mid-channel he met a large shoal of herring followed by a huge whale, blowing loudly and throwing up volumes of water high in the air. The whale terrified him and he was wondering how he could escape if the whale were to swallow him. Would he be expelled from the stomach of the whale as Jonah had been?

He survived, lived to be an old man, dying in his bed aged eighty-eight. He never had an illness and never wore trousers — sitting at his door in the coldest weather, telling his stories with a kilt over his knees and a blue bonnet on his head, bright to the last.

Those with magic in them were at home in the sea. Donald Cameron, much loved and called a 'fool' by the Morvern minister, went a step further than Donald Livingstone. On his submarine journeys, walking along the bottom of the sea from island to island, he visited the wrecks and conducted interviews with the fish he met along the way.

One time, he was coming home along the sea floor from Tiree.

It was very stormy weather, and the walking was difficult, and the road long. I became very hungry at last, and looked out for some hospitable house where I could find rest and refreshment. I was fortunate enough to meet a turbot, an old acquaintance, who invited me, most kindly, to a marriage party, which was that day to be in his family. The marriage was between a daughter of his own, and a well-to-do flounder.

So I went with the decent fellow, and entered a fine house of shells and tangle, most beautiful to look upon. The dinner came, and it was all one could wish. There was plenty, I assure you, to eat and drink, for the turbot had a large fishing bank almost to himself to ply his trade on, and he was too experienced to be cheated by the hook of any fisherman. He had also been very industrious, as indeed were all his family.

So he had good means. But as we sat down to our feast, my mouth watering, and just as I had the bountiful board under my nose, who should come suddenly upon us with a rush, but a tremendous cod, that was angry because the turbot's daughter had accepted a poor, thin, flat flounder, instead of his own eldest son, a fine red rock cod.

The savage, rude brute gave such a fillip with his tail
against the table, that it upset, and what happened, my dear,
but that the turbot, with all the guests, flounders, skate,
haddock, and whiting, thinking, I suppose, that it was a sow
of the ocean (a whale), rushed away in a fright; and I can tell
you, calf of my heart, that when I myself saw the cod's big
head and mouth and staring eyes, with his red gills going
like a pair of fanners, and when I got a touch of his tail, I
was glad to be off with the rest; so I took to my heels and
escaped among the long tangle. Pfui! what a race of hide-
and-seek that was! Fortunately for me I was near the Point of
Ardnamurchan, where I landed in safety, and got to Donald
M'Lachlan's house wet and weary. Wasn't that an adventure?

'Barefooted Lachlan', as he was politely known, was the third of
the great Morvern swimmers.

He lived for hours in the water, and alarmed more than one
boat's crew, who perceived a mysterious object – it might be
the sea-serpent – a mile or two from the shore, now
appearing like a large seal, and again causing the water to
foam with gambols like those of a much larger animal. As
they drew near, they saw with wonder what seemed to be the
body of a human being floating on the surface of the water.
With the greatest caution an oar was slowly moved towards
it; but just as the supposed dead body was touched, the eyes,
hitherto shut, in order to keep up the intended deception,
would suddenly open, and with a loud shout and laugh,
Lachlan would attempt to seize the oar, to the terror and
astonishment of those who were ignorant of his fancies.

There are echoes in that of the terrifying fairy playing dead in the
weed, and although the Morvern minister Norman Macleod tells
it as an amusing tale, with the fearsomeness largely disabled by

the middle of the nineteenth century, there is more to Lachlan's story than this. His japes in the middle of the Sound were enacting something that was even then disappearing. He swam naked and because it was inconvenient in a tidal sea always to return to the point of his departure, would often be seen walking along the Morvern roads without a stitch of clothing on his tanned skin. 'Barefooted Lachlan' was itself a euphemism. 'Society at last rebelled against his judgment,' the minister wrote, and Lachlan was sent to an asylum in the south. There, within a few days of his arrival, 'deprived of his long freedom among the winds and waves of ocean', he died.

Many other tales lie washed up on these shores, of drowning witches, surf-riding sea monsters and potent sea goddesses, many of them to be found in their different versions all along the western seaboards of Britain and Ireland. None is more foundational – or tidal – than the Cailleach, an ancient goddess who among her many adventures wanted to bridge the Sound of Mull at Rhemore, towards the north-western end of Morvern. Before she reached the tide, the strap on her creel broke and she dropped her enormous load of stones in what is now recognised as a Bronze Age cairn, the Carn na Caillich. It is a beautiful, hidden and almost unnoticed place, covered in crumpled rugs of moss and English stonecrop, looking out over a narrow stretch of the Sound, with the height of Ben More on the horizon.

She was one night on the sea with her sons. The night was dark and freezing. The cold pierced to the marrow. She told them to keep themselves warm.

'We cannot,' say they.

'Bail the sea out and in,' says she.

'We cannot do that,' say her children.

'Take the baling scoop, and fill the boat and bail it out again.' They did so and kept themselves warm till morning, till they got a chance to come on land.

Only with a goddess does the tide come and go beside one's feet on the strakes of the hull, and between the thwarts. When asked her age, after bearing 500 children to many fathers, the Cailleach said, 'I have seen the seal-haunted rock of Skerryvore, which is now out in the midst of the sea, when it was a mountain surrounded by fields. I saw the ploughing of those fields, and the barley that grew upon them was sharp and juicy.' She is the goddess of the tide and of time, of erosion and change, of the coming and going of things, of the ways of flux.

All the stories now are as neglected as the sea-tangle itself. Neither they nor the weed are needed for the fertility they might once have brought to life here. The goddesses and the fairies are pushed away into the inert category called 'folklore'. Neither Lachlan's jokes nor Donald's sea-walks nor the other Donald's encounters with the herrings and the whale can animate the lives or spirits of people now. A cultural world in which meaning could cross the tideline and where the connections between sea and land, animal and human, human and fairy were vivid and continuous, has gone. The word 'fairy' has itself become both sweet and toxic; not the embodiment of a potent and unaccommodated spirit abroad in the world but a sentimentalised, sugar-drop version of it; not an enlargement of understanding but a retreat from it.

I now wonder if the haunting of the fairies differed, in any essential way, from the anxieties of the prawns, the winkles or the sandhoppers. All of them experience the ghosts of fear and pain, the imagined or reimagined realities of hurt once suffered and to be suffered again. Life is unsustainable without such wariness. It is one guarantee of survival, telling the organism to be careful in a hostile world. Both fairy and fear banish naivety and create a balance in the mental universe of a person – or animal. Take advantage of the world, it says, and eat its fruits, but recognise the danger that lurks in strange places.

12

Three steps to the modern

I. The tide had crawled up unperceived

By 1850, the earlier world of this bay had been erased. Over three or four centuries, the tide of modernity had eaten away at its foundations. Politics and trade came to matter more than climate or soils. Local adaptations and institutions were overwhelmed. The culture that had developed here was slowly replaced by the demands of a distant market and the growing technological, military and institutional power of the state. The life of most people in Morvern came to seem like an excrescence and, often with carelessness, brutality and humiliation, they were removed.

It was a tragic clash: a modernising, globalising and eventually industrialising world at its most expansive met an essentially pre-modern society whose ways of being and thinking, its *dùthchas*, were subtle, evolved, rich and sustaining, but fragile in front of these demands.

In 1843, 500 radical ministers in the Church of Scotland, responsive to this sense of destruction, had left the church in protest against the Patronage Act by which landowners were able to choose their local minister, a choice in which the people had no say. The protesters set up what they called the Church of

Scotland Free, the 'Free Kirk', and were forced to leave behind any land-based buildings in which to preach.

All over the country they met in the open air. 'Mr Maclean of Tobermory held services on the hillside, often in severe weather.' Some conducted the whole service under heavy rain; others in snow, 'the fall being so heavy that at the close', one minister said, 'I could hardly distinguish the congregation from the ground on which they sat, except by their faces.' One church was built inside a distillery. Many services were held on the verges of the public roads.

People walked fifteen miles across the hills to hear these sermons. These were moments of the deepest emotion; enormous congregations, of 2,000 or more, would be hanging on the lips of the speakers, often dissolving in tears at the redemption that was offered, and with 'deep sobs heard throughout'. In many places, worshippers gathered on the shore and the minister spoke from the bow of a moored boat.

The shore, because it did not belong to the landowners, was a place in-between, the realm of exclusion but also of liberty. At

Just as Christ preached to the fishermen from Peter's boat, ministers of the Free Church, deprived of any land-based building, preached to their congregations when moored in the intertidal.

Strontian on Loch Sunart, the people had built by their own subscription a floating iron church, eighty feet long, in which, anchored to the loch bed, 750 hearers could fit on the benches. The popularity of the preachers could be judged by the depth to which the hull sank in the water, an inch for every hundred extra of the faithful.

At Lochdonhead in Mull, just across the Sound from the bay, beyond Duart, the people were forced to meet in a canvas tent they had put up on the floor of a gravel pit that was on the edge of the sea loch. During one service, the attention of a visiting minister from the Lowlands 'was diverted by an unaccountable commotion among those who were seated within the tent'.

He could not understand what the trouble was. He knew this to be the most attendant of congregations. Then he saw that the minister himself was 'looking towards the ground in an uneasy manner'. The visitor then looked beneath his own chair:

> The tide had crawled up unperceived, and there sat the congregation – not one left his seat – and there stood the preacher, all ankle-deep in the tide, which had thus stealthily crept up to them while they were solemnly engaged in the most sacred rite of the Church. The preacher drew his address to a close, a short parting psalm was sung, for the spot was on the margin of a shallow, land-locked bay, in which the tide rose slowly; the benediction was pronounced, and the congregation, many of them moved to tears, quietly dispersed to their homes.

'Lament at its most extreme will always have to encounter water,' Alice Oswald has said recently and these desperate and touching stories mark the moment when the people of this place were driven into the sea.

II. Survival of the fittest

At the same instant, the love affair between educated Victorian Britain and the edges of the sea was entering its most intense phase. High on the ridge to the west of the bay, a large and beautiful house had been built in the middle of the eighteenth century by a gentleman from Appin, its porch covered in honey-suckle and jasmine, its 'square and sunny' upstairs drawing room looking out over the bay and the Sound towards the Mull hills. Here, as Philip Gaskell, the landlordist historian of Morvern has described, 'rich, cultured foreigners who had no professional interest in the land migrated to the West Highlands for lengthy holidays to walk and shoot and fish and relax in a country of insidious beauty'.

I only realised long after I began to look into the story of this place that the most famous phrase ever used to describe life on earth was written in that house in the late summer of 1864, by a man of enormous fame at the time who is scarcely remembered now, a bachelor-intellectual, in Argyll on holiday, who had been entertaining the other guests and the children of the house with the three aquariums he had set up and for which he had gathered plants and animals from these shores and waters. That summer, he was revising the latest instalment of his giant, all-compre-hending study of man, nature and the world.

In 1860, the bay and its surrounding lands had been bought by Octavius Smith, a vastly successful London distiller who was also part of a self-consciously freethinking, free-market, anti-establishment milieu, intent on changing the conservative habits of mid-Victorian Britain. Energetic, resourceful, full of enter-prise and set against any government interference in the pursuit of his business, Smith was the purest version of a Victorian meritocrat.

He had been introduced to Herbert Spencer, the libertarian (and impoverished) philosopher, whose articles in the *Westminster*

Review and elsewhere had promulgated opposition to what he repeatedly called 'government meddling'. The two became the best of friends, and when Smith bought his Highland estate here, Spencer was usually among the guests for the summer holidays, 'varying in duration as they did from a month to six weeks and even two months'.

Spencer had been born into a highly religious Nonconformist background, from which he had inherited an innate opposition to authority. In time, he lost his faith in God or any form of creator, and became part of that modern philosophical movement which was set on questioning all received ideas. He was no scientist himself, and was thought faintly ridiculous by those who were, but a theoretician of natural law, for whom the principle of evolution became the fundamental fact of existence. Spencer saw a world animated by a steady progress towards an ever more individuated and developed ideal. In nature, in human psychology, in human cultures and societies, there was an imperturbable drive towards that ever finer condition. In 1858 he drew up his 'Outline of a System of Synthetic Philosophy', in which biology, psychology, sociology and ethics were all to be brought together under this single vision of evolution-towards-excellence.

The London distiller felt confirmed by him. 'The ultimate result of shielding men from the effects of folly,' Spencer liked to say, 'is to fill the world with fools.' The great principle was 'the progressive adaptation of constitution to conditions'. The French evolutionist Jean-Baptiste Lamarck had envisaged the necessary mechanism: in any body, any mind or any society, 'the increase or decrease of structure [was] consequent on increase or decrease of function'. If a giraffe stretched for the highest leaves on a tree, its progeny would be born with longer necks. Northerners who moved to sunny countries would have dark-skinned children. Puppies born to hounds already knew what had been taught to their parents. How this actually happened, Spencer could not say, but the assumption was that any transformation of a body, a

Herbert Spencer (1820–1903).

mind or a 'social organism' would be transmitted to its successors and descendants. The giant System of Synthetic Philosophy would demonstrate the coherence of this idea in all conceivable dimensions.

It was, in a sense, a form of self-justification: Spencer and his friends had emerged from non-establishment, relatively humble backgrounds to dominate their world. He had become better than those he saw around him, and what he was, his descendants would surely also be.

An unaddressed hole lurked in the centre of the proposed world-system: there was no identified means by which this idea of evolution operated. Then, in July 1858, a composite paper by Charles Darwin and Alfred Wallace was read at the Linnean Society in London and the idea of natural selection as the origin of species burst on the world. The presence of death was revealed as the shaper of life. Just as a breeder of hens or hounds would choose the best for their purposes, death in nature would select the survivors. Environment, predation and competition made the selection, preserving, as Darwin said, only the 'favoured races in the struggle for life'.

A new candidate had surfaced for the greatest idea in Victorian England. Spencer, in his mid-forties and now a desperate hypochondriac, was on holiday here when the paper was read. 'I have but a vague impression of the way in which this event became known to me; but my belief is that I remained in ignorance of it until my return to town in October.'

It was a devastating moment: someone else had understood the mechanism by which evolution happened. Spencer 'held that the sole cause of organic evolution is the inheritance of functionally produced modifications', but he was wrong. There was no grand spirit of progress pushing creation towards ever more evolved forms. Change did not come about by inheritance from antecedents. Chance mutation, acted on and selected by the demands of the environment, was the way that life diversified.

Then Spencer remembered something: this idea had already 'occurred to me in the course of a country ramble with Mr. G. H. Lewes in the autumn of 1851. The thesis was that organic forms in general, vegetal and animal, are determined by the relations of the parts to incident forces.' He kicked himself that he had not developed the idea more fully at the time and now Darwin had scooped the prize.

Money worries, the fight against the church establishment, the struggle to establish a coherent vision of existence, the pervasiveness of change: from all of this Spencer was suffering. 'I was able to work at the best only three hours a day, and often not that;

and there occasionally came relapses which forced me to leave off for a time entirely.' He was wrapped in his own solitary struggle: 'I once discovered to my dismay that I sometimes passed those living in the same house with me, and, though I looked them in the face, remained unconscious that I had seen them.' He often could not sleep and had regular 'recourse to one or other preparation of opium'.

The strain of writing overtaxed him and his habit now was to dictate his prose. En route to the bay, in Oban, he had found 'a youth of some eighteen or so, sufficiently educated to serve as amanuensis' and when on holiday here liked to spend his afternoons 'paddling about in Ardtornish Bay, and dictating while I rowed'. His working papers do not survive but it is not inconceivable that the most famous phrase in biological thought was coined when out on the water of the bay itself.

'The coast is very rich, and I expect to get many novelties,' he wrote to his mother, and years later in his autobiography described his happiness here, setting up the aquariums, showing the other guests how to use a microscope, fishing in the rivers and walking on the cliffs, loving 'the gorgeous colours of clouds and sky' while listening to Beethoven sonatas played by the girls on the house piano.

In the late summer of 1864, he was revising that part of his *Principles of Biology* that was to be published the following October. He had come to the point where he had to admit Darwin's discovery. Perhaps, much as a starfish absorbs the meat of a mussel, Spencer could absorb natural selection into his own system.

A man writing by dictation tends to long-windedness and so you must imagine him out in the bay as he pulls gently on the oars, the young boy sitting in the stern-sheets taking down the precious words: 'Doubtless many who have looked at Nature with philosophic eyes, have observed that death of the worst and multiplication of the best, must result in the maintenance of a constitution in harmony with surrounding circumstances.' The destruction of the weak will always demonstrate that 'organisms which live thereby prove themselves fit to live, in so far as they have been tried; while organisms which die, thereby prove themselves in some respects unfitted for living ... This self-acting purification of a species must tend ever to insure adaptation between it and its environment.'

He has by now rowed across the bay to Rubha an t-Sasunnaich, has turned the boat and is slowly making his way back towards the house, tea, Beethoven and companionship. 'Applying alike to the lowest and the highest forms of organization, there is in all cases a progressive adaptation, and a survival of the most adapted.'

That was the first run at it, but he then came to the final wording:

> This survival of the fittest, which I have here sought to express in mechanical terms, is that which Mr Darwin has called 'natural selection, or the preservation of favoured races in the struggle for life'.

Darwin had not used 'survival of the fittest' as a phrase. Many of his followers disliked the term 'natural selection', as it implied an agency doing the selecting, and preferred Spencer's term as it encapsulated the blindness of the process. In time, and in later editions of *On the Origin of Species*, Darwin, who considered Spencer full of 'dreadful hypothetical rubbish', would nevertheless adopt 'survival of the fittest' as the truth at the heart of the evolution of life.

For all the precision of his words, Spencer could not accept that natural selection was the only mechanism by which life evolved. Doggedly, he held on to the idea of the inheritance of acquired characteristics. Perhaps he had to. Darwin's idea represented a peculiarly modern anarchy, while Spencer's cherished idea of evolution-towards-excellence was deeply connected to his mid-nineteenth-century view of the reality of progress. Gradually, in the second half of his life, that view came to seem not only biologically wrong but naively optimistic, the need of a lonely, sickening man to systematise the whole of experience, to give it the comfort blanket of a single enveloping principle by which the better and the best, like Spencer and Octavius Smith and all the brilliant Smith children, would always emerge on top.

But life was not on a relentless drive towards the perfect. The general crisis of the early twentieth century and the devastations of the Great War finally revealed the comfort and self-assurance of this Spencerian vision to have been hopelessly wrong. Evolution-towards-excellence was not the ultimate truth but the delusion of successful Victorians who imagined they were the natural outcome of laws that governed the universe.

III. Being-with

I also rowed out in the bay, looked at creatures in my aquarium and peered down into the pools to find there the subtle structures of animal and vegetable life. I felt a million miles from Spencer's expectation of evolution-towards-perfection, but what to replace it with? Floating out on the bay, I instead read a short and brilliant book by George Steiner about a very different figure from a very different time.

A small boat on a calm autumn sea is a beautiful and easy place to read and gently absorb Steiner's unfolding of the difficult and opaque ideas of the great early-twentieth-century German philosopher Martin Heidegger. My expectations were not high because Heidegger comes with the darkest of clouds hanging over him. He was a Nazi, promoted by the Nazis, promulgating the virtues of Nazism to his students and, after the hellish revelations of Belsen and Auschwitz, never once explaining or apologising for his involvement with the Nazi cause.

The beauty and marvel of Steiner's book is its ability to find in Heidegger, alongside the 'active partisan in barbarism', a man he could also call 'a philosopher of towering stature'. Slowly, page by page, I followed Steiner searching for wisdom and understanding in the works of a man he confronts as a lifelong anti-Semite, who in the 1930s had been 'caught up in the electric trance of Nazism' and who after the war lurked in a long, dark and ugly silence.

For Steiner, born in 1929 in Paris to Viennese Jewish parents, to have written this book seemed increasingly to me an act of courage and grace, not of forgiveness, as there can be no forgiveness for the crimes of a Nazi vision that in many ways acted out the most wicked assumptions of a Spencerian imposition of excellence, but of generosity and civilisation. By sheer chance, I had met Steiner a year or two before he wrote this book. I was eighteen and he came to speak to some of us at school. I was asked

Martin Heidegger (1889–1976).

to look after him, and I remember now his sheer brightness, as small-boned as a bird, looking up at us and asking about our lives and ideas. As I took him back to the Head Master's house, he turned and said, 'Never forget the beauty of what you now are,' words that seemed more than strange at the time, but wonderful in retrospect, a measure of the generosity and scale of spirit that animated him.

And so Steiner as much as Heidegger was out with me in the bay and on Rubha an t-Sasunnaich, all three of us there in our ragged waterproofs and tattered waders. During the terrible troubles in Germany after the end of the Great War, years filled with poverty, violence and despair, Heidegger's ambition was to reshape the whole of Europe's intellectual heritage. He saw it, in a way, quite simply. Two streams had descended to us from ancient Greece: from Plato, who wanted to find ultimate reality and value beyond this world, in a realm of ideal forms of which mundane existence was only a weak and shadowed projection; and from Aristotle, who wanted to find meaning in the actuality and mechanics of the physical world as it was.

From Plato came the long and grand tradition of metaphysics, of considering this life less than another to which we have no real access; from Aristotle came the world of science, which excludes the questions of ultimate meaning and attends only to the facts as they are. For centuries, Europe had been in thrall to the first, the centuries of religion; the modern industrialised world of technology and the exploitation of nature is in thrall to the second.

Both visions for Heidegger are inadequate, either condemning life on earth to an empty shadow-play or turning us into predatory users of our world. Both are empty and eviscerated. Both are unhappy. Both are diminishing and destructive. Heidegger's word for this is 'privative'.

These traditional understandings of life take away the heart of existence. By emphasising either the other-worldly or the exclusively material, they induce in us a forgetting of being. Heidegger thought that, since ancient Greece, we had 'forgotten how to be in the world', one of those phrases that produced in me the strange and enlarging experience of learning something new that nevertheless seemed to articulate what I had always half-thought, even if in an inchoate and unexpressed way, but which now appeared fully illuminated.

That was the recognition-of-what-I-had-always-known given me by Heidegger–Steiner on the rocks. I have always thought that neither science nor religion is good enough. But what to put in their place? The Heideggerian answer is something Steiner translates as 'total thereness', a life which is 'soul- and spirit-deep in that which is'. Phrases circling that idea come rolling round again and again: 'the luminous thereness of what is'; 'the highest densities of meaning lying in the immediate'; 'being is not a chance or a choice because being-in-the-world is as it is'; 'to be at all is to be worldly'; 'the radiant autonomy of organic and inorganic objects'; the revelatory nature of 'real concreteness'.

These glowing realities add up to what Heidegger calls the 'house of being'. But what, really, is that underlying being, the thereness to which we must commit our lives? Neither Heidegger nor Steiner can finally say, but Steiner finds a beautiful analogy. We know what this reality of being is, the Being beyond the surface manifestations of being, when listening to music. 'Music,' Steiner says, '"enters" the body and mind at manifold and simultaneous levels,' but how or why it does that eludes us.

'Wherever possible we consign the question either to technicality or the limbo of the obvious. Yet we *know* what music is. We know it in the mind's echoing maze and in the marrow of our bones. We assign to it an immensity of meaning. What does it mean? When Schumann was asked what one of his compositions meant, his answer was to play it again. In music being and means-of-being are inextricable.'

This is not metaphysical, not about any other world than this. Heidegger–Steiner's description is of this world, the world as it is, full as it is of 'contradictory simultaneities' and repeated chances of ecstatic encounter. Neither Plato, thinking reality is elsewhere, nor Aristotle, attached to the atomised physical, could know about it. Nor is it any form of balm, relieving one of the anxiety and difficulty of being, as the Platonic dream or the Aristotelian forgetting of wider significance, might have done.

Heidegger's world recognises the reality of anxiety, and above all the reality of death, our own 'finitude', as the condition of life. We can live only in the uncertainty of our reality. We must be patient because 'to know how to wait is to know how to question being'. Steiner paraphrases the Heideggerian tangle: 'thought must descend humbly to the poverty of its tentative condition'. Here now, beside the pools, Heidegger–Steiner approached the core of the idea. The way to be in the world is 'being-with'. To understand the presentness of all others is to exist. Being with others makes us who we are and the acceptance of others enlarges us. The co-presence of others, both given and received, becomes the frame in which knowledge is possible.

Concern for them is the central connective tissue, and only the recognition of the reality of individual death, the limited nature of individual life, can lead to an engagement with what is here now. Only a life that recognises the actual and the daily can hope to be true. And so Heidegger arrives at a vast and humane vision, in a thought that encapsulates what Steiner calls his 'vehement humanity': 'I care therefore I am.'

This central concern is for more than humanity; it is care for all that is and as such is the opposite of Descartes's idea that he is because he thinks. The world exists beyond any knowing you might have of it. 'Knowing is not a process of returning with one's booty to the "cabinet" of consciousness. It is on the contrary a form of being-with, a concern, a lingering alongside.' That for Heidegger is the paradoxical condition of true liberty: knowing your life is limited, with 'a bracing awareness of one's finitude' you will care for all others, coming alongside them and being-with the world in 'a freedom which is both certain of itself and anxious'.

It is one of the great statements of the marvellous. Death is not an event but an aspect of being; and its principal effect is not, eventually, to kill you but to generate a life lived in the awareness and recognition of all others. 'Care,' Heidegger says, in summation, 'is the primordial condition.' Care and true being are indivisible.

These great and revolutionary thoughts are almost a century old. They seem scarcely to have been absorbed by the culture, but they came to shape my time at the rock pools. The coexistence with the things of the pool, the being-with them, a total co-presence with them, came to seem like a way of establishing my own being in the world. To be-with is the only way to be. Not-being-with – to be in real isolation – and allowing no penetration of the You into the I can only be a form of non-being, a gravity-less floating in an atomised and disconnected universe which has lost all significance beyond the 'service' it is said to provide for an I-fixated humanity.

Service! You have to ask what service the prawn had in mind when it was selected for the sandwich? Or the crab for its mayonnaise? No creature, no set of creatures and no networked relationship of creatures provide any service to us. We prey on them. The ego is essentially predatory. We take and use the world, carelessly destroy the conditions for which its inhabitants have evolved, and casually engineer another world-destroying crisis equivalent to the disaster that made the lifeless rocks on Rubha an t-Sasunnaich some 200 million years ago.

An understanding of Heidegger's care, Heidegger's being-with and Heidegger's diminution of the thinking self is the only way we can change the way we think of our own being. Confronted with the grand crisis of nature, Heidegger provides the most powerful set of ideas: an all-pervading consciousness of the autonomy of other life; a recognition, at this most enveloping of philosophical levels, that we cannot exist unless embedded in it; the need to remain anxious at its unsettlingness, not as a failure to resolve problems but as a recognition of their reality; and our own finitude beside it.

The pointlessness of making the pools – so many people asked 'But what are they for?' – was their value. They were for nothing. Making the pools was not the point. Being there while making them, what Heidegger calls 'lingering with being' was what was valuable, an inadvertent and marginal benefit that strikingly bears the same relationship to making something useful as the shore does to the sea itself: a revelatory edge that by definition is no good for shipping.

There is much to be said about the state of the world's seas, the levels of destruction, the hypocrisies of policymakers, the empty designations of sea areas that are meant to be protected but which are unpoliced and effectively unprotected, our inability to confront our own rapaciousness – but behind those destructive behaviours is a deeper and more fundamental question about our sense of who we are, what it is to be and what it is to understand. The things of the world exist whether we are with them or not; and our presence with them is made significant only by their being-with us. Nature is more than a quarry to be eaten away at by our own ego-fixated technologies.

'I do not want to be reflective any more,' Louis MacNeice wrote a few years after Heidegger was thinking about these things.

> The tide comes in and goes out again, I do not want
> To be always stressing either its flux or its permanence,
> I do not want to be a tragic or philosophic chorus
> But to keep my eye only on the nearer future
> And after that let the sea flow over us.

Come then all of you, come closer, form a circle,
Join hands and make believe that joined
Hands will keep away the wolves of water
Who howl along our coast. And be it assumed
That no one hears them among the talk and laughter.

Be with the shore, be with its others, be with everyone there.
Listen to the wolves, consider 'the nearer future' and fill it with
talk and laughter.

CONCLUSION

The last pool

As winter came on, I built a third pool, further down the tide, in the richer and fiercer environment of the lower shore. It was to be different from the others: not dug in with a pickaxe, nor made by damming a hollow but by forming a MacNeicean circle next to a rock buttress, down in amongst the weed. When I first saw a place that might work, at the far eastern end of Rubha an t-Sasunnaich, a storm was blowing and the winter sea was

The site of the last pool in winter, satisfactorily far down the tide.

A computer sketch of the last pool, making a circular enclosure
against a rock buttress.

surging to and fro across it, the fronds of the weed whiplashed in
the waves, the wolves of water howling on the shore.

As soon as it calmed, I got the foundations in: no measure-
ments, scraping at the limestone to get a good bedding for the
wall, but leaving the seaweeds around it, so that the pool would
start not as a raw and empty rock-dish but an enclosed part of
the seabed, a park more than a garden. I would make the boundaries and the sea and its life could wander in. I saw it now as a
frame for being-with.

Every day, squeezing the work into the hour or two it was
open on either side of low tide, I added concrete to the wall.
Within a week it was done and I knew then I had to be patient.
I left it to rest so that it would have time to become itself, thinking I would return in the spring. Then life disrupted all plans, the
pandemic of 2020 struck and the shore was out of bounds for
months.

The circular wall emerges from the weed.

And the pool sinks beneath the tide.

It was high summer before Sarah and I came back. We were too impatient to wait for low tide and as soon as we could we took the boat across to the headland. It was the most perfect of days, the tide slipping easily out across the weeds of the upper shore. The sea had yet to drop. Water flowed seamlessly between the inside and outside of the pool, blurring the concrete, and the pool looked exactly as I had imagined it all winter and spring, half-visible, buried in the sea, sunk like a memory.

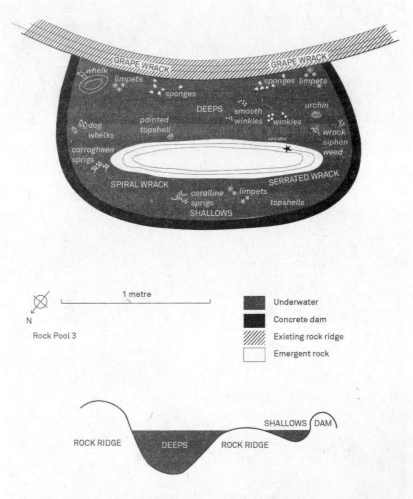

The third pool and its inhabitants: grey shows water in the pool, white emergent rock, black the concrete dam.

As the tide fell, the wall and pool emerged: a cupping of the sea, a stilling. Already, unvisited, multiple life forms had taken up residence in it and over the weeks of the summer I made a map of what was there.

It varied all the time. The weeds, the sponges, the limpets and tiny, newly seeded barnacles were all fixed and remained constant but other animal life came in on one tide and left on the next. Sometimes the pool was nearly bereft of creatures; at others it met me with spectacular surprises. I felt like a child when I arrived one day to find a starfish sprawled in the one-foot depths of the central channel, its arms looking as sugar-crusty as an Eccles cake, covered in the tiny self-cleaning organs, the pedicellariae, with which it picks away any weed or creature that tries to colonise its surface. Only because of the pedicellariae is the starfish so bright. Its wavering tube-feet reach out to the stones around it like the fingers of a man looking to know where he is in the dark. Then, on one unforgettable day, the common sea star spread its twelve pink and white tuft-encrusted limbs across

Visitors – a starfish …

... a common sea star ...

the sunlit edges of the shallows, as brilliant as if it were newly made, just as assiduous as its cousin in cleaning its own body, so that it looked more like a dish of strawberries and cream that had arrived from Mars than a thing of the Scottish seas, or a coral reef steadily on the move, as huge and deliberate as the giant tracked vehicles that transport rockets to the launch pad at Cape Canaveral, a bi-colour garden, the prettiest of dresses, a tooth-brush from paradise, a radiant morning gleaming from the shallows. It was there for one tide only and never returned.

I picked the near-perfect, Venetian spiral of a painted topshell out of the bottom of the deeps. I watched the barnacles filtering life from water. And the carnivorous little dog whelks looking for their own meaty rewards. Sometimes I found their empty victims, the shells of other creatures neatly bored with a single hole drilled through them for the whelk to get its meat.

It was a time of absorption, the shore animals putting on their cavalcade at every turn. This wasn't fixity but something happening, oscillating not only with the tide but from one day to the next, each manifestation of the pool a different patch of life over time.

An urchin was there one day, perhaps washed in from lower down the tide, a pink pompom but clearly the cousin of a starfish, its five arms still marked on the globe of its body but as surface gestures, memories of the limbs its ancestor had once possessed. Like the starfish the urchin was moving through its world with its hundreds of tube-feet, beautiful dancer-arms emerging from between its spines, extending their fingers into the surrounding weed and sea, and equipped like the starfish with the pedicellariae that keep it bright.

... and a sea urchin.

I had read something by Graham Harman, who teaches philosophy at SCI-Arc in Los Angeles. He had written about Kant's distinction between phenomena – 'everything that humans are able to encounter, perceive, use or think about' – and noumena which 'by contrast, are things-in-themselves that we never experience directly, since we remain trapped in the conditions of human experience'.

All we can know are phenomena, what we know, or think we know, of other beings. Those beings themselves are unknowable. The underlying nature of reality is beyond our grasp. It remains inevitably and permanently enclosed in its noumenal distance. And so we do not have access to creatures-in-themselves. We can encounter the phenomenal side – the brightness, the smoothness, the wrinkliness, the brilliance – but we have no access to what they are beyond these surface qualities.

The mystery of things is not metaphysical but implicit in the existence of everything that is. I would never know the animals, nor the rocks on which they lived. All I could know is what my senses and the sciences told me of these strangers' qualities.

Harman talked later about what he called the 'object/qualities rift'. The sensed object is not a bundle of qualities. The thing simply is. What the object *is* is more than its qualities. And this is a universal condition. We share this unknowing with all existence but there is no hierarchy here. If we share ignorance, we also share a kind of undeniable being. All is equally and gleamingly present. An ice boulder, the rigidified basalt, the flooding sea, the gulls standing looking bereft in the sunshine, the slow, feeling tube-arms, hydraulically driven, of the starfish, the urchin and the sea star: we are all equally, marvellously here, even as the tide laps up around our knees.

The pool was that cup of wonder for me, as I made the daily trip across the bay to find it again, anchoring the boat to the rock and letting the breeze drift it out to the length of its rope into the sea, and then looking again into the shallow depths. Shallow depths! That was everything this year had been about: the fractal way in which unknowability can be found in the shallows of a pool, where layers of complexity constitute 'the lovely puzzles' Stephen Jay Gould had described. Plato said that 'wonder is the feeling of a philosopher, and philosophy begins in wonder' but the sense of the word in Greek is not 'awe' or 'amazement' – the inadvertent wow when meeting the beautiful – but the sense of 'puzzlement', the perplexity of realising that you do not know at some level what is true. The tens of thousands of scientific papers devoted to this life can only concentrate on *how* it is, the workings of life, but that presence of the puzzling-wonderful is surely the engine behind it all.

They were magical weeks. Categories seemed to fuse. Perhaps it was the circumstances: the distant, human world held in the grip of its own viral infection; me here now, away from that trouble, embedded in the subtle and expressive life of the pools. I felt such gratitude. The existence of things seemed to be continuous with the ways that existence made itself apparent; the phenomenal surface seemed for a moment like a route to the noumenal, to the undeniable reality of things as they are.

I explored the low shore around the pool and came to see that I had merely built another patch in it, in an environment that was already patchy. Every different turn and wrinkle of the rock created a different place, different in its exposure to storm waves, different in depth and so in length of submersion, different in the ability of plants and animals to live there. Patchiness was the essential quality of this world.

Would it be possible to detect the tensions at work within it?

At first, it does not look tensed at all. This pool is on the lip of the very lowest spring tides. From here I can look back up at a well-ordered shore, a plain staircase of seaweeds, the same as on any northern rocky coast, stepping down towards me from dry land.

At the very top, next to the grass and in a place where fresh water runs off the land, is some bright green gutweed, fresh, transient and fragile. Below that is the channelled wrack, or channel wrack, so-called because each sprig of each frond encloses a shallow channel, just narrow enough for the seawater to be held in there by its own surface tension when the tide drops away, so that these channels make miniature rock pools for the weed, ensuring that it stays damp on a hot afternoon.

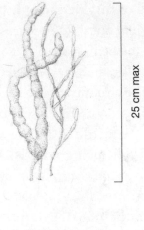

Gutweed

25 cm max

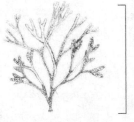

Channelled wrack

15 cm max

Just below it is the spiral wrack, slightly darker, in whose twisting and turning lobes the water will also remain between the tides. Both spiral and channel wrack are able to rehydrate

Spiral wrack

more quickly and more thoroughly and after a deeper desiccation than all the other weeds. They are made to thrive on the upper shore.

Below them comes bladderwrack, living for far longer below the tide, supplied with air bladders that lift it towards the light when submerged.

Its larger cousin, grape or knotted wrack, comes next, right down to the pool itself, mixed in there with the serrated wrack, its leaves more robust, thicker and more difficult to tear than the others, with its margins cut away, perhaps so that it can better

Bladderwrack

60 cm max

Serrated wrack

survive the thrashing given it by storm waves out here on these exposed rocks. A red parasitic weed called wrack siphon weed attaches itself to the hanks of grape wrack.

120 cm max

10 cm max

Knotted wrack and
wrack siphon weed

Below those wracks and just below the pool I had made come the kelps, exposed to the air only at exceptionally low tides: giant bladed brown weeds, some as single longer fronds, others, further out and more exposed, wrinkled or divided into many fingers, also as a protection against storm waves, whose energy is broken

300 cm max

Kelp

by the multiple surfaces of the wrinkled kelp and the many fingers of its digitated cousin.

At the very lowest of the tide, when you wade around within the serrated wrack and the kelps, pulling aside the dark of their shade, you find the dulse, growing on the rock near and under the kelps, or attached to the kelps themselves, a soft red weed that tastes of hazelnuts. At their feet and in among the claw-like holdfasts of the kelp are the rock-encrusting corallines, pink

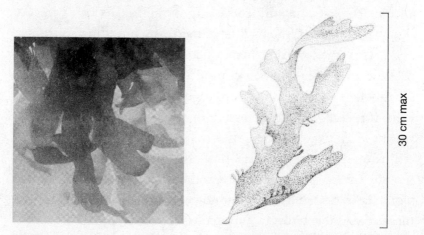

30 cm max

Dulse

7 cm max

Coralline

weeds that generate their own limy protective skin, some hugging the rock itself as a crust, others tufty in what look like little, pink brittle forests. Except they are not brittle: those tufted corallines are provided with their own calcium carbonate armour to resist predators; but look close and you will see that their stems are bobbled, the strong protected lengths regularly interrupted with soft, flexible joints, like the elbows or knees in a suit of armour, so that storm waves will not break them.

What could be better organised than this? At least ten different sorts of seaweed are here, each laid out as if in a library, neatly within its place, happily coexisting alongside its companions. But that is not true. Heraclitus remains the presiding spirit here and translocation experiments have shown that this is not a picture of order but of competition between the weeds. Channelled wrack would happily grow all the way down to the kelps if it could, but a succession of rivals from spiral to bladder and knotted wrack all do better than it and shut it out. Mutual exclusion is the overriding process. Bladderwrack can grow happily where spiral wrack covers the rocks but the spiral wrack won't let it. Serrated wrack would grow higher up the shore but bladderwrack won't let it. Serrated wrack outcompetes the kelps. All of them shade out their lower neighbours. Look at one of

312

these soggy, slithery shores and you are looking at a battle of the weeds. Any constancy here is only the stability of a whirling top, held in place by the interaction of forces in tension. Should one of those forces drop away, the system goes into crisis.

Few events have been more revealing than the wrecking in March 1967 of the *Torrey Canyon*, one of the early supertankers, on the rocks of the Seven Stones reef, between Land's End in Cornwall and the Scilly Isles. The ship was on a tight deadline to arrive at the oil refineries in Milford Haven in Pembrokeshire, where it was to discharge its cargo of 117,000 tons of Kuwaiti crude. The bridge was without a complete set of charts, had an out-of-date navigation system and the captain was asleep while the first officer made bad navigational decisions when avoiding a fleet of fishing boats near Scilly. These vast ships, almost 1,000 feet long, travel fast and the *Torrey Canyon* struck the reef at seventeen knots, tearing open six of her eighteen storage tanks and damaging the others. Over the next six weeks, she broke up, partly as storms tore at the hull, partly when the Royal Air Force and Royal Navy bombed the wreck, setting fire to the oil. By the end of April, the tanks were empty and the oil had spread over 270 square miles of sea. About 20,000 seabirds were killed.

The British government was acutely conscious of the holiday beaches in Cornwall and authorised the use of some highly toxic chemicals that had been developed to clean oily surfaces in ships' engine rooms. About 14,000 tons of oil came ashore on ninety miles of the Cornish coast and 10,000 tons of these dispersants were applied to them. Nothing could have been worse. The dispersants combined with the oil to make long-lasting and deeply poisonous scums, far more toxic and more ingestible by shore-life than the undispersed oil would have been.

In some remote and inaccessible beaches, drums of neat dispersant were rolled over the edges of the cliffs and allowed to split open on the rocks below. At Godrevy near St Ives, the headland was owned by the National Trust who were anxious about the effect of the chemicals on the seals and so they were not applied there. To everyone's surprise, the common limpets at Godrevy began to browse on the untreated oil, helping to clear the rock surfaces of the slick that had come ashore.

Elsewhere, the damage was catastrophic. Vast areas of seaweed were killed, along with the fish, crabs, winkles, topshells, mussels and barnacles that lived among them. The limpets in particular were poisoned and died in uncounted numbers.

Along this coastline, the life of the shore and all its interrelationships had been destroyed and, in response, it went into extraordinary spasms of reaction and recovery. The absence of the limpets, which had grazed on the weed, resulted, in that first summer, in a sudden flush of bright green gutweed and sea lettuce, whose spread had previously been held down by the limpet grazers. That was followed by a secondary, more long-lasting flush of the various brown wracks which outcompeted the green weeds and established a dense canopy in whose shade all the surviving barnacles died, smothered by weed, eaten by dog whelks or plucked off the rocks when the big stands of wrack that were growing on them were torn away in storms.

Nothing was stable. The shore had become a place of wild oscillations, a deregulated world in which the mutual government of weed and grazer had been suspended and successive life forms tyrannised their surroundings. The wrack was growing in places it had never been seen before, blanketing what had been weed-free coastline. Ironically, that heavy cover of serrated, bladder and knotted wrack then created an ideal nursery for young limpets coming in as plankton from the open sea. A huge number of limpets populated the wrack forest, and by 1973 they had eaten most of it away. The limpets then starved, abandoning their normal lives and 'migrating in a lemming-like front across the shore before many of them died'. Because there had been such a huge number of adult limpets, no young limpets had been able to find a place to live among the weed and so when this generation starved to death in the early 1980s, there were no others to take their place and the wrack forest boomed again.

This alternate pulsing of heavy weed and a heavy limpet presence, followed by the death of the weed and then the death of limpets, continued on into the 2000s, the boom-bust graph of their fluctuations scarcely diminishing over time, but ricocheting between alternative unstable states, still unsettled fifty years after the tanker was wrecked and the shore had been drenched with the dispersants.

Why do these chaotic oscillations not happen here? How come there is usually a constancy on these shores? The answer is that the system remains tense. Its inner tautness has not been slackened by any pollutant catastrophe. When I look deep down among the serrated wrack and the kelp I can find a still-coherent world in which neither the grazers (largely limpets and below them the urchins) nor the grazed (the young wracks and kelp)

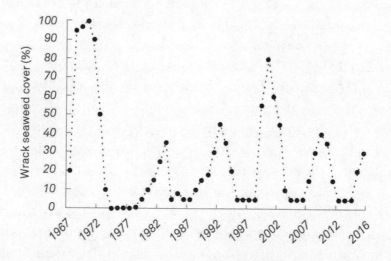

The boom-bust of the wrack seaweeds at Porthleven in Cornwall
after the oil dispersants had been applied to the shore in 1967.
The giant surge in the early 1970s was followed by a series of peaks
over the following decades that only hesitantly moved towards
a more stable system.

have outcompeted each other. Urchins are plucked off by storms. Total overgrowth by the weeds is kept in check by the grazers. The result is the open ground over which the corallines spread to make the pink and vermilion ballrooms on which these giants browse. It feels like an old and continuous world down here where the mussels and the sea stars have been known to live for at least twenty years, the urchins up to sixteen, the sponges and corallines to an age no one has yet been able to compute, all of them at home in the shadows of their polychrome groves.

The limpet is the governor. They are long-livers too and some mark the stages of their growth by the regular rings of barnacles that have attached themselves to the shell, stage by stage as the limpet grew.

They are adaptable: those higher up the shore are usually taller, with shells tending towards witches' hats, probably so that when they are out of the water at low tide, they do not get hot. Those lower down the shore are flatter, perhaps because they have less need to cool down and because a flatter shell is less vulnerable to being knocked off by a wave. Those in the middle shore have forms in between. Often I used to take them back to my aquarium in the house still attached to the rocks on which I had found them and watch them wandering around their world, their two forward-facing antennae supplemented by tiny hair-like cilia around the rim of their shells, keeping a look out to the side and behind, as delicate as eyelashes on a whale.

Limpets have embedded in them a tidal clock and so as the tide falls outside, even though the water level in the aquarium remains constant, they would begin their expeditions. The foot of the animal has a set of muscles through which it can send sequential ripples to create a forward movement. If it wants to turn on the spot, or if it has detected a predator, the muscles on one side can move in a way opposite to the other and so the limpet rotates like a tank with its tracks turned to forward on the left and reverse on the right.

A limpet can accommodate a new generation of barnacles with each extension of its own shell.

In exposed situations, its shell will be flattish.

In half-sheltered nooks, they can grow almost globular.

And in the comfort of a pool, as tall as a steeple.

They are capable of moving four inches or even more in a minute, always along the same paths, using their iron-tipped teeth to mow up the micro-algae and other vegetable food that has stuck to the mucus trail which their previous journeys applied to the rock. Tests have shown that this stickiness is deliberate. The trails left by carnivorous dog whelks, which have no need to attract the detritus floating in the water, are less sticky and end up far less nutritious than those of the limpets. Some limpets deliberately garden their surroundings, keeping patches of rock near them in such a good mucus-sticky and nutritious state that small pioneer algae, of the best tiny-vegetable kind, will grow there. This is no chance behaviour: limpets will defend their gardens from others by standing high (an act called 'mushrooming') to more than twice the height of their shell when at rest, and stamping on the invader. The starfish that try to attack them can have their toes cut off this way.

Most of my limpets were apparently solitary but on some rocks out on the shore they lived in quite large aggregations which are thought to be defensive. If an oystercatcher attacks one limpet on the edge of a crowd, the rest settle down tight to make sure the bird will have no chance of getting under their shells. No one has worked out how a limpet knows that another of its kind two feet away is being attacked but it is probably the vibrations coming up through the rock. Limpets feel through the soles of their feet the giant birds trying to eat their neighbours.

They are the shore engineers. Wherever I could find the beautiful and open coralline patches around the pool, I could know that the gardening of the limpets was at work, a reduction through their grazing of the weeds that would otherwise overgrow the rocks. There are subtleties here, because the coralline is dependent on the shade provided by the big wracks or kelp. And so the system is held in a delicate and poised condition. The coralline needs the wrack for its shade but not too much of it. The limpet needs to eat the young weeds and so needs them to seed the coralline but must make sure that open coralline-rich ground remains as a viable garden and does not get overgrown. The big wracks need some space on which their holdfasts can anchor them to the rock so they are not destroyed in storms. Each organism needs something of a halfway house and for the others not to become too dominant.

Biologists looking at the shore have seen that this condition of mutual tolerance-cum-control depends on what they have called 'intermediate disturbance'. If there is too little interference, by storm or predator, as at the quiet head of the bay, there will be little chance for a diversity of life to thrive. That is also true if there is too much, as on the point of headland where the rocks are often covered in little but limpets and barnacles, because storm waves make life impossible for the weeds. In winter storms the fronds of the wrack sweep most animals away from the rock. Weeds that have begun to grow on barnacles are poorly attached and can be taken away with the underlying barnacles. In those circumstances, limpets must largely prey on their barnacle neighbours. Only in the middle ground, as here in the half-protected limb of a headland, away from the dominant south-westerlies, is there a chance of riches.

Professor Stephen Hawkins, who for decades led research into these relationships at marine laboratories in Liverpool and Southampton, summarised them in a diagram.

The wild tip of a headland will have relatively small-scale successions of different forms of life, most of them the hard survival-champions of the limpets and the barnacles. The quiet head of the bay will be an equally reduced weedy place where the wracks will luxuriate in simplified quiet. Only here, on moderately exposed places like the eastern edge of Rubha an t-Sasunnaich, will shore life achieve its full and beautiful complexity.

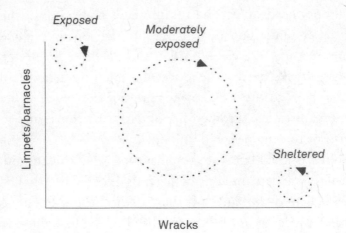

Professor Stephen Hawkins's concise guide to life on the shore. On an exposed headland there will be mostly limpets and barnacles, clinging tightly to the rocks, alternating a little with the seaweeds. In the deep shelter of a bay, there will be mostly easy-living seaweeds and only a little alternation with limpets and barnacles. In the middle, moderately exposed ground, life is dynamic and both seaweeds and limpets and barnacles regularly take each other's place in a big, vital, multiplicitous and unending churn.

The wild oscillations after the *Torrey Canyon* episode do not occur here because much smaller and more regular catastrophes are happening all the time. A storm will tear off a hank of weed which may take the barnacles and even the coralline with it. A sudden settlement of barnacles will colonise the shore where a gap has opened up. There might have been a slight variation in temperature, even a frost, which killed off a generation of limpets. It is a tickering, flickering landscape, at a scale which we scarcely notice unless we look. But do look. Look at it slowly and the shore ripples like an oscilloscope with the interlocking and over-lapping patterns of unceasing change. The sea is not made of water, nor a medium in which to swim but a world to come alongside, to be-with in ways that go beyond the predatory.

These oscillations are patches in time, just as the patches on the rock are oscillations in space. Micro-tides flood and ebb across every dimension of their world. Their micro-catastrophes and micro-blooming are the guarantee of calm. Life is unsealed. There is no distinction between flux and stillness; they are one. The core of being is interplay, and its give-and-take of quick and still is the animation of life.

NOTES

Introduction: The marvellous

2 'these unruffled wells': Philip Gosse, *Evenings at the Microscope; or, researches among the minuter organs and forms of animal life* (1859), p. 375.

2 half-remembering the children's rhyme: 'Adam and Eve and Pinch-Me' was already alive in English playgrounds in the 1850s: Iona Opie, in Peter Hunt, Sheila G. Bannister Ray, *International Companion Encyclopedia of Children's Literature* (Taylor & Francis, 1996), p. 180.

2 'Adam and Eve': Edmund Gosse, quoting his father in *Father and Son: A Study of Two Temperaments* (1907; Penguin, 1949), pp. 110–11.

2 like gardens of prelapsarian bliss: Amy M. King, 'Tide Pools', *Victorian Review*, Vol. 36, No. 2, Natural Environments (Fall 2010), 40–5; Jonathan Smith, *Charles Darwin and Victorian Visual Culture* (CUP, 2006).

3 inner structures of the barnacle: Rebecca Stott, *Darwin and the Barnacle* (Faber & Faber, 2003).

3 'The soul wants to be wet': Guy Davenport, *Seven Greeks* (New Directions, 1995), Fragment 47, p. 163.

3 'running deep': R. L. Stevenson, *Kidnapped* (1886; Dent, 1960), p. 118; David Stevenson, *Highland Warrior: Alasdair MacColla and the Civil Wars* (1980; Birlinn, 2014), p. 208.

4 The whole riven province: All but seven miles of a boundary that is roughly seventy miles long (when measured in one-mile lengths).

8 '*Cha tàinig tràigh*': From the song 'Mo Rùn Geal Dìleas'. With thanks to James Westland @geologymull; and Roddy Murray for discussion of its terms.

8 story of a vixen: A. R. Forbes, *Gaelic Names of Beasts etc.* (Oliver & Boyd, 1905), p. 161.

8 'drowned with its paw': Ibid., p. 208.

9 'dead kittiwake': Reverend Alexander Stewart (Nether

Lochaber), *The Natural History, Legends, and Folk-lore of the West Highlands* (Kindle Locations 3835–52).

9 'the challenge the ocean': Steve Mentz, *At the Bottom of Shakespeare's Ocean* (Continuum, 2009), p. ix; Melville in *Moby-Dick* thought that in 'oceans we see the image of the ungraspable phantom of life'.

9 'menace and caress': From T. S. Eliot, *Four Quartets*, 'III: The Dry Salvages', line 31.

9 'Full fadom': *The Tempest*, 1.2.397–403, 405 (First Folio text, 1623).

10 'What care these': Ibid., 1.1.24–5. See Mentz, *At the Bottom of Shakespeare's Ocean*, for a brilliant analysis of Shakespeare's relationship to the sea on which these paragraphs draw.

10 'makes a still-stand': *Henry IV Part II*, 2.3.63.

11 'that part of the land': John MacAskill, *Scotland's Foreshore* (Edinburgh University Press, 2018), p. 1.

11 paid the landowners rent: John MacAskill, '"The Most Arbitrary, Scandalous Act of Tyranny": The Crown, Private Proprietors and the Ownership of the Scottish Foreshore in the Nineteenth Century', *Scottish Historical Review*, Vol. 85, No. 220, Part 2 (October 2006), 277–304.

12 'swimming, sunbathing': Scottish Law Commission Report on the Law of the Foreshore and Sea Bed March 2003 paras 3.12–3.17, pp. 40–2, quoted in MacAskill, *Scotland's Foreshore*, p. 237.

13 'things overflow': In David Thomson, *The People of the Sea* (1954), introduction to Canongate Classics edition, 1996, p. xi.

14 'Shoes /': Emily Dickinson, 'By the Sea', lines 19–20.

15 'We stand, then': William Golding, 'In My Ark', review of Gavin Maxwell, *Ring of Bright Water*, *Spectator* (16 September 1960), reprinted in William Golding, *The Hot Gates* (Faber & Faber, 1965), p. 105.

15 'upsurging presence': See G. Steiner, *Martin Heidegger* (1978; University of Chicago Press, 1991), p 137; M. Heidegger, *The Beginning of Western Philosophy*, tr. R. Rojcewicz, Indiana UP, 2015, 16.

1 Sandhopper

21 Colonel George Montagu: R. J. Cleevely, 'Montagu, George, (1753–1815)', ODNB online, https://doi.org/10.1093/ref:odnb/19017.

21 Montagu spent his days: From: https://www.conchology. be/?t=9001&id=25237.

22 'burrowing under':'Mr Montagu's Description of several Marine Animals', *Transactions of the Linnean Society*, Vol. IX (1808), 95–7.

23 Sandhoppers' genes: P. M. Driver and David A. Humphries, 'Protean Defence by Prey Animals', *Oecologia*, Vol. 5, No. 4 (1970), 285–302.

24 Those back legs: A. I.
Bulycheva, Морские блохи
морей СССР и
сопредельных вод
(Amphipoda-Talitroidea);
'Marine fleas of the seas of
USSR and surrounding waters',
Opredeliteli po faune SSSR
65:1–186.1957 (MS
translation by T. Pidhayny,
Foreign Languages Division,
Dept. of Canada; kindly lent
by Dr E. L. Bousfield).

24 filmed the whole performance:
G. Bracht, 'Das
Verbreitungsbild von Orchester
cavimana Heller, 1865
(Crustacea: Amphipoda:
Talitridae) in
Nordwestdeutschland',
Gewässer und Abwässer 66/67
(1980), 119–29; G. Bracht,
'The jump of *Orchestia
cavimana* Heller, 1865
(Crustacea: Amphipoda:
Talitridae)', *Experientia* 36
(1980), 56–7.

25 A lighter shell: D. M. Reid,
'Talitradae (Crustacea:
Amphipoda)', *Synopses Br.
Fauna* 7 (1947), 1–25.

26 their protective coat: P. G.
Moore and C. H. Francis, 'On
the water relations and
osmoregulation of the beach-
hopper *Orchestia gammarellus*
(Pallas) (Crustacea:
Amphipoda)', *J. Exp. Mar.
Biol. Ecol.* 94 (1985), 131–50.

26 I went looking: Ibid.

27 'the internal milieu': S. J.
Holmes, 'Death feigning in
terrestrial amphipods', *Biol.
Bull. Mar. Biol. Lab.*, Woods
Hole 4 (1903), 191–6; J. G.

Holmquist, 'The functional
morphology of gnathopods:
importance in grooming and
variation with regard to habitat
in Talitroidean amphipods', *J.
Crust. Biol.* 2 (1982), 159–79.

27 With unforced lucidity:
Floriano Papi, 'Leo Pardi
(1915–1990)', *Tropical Zoology*
4:1 (1991), 153–6.

28 Pardi found: Guido Caniglia,
'Understanding Societies from
Inside the Organisms. Leo
Pardi's Work on Social
Dominance in Polistes Wasps
(1937–1952)', *Journal of the
History of Biology*, Vol. 48, No.
3 (Fall 2015), Harvard Fatigue
Laboratory, 455–86.

28 As the tide floods: R. C.
Newell, *The Biology of Intertidal
Animals* (3rd edn; Faversham,
1979), p. 299; E. Dahl, 'The
Amphipoda of the Sound. I:
terrestrial Amphipoda', *Acta
Universitatis Lundensis* 42
(1946), 1–53; L. Geppetti and
P. Tongiorgi, 'Ricerche
ecologiche sugli Artropodi di
una spiaggia sabbiosa del
littorale tirrenico, II. Le
migrationi di *Talitrus saltator*
(Montagu) (Crustacea-
Amphipoda)', *Redia* 50,
309–36.

29 Photograph of von Frisch, Papi
and Pardi: Reproduced in
Canigia, 'Understanding
Societies from Inside the
Organisms', op. cit.

30 If *Talitrus* was kept: F. Papi,
'Orientation by night: the
moon', *Cold Spring Harbor
Symp. Quant. Biol.* 25 (1960),
403–12; Alberto Ugolini,

Tiziana Fantini and Riccardo Innocenti, 'Orientation at Night: An Innate Moon Compass in Sandhoppers (Amphipoda: Talitridae)', *Proceedings of the Royal Society B: Biological Sciences*, Vol. 270, No. 1512 (7 February 2003), 279–81; Alberto Ugolini, Claudia Melis, Riccardo Innocenti, Bruno Tiribilli and Carlo Castellini, 'Moon and Sun Compasses in Sandhoppers Rely on Two Separate Chronometric Mechanisms', *Proceedings of the Royal Society B: Biological Sciences*, Vol. 266, No. 1420 (7 April 1999), 749–52.

30 Thirsty sandhoppers: R. F. Hartwick, 'Beach Orientation in Talitrid Amphipods: Capacities and Strategies', *Behavioral Ecology and Sociobiology*, Vol. 1, No. 4 (1976), 447–58.

32 And when exposed: F. Papi and L. Pardi, 'Ricerche sull'orientamento di *Talitrus saltator* (Montagu) (Crustacea: Amphipoda) II. Sui fattori che regolano la variazione dell'angolo di orientamento nel corso del giorno. L'orientamento di notte. L'orientamento diurno di altre populatione', *Z. vergl. Physiol.* 35 (1953), 490–518; F. Papi and L. Pardi, 'On the lunar orientation of sand hoppers (Amphipoda: Talitridae)', *Biology Bulletin* 124 (1963), 97–105; L. Pardi, 'Modificazione sperimentale della direzione di fuga negli anfipodi ad orientamento solare', *Z. Tierpsychol.* 14 (1957), 261–75; L. Pardi and M. Grassi, 'Experimental modification of direction finding in *Talitrus saltator* (Montagu) and *Talorchestia deshayesei* (Aud.) (Crustacea: Amphipoda)', *Experientia* 11 (1955), 202–5; L. Pardi and F. Papi, 'Ricerche sull'orientamento di *Talitrus saltator* (Montagu) (Crustacea: Amphipoda) I. L'orientamento durante il giorno in una populazione del litorale Tirrenico', *Z. vergl. Physiol.* 35 (1953), 459–89.

32 Pardi and his colleagues: Hartwick, op. cit.

32 'What reason': Thomas Browne, *Religio Medici* (1645), Part 1, Section 14, p. 29.

33 Scientists at the University of Plymouth: D. J. Hodgson, A. L. Bréchon, R. C. Thompson, 'Ingestion and fragmentation of plastic carrier bags by the amphipod *Orchestia gammarellus*: Effects of plastic type and fouling load', *Marine Pollution Bulletin*, Vol. 127 (2018), 154–9.

2 Prawn

36 'I remember lying': Hermione Lee, *Virginia Woolf* (Chatto & Windus, 1996), p. 379.

36 'sheeting the body': Virginia Woolf, *The Waves* (Penguin, 1992), p. 18.

37 'It seems as if': Ibid., p. 27.

37 'is of lying half asleep': Lee, *Virginia Woolf*, pp. 22–3.

38 'The blind was thin yellow': Ibid., pp. 23–4.

38 Sparkled lines: These extraordinary pores are within the body under the shell of the prawn, their shifting colour and luminosity visible through the translucent shell.

40 'Hardly a natural historian': Stephen Jay Gould, *The Structure of Evolutionary Theory* (Harvard University Press, 2002), p. 1338.

42 these animals can be identified: A. R. Forbes, *Gaelic Names of Beasts etc.* (Oliver & Boyd, 1905).

43 'I felt happy enough': Melanie Challenger, *How to Be Animal* (Canongate, 2020), pp. 173–4.

43 'the mysterious': Ibid., pp. 174, 175.

44 How much nearer: Ibid., p. 182.

44 When some rock-pool prawns: Edward Fahy, Niamh Forrest and Paul Gleeson, 'Estimates of the Contribution of *Palaemon elegans* Rathke to Commercial Shrimp Landings in Ireland and Observations on Its Biology', *The Irish Naturalists' Journal*, Vol. 26, No. 3/4 (1998), 93–8; A. C. Taylor and J. I. Spicer, 'Metabolic responses of the prawns *Palaemon elegans* and *P. serratus* (Crustacea: Decapoda) to acute hypoxia and anoxia', *Marine Biology* 95 (1987), 521–30; Rohan M. Brooker and Danielle L. Dixon, 'Intertidal crustaceans use seaweed-derived chemical cues to mitigate predation risk', *Behavioral Ecology and Sociobiology* (2017) 71:47.

45 after as much as twelve hours: Taylor and Spicer, op. cit.

46 In a well-developed pool: David L. Evans and Maha Shehadi-Moacdieh, 'Body size and prior residency in staged encounters between female prawns, *Palaemon elegans* rathke (decapoda: palaemonidae)', *Animal Behaviour*, Vol. 36, Iss. 2 (April 1988), 452–5; Maha Shehadi-Moacdieh, 'Aspects of the agonistic and escape behaviour of the prawn *Palaemon elegans*', MSc Dissertation, American University of Beirut, 1985; see also A. Berglund, 'Niche differentiation between two littoral prawns in Gullmar Fjord, Sweden: *Palaemon adspersus* and *P. squilla*', *Holarctic Ecology* 3 (1980),11; A. Berglund, 'Coexistence, size overlap and population regulation in tidal vs non-tidal *Palaemon* prawns', *Oecologia* 54 (1982), 1–7.

48 The fight ended: Christoph Goessmann, Charlotte Hemelrijk and Robert Huber, 'The formation and maintenance of crayfish hierarchies: behavioral and self-structuring properties', *Behavioral Ecology and Sociobiology* (2000) 48:418–28.

48 It came to understand: Ibid.

51 At the other end: Daniel K. Maskrey et al., 'Who dares doesn't always win: risk-averse rock pool prawns are better at controlling a limited food resource', *Animal Behaviour* 140 (2018), 187–97.

51 Is it possible: C. A. G. Wiersma, 'Giant nerve fiber system of the crayfish. A contribution to comparative physiology of synapse', *Journal of Neurophysiology* 1 (January 1947); Jeffrey J. Wine and Franklin B. Krasne, 'The organization of escape behaviour in the crayfish', *Journal of Experimental Biology* 56 (1972), 1–18.

53 It is a flash: Jens Herberholz and Gregory D. Marquart, 'Decision-making and behavioral choice during predator avoidance', *Frontiers in Neuroscience* (28 August 2012).

53 'by gradual pinching': Wine and Krasne, op. cit.

53 'intensity is not': Ibid.

54 'non-giant reactions': Ibid.

54 'considered, in a way': Herberholz and Marquart, op. cit.

55 'freezing': Francesco Filiciotto et al., 'Underwater noise from boats: Measurement of its influence on the behaviour and biochemistry of the common prawn (*Palaemon serratus*, Pennant 1777)', *Journal of Experimental Marine Biology and Ecology* 478 (May 2016), 24–33.

56 as Herberholz and others: W. H. Liden and J. Herberholz, 'Behavioral and neural responses of juvenile crayfish to moving shadows', *Journal of Experimental Marine Biology and Ecology* 211 (2008), 1355–61; William H. Liden, Mary L. Phillips and Jens Herberholz, 'Neural control of behavioural choice in juvenile crayfish', *Proceedings of the Royal Society B: Biological Sciences* 277 (2010), 3493–500.

56 'Crayfish calculate': Liden, Phillips and Herberholz, op. cit.

57 No one understands: R. F. Bowerman and J. L. Larimer, 'Command fibres in the circumoesophageal connectives of crayfish. I. Tonic fibres', *Journal of Experimental Biology* 60 (1974), 95–117.

58 'are aware': Colin Klein and Andrew B. Barron, 'Crawling around the hard problem of consciousness', *Proceedings of the National Academy of Sciences of the United States of America*, Vol. 113, No. 27 (5 July 2016), E3814–5.

59 'The lower animals': Charles Darwin, *The Descent of Man and Selection in Relation to Sex* (John Murray, 1871), p. 39, quoted in Marian Stamp Dawkins, 'Through animal eyes: What behaviour tells us', *Applied Animal Behaviour Science* 100(1–2) (2006), 4–10.

59 'The largest of decapod': European Food Safety Authority, 'Opinion of the Scientific Panel on Animal Health and Welfare (AHAW) on a request from the Commission related to the aspects of the biology and welfare of animals used for experimental and other scientific purposes', EFSA-Q-2004-105, *EFSA Journal* 292 (2005), 1–46.

59 Switzerland has included: https://www.blv.admin.ch/blv/de/home/tiere/tierschutz/revision-verord nungen-veterinaerbereich.html.

59 Many attempts: Details in B. K. Diggles, 'Review of some scientific issues related to crustacean welfare', *ICES Journal of Marine Science* (June 2018), 68, 71.

60 'electric shocks': Ibid., 67.

60 'insects … eating': Ibid., 74.

60 running of a big brain: Shelley Anne Adamo, 'Consciousness explained or consciousness redefined?', *Proceedings of the National Academy of Sciences of the United States of America*, Vol. 113, No. 27 (5 July 2016), E3812.

62 Pascal Fossat's record of crayfish tracks: Pascal Fossat et al., 'Anxiety-like behavior in crayfish is controlled by serotonin', *Science* 344, 1293 (2014); Pascal Fossat et al., 'Measuring Anxiety-like Behavior in Crayfish by Using a Sub Aquatic Dark-light Plus Maze', bio-protocol.org/e1396 Vol. 5, Iss. 3 (5 January 2015); Julien Bacqué-Cazenave et al., 'Do arthropods feel anxious during molts?', *Journal of Experimental Biology* (21 January 2019).

63 'In this context': Pascal Fossat et al., 'Anxiety-like behavior in crayfish is controlled by serotonin', *Science* 344, 1293 (2014); Pascal Fossat et al., 'Measuring Anxiety-like Behavior in Crayfish by Using a Sub Aquatic Dark-light Plus Maze', bio-protocol.org/e1396

Vol. 5, Iss. 3 (5 January 2015); Julien Bacqué-Cazenave et al., 'Do arthropods feel anxious during molts?', *Journal of Experimental Biology* (21 January 2019).

3 Winkle

64 essays by Tim Robinson: Tim Robinson, *Setting Foot on the Shores of Connemara and other writings* (Lilliput, 1996).

65 He had been alerted: Benoît B. Mandelbrot, 'How long is the coast of Britain? Statistical self-similarity and fractional dimension', *Science* 156 (1967), 636–8.

65 'the idea that': Tim Robinson, *Setting Foot on the Shores of Connemara and other writings*, p. 81.

66 'luminously its own thing': David Thomson, *The People of the Sea* (1954; Canongate Classics, 1996), p. ix.

66 'strange geography': Robinson, *Setting Foot on the Shores of Connemara*, p. 18.

67 'surprises us': Ibid., p. 86.

67 'coastline length': Benoît B. Mandelbrot, *The Fractal Geometry of Nature* (W. H. Freeman, 1983), p. 28.

68 'Every atom belonging': Walt Whitman, "Song of Myself," *Leaves of Grass* (David McKay, 1892).

68 'is to estimate': Robinson, *Setting Foot on the Shores of Connemara*, p. 95.

69 'Suppose someone': Plato, 'Theaetetus', in *The Dialogues of Plato*, trans. Jowett (2 vols, 1937), 2:202 (adapted).

72 'the shorey shore-things': For Scotland the latest (hopelessly inaccurate) harvest figures for winkles are from 1994: 2,053 tons picked, worth £1.5 million, in D. W. McKay and S. L. Fowler, 'Review of the exploitation of the winkle *Littorina littorea* (L.) in Scotland' (1996); Report to Scottish Natural Heritage from the Nature Conservation Bureau; for Ireland from 2000, an estimate of c.4,000 tons picked, worth c.£7 million, in Valerie Cummins et al., 'An Assessment of the Potential for the Sustainable Development of the Edible Periwinkle, *Littorina littorea*, Industry in Ireland' (Final Report, 2002).

73 If strained and drunk: A. R. Forbes, *Gaelic Names of Beasts etc.* (Oliver & Boyd, 1905), pp. 377–8.

74 Would Achilles: Reverend Alexander Stewart (Nether Lochaber), *The Natural History, Legends, and Folk-lore of the West Highlands* (Kindle Locations 3835–52), https:// electricscotland.com/history/ lochaber/chapter43.htm.

75 'biofilms are found': Julian Cremona, *Seashores: An Ecological Guide* (The Crowood Press, 2014), p. 17.

75 'becomes a complex': Ibid., p. 18.

76 Those that live: R. C. Newell et al., 'Factors affecting the feeding rate of the winkle L. Littorea', *Marine Biology* 9(2) (1971), 138–44.

77 They know to escape: A. M. Mackie and P. T. Grant, 'Interspecies and intraspecies chemoreception by marine invertebrates', in P. T. Grant and A. M. Mackie (eds), *Chemoreception in marine organisms* (Academic Press, 1974), pp. 105–41.

77 In 1980: Robin P. Hadlock, 'Alarm Response of the Intertidal Snail *Littorina littorea* (L.) to Predation by the Crab *Carcinus maenas* (L.)', *Biological Bulletin*, Vol. 159, No. 2 (October 1980), 269–79.

80 Each winkle population: Ibid.

81 Its preferred seaweed: Colin Little and J. A. Kitching, *The Biology of Rocky Shores* (OUP, 1996), p. 83.

82 Jane Lubchenco revealed: Jane Lubchenco, 'Plant Species Diversity in a Marine Intertidal Community: Importance of Herbivore Food Preference and Algal Competitive Abilities', *The American Naturalist*, Vol. 112, No. 983 (January– February 1978), 23–39.

83 Both are stable states: R. C. Lewontin, 'The meaning of stability' in Diversity and Stability in Ecological Systems, in Brookhaven Symposia in Biology (1969), 13–24; Nancy Knowlton, 'Multiple "stable" states and the conservation of marine ecosystems', *Progress in Oceanography* 60 (2004), 387–96.

83 Geoffrey Trussell: Geoffrey C. Trussell, Patrick J. Ewanchuk, Mark D. Bertness and Brian R. Silliman, 'Trophic Cascades in

Rocky Shore Tide Pools: Distinguishing Lethal and Nonlethal Effects', *Oecologia*, Vol. 139, No. 3 (May 2004), 427–32.

86 It is almost certainly: Andrew K. Wilbur and Robert S. Steneck, 'Polychromatic Patterns of *Littorina obtusata* on *Ascophyllum nodosum*: Are Snails Hiding in Intertidal Sea Weed?', *Northeastern Naturalist*, Vol. 6, No. 3 (1999), 189–98.

86 A decade after: Robin Hadlock Seeley, 'Intense Natural Selection Caused a Rapid Morphological Transition in a Living Marine Snail', *Proceedings of the National Academy of Sciences of the United States of America*, Vol. 83, No. 18 (15 September 1986), 6897–901.

87 'to the spread': Geerat J. Vermeij, 'The limits of adaptation: humans and the predator–prey arms race', *Evolution*, Vol. 66, No. 7 (July 2012), 2007–14.

88 the young winkles: Ruth Bibby et al., 'Ocean acidification disrupts induced defences in the intertidal gastropod *Littorina littorea*', *Biol. Lett.* 3 (2007), 699–701.

90 The toxic sea: Ibid.; Brittany M. Jellison, Aaron T. Ninokawa, Tessa M. Hill, Eric Sanford and Brian Gaylord, 'Ocean acidification alters the response of intertidal snails to a key sea star predator', *Proceedings of the Royal Society B: Biological Sciences*, Vol. 283,

No. 1833 (29 June 2016), 1–8; Sue-Ann Watson et al., 'Marine mollusc predator-escape behaviour altered by near-future carbon dioxide levels', *Proceedings of the Royal Society B: Biological Sciences*, Vol. 281, No. 1774 (7 January 2014), 1–9.

4 Crab

91 'Music as desolate': Ewen MacCaig (ed.), *The Poems of Norman MacCaig* (1997; Polygon, 2009).

95 'One might start': Iris Murdoch, 'On "God" and "Good"', *Existentialists and Mystics: Writings on Philosophy and Literature* (Chatto & Windus, 1997), pp. 347–8.

95 'occasions of unselfing': Iris Murdoch, *The Sovereignty of Good* (Routledge & Kegan Paul, 1970), p. 85.

96 'intolerably chancy': Ibid., p. 87.

96 'We take a self-forgetful': Iris Murdoch, 'The Sovereignty of Good Over Other Concepts', *Existentialists and Mystics*, pp. 369–71.

97 'The self': Murdoch, *Sovereignty of Good*, p. 93.

97 'Love': Iris Murdoch, 'The Sublime and the Good', *Existentialists and Mystics*, p. 215.

104 As aggressive: James T. Carlton and Andrew N. Cohen, 'Episodic Global Dispersal in Shallow Water Marine Organisms: The Case History of the European Shore Crabs *Carcinus maenas* and *C. aestuarii*', *Journal of*

Biogeography, Vol. 30, No. 12 (December 2003), 1809–20; Peter J. Hayward, *Seashore* (Collins, 2004), p. 139.

104 Inspectors arrived: J. P. O'Connor and J. M. C. Holmes, 'The Shore Crab *Carcinus maenas* L., an Indoor Pest in Dublin City', *The Irish Naturalists' Journal*, Vol. 24, No. 2 (April 1992), 82.

105 Map: Adapted from James T. Carlton and Andrew N. Cohen, 'Episodic Global Dispersal in Shallow Water Marine Organisms: The Case History of the European Shore Crabs *Carcinus maenas* and *C. aestuarii*', *Journal of Biogeography*, Vol. 30, No. 12 (December 2003), 1809–20.

105 'When found': Ibid.

105 eating other animals: Geerat J. Vermeij, 'The Limits of Adaptation: Humans and the Predator–Prey Arms Race', *Evolution*, Vol. 66, No. 7 (July 2012), 2007–14.

105 The greedy die young: I. Johnstone and K. Norris, 'Not all oystercatchers *Haematopus ostralegus* select the most profitable common cockles *Cerastoderma edule*: a difference between feeding methods', *Ardea* 88 (2000), 137–53.

106 'It would seem': Isabel M. Smallegange and Jaap Van Der Meer, 'Why Do Shore Crabs Not Prefer the Most Profitable Mussels?', *Journal of Animal Ecology*, Vol. 72, No. 4 (July 2003), 599–607.

107 Male crabs fight: Lynne U. Sneddon, Felicity A. Huntingford and Alan C. Taylor, 'Weapon Size versus Body Size as a Predictor of Winning in Fights between Shore Crabs, *Carcinus maenas* (L.)', *Behavioral Ecology and Sociobiology*, Vol. 41, No. 4 (1997), 237–42.

108 The Norwegian ecologist: G. I. Sekkelsten, 'Effect of handicap on mating success in male shore crabs *Carcinus maenas*', *Oikos* 51 (1988), 131–4; Sekkelsten was Gro I. Van Der Meeren's maiden name.

109 She sends out: Ralf Bublitz, Bernard Sainte-Marie, Chloe Newcomb-Hodgetts, Nichola Fletcher, Michelle Smith and Jörg Hardege, 'Interspecific Activity of the Sex Pheromone of the European Shore Crab (*Carcinus maenas*)', *Behaviour*, Vol. 145, No. 10 (October 2008), Bioactive Water-Borne Chemicals: Pheromones and Welfare Indicators: The 'Faro Workshop', 1465–78.

109 It was thought: T. S. Cheung, 'An observed act of copulation in the shore crab, *Carcinus maenas* (L.)', *Crustaceana* 11(1) (1966), 107–8.

111 Afterwards, she turns: Michael Berrill and Michael Arsenault, 'Mating behavior of the green shore crab *Carcinus maenas*', *Bulletin of Marine Science* 32(2) (1982), 632–8.

111 Once a week: Gro I. Van Der Meeren, 'Sex- and Size-Dependent Mating Tactics in a Natural Population of Shore Crabs *Carcinus maenas*',

Journal of Animal Ecology, Vol. 63, No. 2 (April 1994), 307–14.

115 'Professor Slabber': John Vaughan Thompson, *Zoological Researches and Illustration: Or, Natural History of Nondescript Or Imperfectly Known Animals, in a Series of Memoirs* (King and Ridings, 1828), pp. 4–5.

115 He became an army surgeon: For Thompson's life see Alwyne Wheeler, 'Thompson: Marine Biologist', *British Medical Journal* 3 (1975), 534–6; David M. Damkaer, 'John Vaughan Thompson (1779–1847), Pioneer Planktonologist: a life renewed', *Journal of Crustacean Biology*, 36(2) (2016), 256–62.

115 'throw out': J. V. Thompson, 'Memoir I. On the metamorphoses of the Crustacea, and on zoea, exposing their singular structure and demonstrating that they are not, as has been supposed, a peculiar genus, but the larva of Crustacea!!', *Zoological Researches* 1 (1828), 3.

116 'to his great surprise': J. V. Thompson, 'Memoir IV. On the cirripedes, or barnacles; demonstrating their deceptive character; the extraordinary metamorphosis they undergo, and the class of animals to which they indisputably belong', *Zoological Researches* 3 (1830), 75–6.

116 'when it died': Thompson, *Zoological Researches and Illustration*, p. 8.

117 'the *Crustacea Decapoda*': Ibid., p. 9.

118 '"supposed" *Zoeae*': J. O. Westwood, 'On the supposed existence of Metamorphoses in the Crustacea', *Philosophical Transactions of the Royal Society of London* 2 (1835), 311–28.

119 'a small translucent': Thompson, *Zoological Researches and Illustration*, p. 76.

119 'the author had': Ibid., p. 78.

119 'Thus then': Ibid.

120 'capital discovery': C. Darwin, *A Monograph on the Sub-Class Cirripedia, With Figures of All the Species. The Lepadidae; or, Pedunculated Cirripedes* (Ray Society, 1851), p. 8.

120 'the pecuniary loss': Quoted in Damkaer, op. cit., 260.

120 A portrait was made: Portrait by Maurice Despland Roux, painted in 1835 in London, now in Port Macquarie Museum, New South Wales.

120 This great: Quoted in Damkaer, op. cit., 262.

122 'These tidal clocks': Chaoshu Zeng and Ernest Naylor, 'Endogenous tidal rhythms of vertical migration in field collected zoea-1 larvae of the shore crab *Carcinus maenas*: implications for ebb tide offshore dispersal', *Marine Ecology Progress Series* 132 (1996), 71–82.

123 'endogenously controlled': Ibid.

124 'notwithstanding the advantages': Ibid.

125 Most of the plankton: O. Larink and W. Westheide, *Coastal Plankton* (AWI Handbooks on Marine Flora and Fauna, eds K. H. Wiltshire and M. Boersma, 2006), p. 9.

5 Anemone

128 It is the world-excluding: Harvard University, Houghton Library, modbm_ms_am_2560_163.

129 'peering through': T. S. Eliot, 'Wordsworth and Coleridge', Charles Eliot Norton Lectures at Harvard, 1932–3, in *The Use of Poetry and the Use of Criticism* (Faber & Faber, 1933), pp. 78–9.

130 're-appear transformed': Ibid.; Jennifer Formichelli, 'Childhood in Twain and Eliot', *Literary Imagination*, Vol. 16, Iss. 2 (July 2014), 125–34.

130 'The salt is': T. S. Eliot, *Four Quartets*, 'III: The Dry Salvages', lines 26–7.

130 All of it surfaced: Eliot, *The Use of Poetry and the Use of Criticism*, p. 70.

130 'a simple experience': Ibid., p. 79.

131 'fingers meet': Gwen Harwood, 'The Sea Anemones', in *Mappings of the Plane: New Selected Poems* (Carcanet, 2009), p. 83.

133 Very nearly: J. Davenport, T. V. Moloney and J. Kelly, 'Common sea anemones *Actinia equina* are predominantly sessile intertidal scavengers', *Marine Ecology Progress Series*, Vol. 430 (2011), 147–55.

133 Both were beadlet: Phillip C. Watts and A. Louise Allcock, 'An analysis of the nematocysts of the beadlet anemone *Actinia equina* and the green sea anemone *Actinia prasina*', *Journal of the Marine Biological Association of the UK* (August 2000).

135 The acrorhagi: W. Rapp, 'Uber die Polypen in Allgemeinen und die Aktinien im Besonderen', Verlage des Grofsherzogl. Sachs. privileg. Landes-Industrie-Comptoirs, Weimar, 1829.

135 But should a: Roger Lubbock, 'Clone-specific cellular recognition in a sea anemone', *Proceedings of the National Academy of Sciences of the United States of America*, Vol. 77, No. 11 (November 1980), 6667–9.

135 All life: D. B. Dusenbery, *Sensory Ecology* (W. H. Freeman, 1992).

136 The chemical basis: Lucia F. Jacobs, 'From chemotaxis to the cognitive map: The function of olfaction', *Proceedings of the National Academy of Sciences of the United States of America*, Vol. 109, Supplement 1: In the Light of Evolution VI: Brain and Behavior (26 June 2012), 10693–700; Roy E. Plotnick, Stephen Q. Dornbos and Junyuan Chen, 'Information landscapes and sensory ecology of the Cambrian Radiation', *Paleobiology*, Vol. 36, No. 2 (Spring 2010), 303–17.

136 Driven by these: Jacobs, op. cit.; Plotnick et al., op cit.

138 Those cut surfaces: V. L. G. Turner, S. M. Lynch, L. Paterson, J. L. León-Cortés, J. P. Thorpe, 'Aggression as a function of genetic relatedness in the sea anemone *Actinia equina* (Anthozoa: Actiniaria)', *Marine Ecology Progress Series*, Vol. 247 (2003), 85–92.

138 The result is clusters: W. H. Hildemann, I. S. Johnson and P. L. Jokiel, 'Immunocompetence in the lowest metazoan phylum: transplantation immunity in sponges', *Science* 204(4391) (1979), 420–2; L. W. Buss, 'Somatic cell parasitism and the evolution of somatic tissue compatibility', *Proceedings of the National Academy of Sciences of the United States of America*, Vol. 79, No. 17 (1982), 5337–41.

138 An anemone is: Richard K. Grosberg, 'The Evolution of Allorecognition Specificity in Clonal Invertebrates', *The Quarterly Review of Biology*, Vol. 63, No. 4 (December 1988), 377–412.

138 The one thing: Ibid.

141 'the reproductives': D. J. Ayre and R. K. Grosberg. 'Aggression, habituation, and clonal coexistence in the sea anemone *Anthopleura elegantissima*', *The American Naturalist* 146(3) (1995), 427–53.

141 Attacks are coordinated: D. J. Ayre and R. K. Grosberg, 'Effects of social organization on inter-clonal dominance relationships in the sea anemone *Anthopleura elegantissima*', *Animal Behaviour* 51(6) (1996), 1233–45; D. J. Ayre and R. K. Grosberg, 'Behind anemone lines: factors affecting division of labour in the social cnidarian *Anthopleura elegantissima*', *Animal Behaviour*, 70(1) (2005), 97–110.

142 Anemones, it seems: Fabian S. Rudin and Mark Briffa, 'The logical polyp: assessments and decisions during contests in the beadlet anemone *Actinia equina*', *Behavioral Ecology*, Advance Access publication, 11 July 2011.

6 Heraclitus on the shore

145 And an adored: A collection of essays to commemorate his life was privately published in 1981 as *John Raven by his Friends*.

145 *The Presocratic Philosophers*: G. S. Kirk, J. E. Raven and M. Schofield, *The Presocratic Philosophers: A critical history with a selection of texts* (CUP, 1983).

146 In the radically tidal: Ibid., pp. 181–213.

146 'that there is no solidity': Plato, *Cratylus*, 440c-d, online at http://www.perseus.tufts.edu/.

147 'Man's life': Kirk and Raven, *The Presocratic Philosophers*, p. 203.

148 'the physical world': F. Capra, *The Web of Life: A New Scientific Understanding of Living Systems* (1996; Flamingo, 1997), p. 39.

148 'In a living system': Ibid., p. 155.

149 'whirlpools': Quoted in ibid., p. 51.

149 'They do not understand': Kirk and Raven, *The Presocratic Philosophers*, p. 192.

150 'the victor': Ibid., p. 194.

150 'I have reason': C. Darwin, *On the Origin of Species by Means of Natural Selection, or the Preservation of Favoured Races in the Struggle for Life* (2nd edition, John Murray, 1860), pp. 73–4.

152 'Why is the world green?': Nelson G. Hairston, Frederick E. Smith and Lawrence B. Slobodkin, 'Community Structure, Population Control, and Competition', *The American Naturalist*, Vol. 94, No. 879 (November–December 1960), 421–5.

152 Beneath him: From an interview with Paine in Cristina Eisenberg, *The Wolf's Tooth* (Island Press, 2010), p. 27.

154 'would be a delicate': Stephen R. Palumbi, James A. Estes, Peter Kareiva, Simon A. Levin, Jane Lubchenco and Mary E. Power, 'Robert Treat Paine III (1933–2016)', *Proceedings of the National Academy of Sciences of the United States of America*, Vol. 114, No. 27 (3 July 2017), 6881–2.

154 'when in action': R. T. Paine, 'Food webs: linkage, interaction strength and community infrastructure', *Journal of Animal Ecology* 49(3) (1980), 667–85.

156 'This changes everything': Quoted in James A. Estes, Paul K. Dayton, Peter Kareiva, Simon A. Levin, Jane Lubchenco, Bruce A. Menge, Stephen R. Palumbi, Mary E. Power and John Terborgh, 'A keystone ecologist: Robert Treat Paine, 1933–2016', *Ecology*, Vol. 97, No. 11 (November 2016), 2905–9.

156 'keystone species': R. T. Paine, 'A Note on Trophic Complexity and Community Stability', *The American Naturalist*, Vol. 103, No. 929 (January–February 1969), 91–3.

156 'trophic cascade': Paine, 'Food Webs', op. cit.

157 'is arguably': James A. Estes et al., 'Trophic Downgrading of Planet Earth', *Science* 333 (2011), 301.

157 The disastrous cascade: D. Fortin, H. L. Beyer, M. S. Boyce, D. W. Smith, T. Duchesne and J. S. Mao, 'Wolves influence elk movements: behavior shapes a trophic cascade in Yellowstone National Park', *Ecology* 86 (2005), 1320–30.

157 but no instance: James A. Estes and John F. Palmisano, 'Sea Otters: Their Role in Structuring Nearshore Communities', *Science*, New Series Vol. 185, No. 4156 (20 September 1974), 1058–60; J. A. Estes, M. T. Tinker, T. M. Williams and D. F. Doak, 'Killer Whale Predation on Sea Otters Linking Oceanic and Nearshore Ecosystems', *Science*,

New Series, Vol. 282, No. 5388 (16 October 1998), 473–6; Robert G. Anthony, James A. Estes, Mark A. Ricca, A. Keith Miles and Eric D. Forsman, 'Bald Eagles and Sea Otters in the Aleutian Archipelago: Indirect Effects of Trophic Cascades', *Ecology*, Vol. 89, No. 10 (October 2008), 2725–35.

158 An organism: Daniel Barrios-O'Neill, Camilla Bertolini and Patrick Colman Collins, 'Trophic cascades and the transient keystone concept', *Biological Conservation* 212 (2017), 191–5.

160 'You can tip': Elizabeth Kolbert, 'The Climate of Man – I Disappearing islands, thawing permafrost, melting polar ice. How the earth is changing', *New Yorker Annals of Science* Issue (25 April 2005).

161 These gobies: J. Bjelvenmark and E. Forsgren, 'Effects of mate attraction and male-male competition on paternal care in a goby', *Behaviour* 140(1) (2003), 55–69.

7 Tide

166 'the sea on a cosmic leash': R. Blythe, *The Time by the Sea* (Faber & Faber, 2013), p. 20.

166 'see something falling up': Hugh Aldersey-Williams, *Tide* (Penguin, 2017), p. 154.

167 'Her power penetrates': Quoted in D. I. Radin and J. M. Rebmam, 'Lunar correlates of normal, abnormal and anomalous human behavior',

Subtle Energies & Energy Medicine Journal Archives 5(3) (1994).

167 'rude philosophy': James George Frazer, *The Golden Bough: A Study in Magic and Religion* (1890; Cosimo, 2009), p. 34.

167 In the West Highlands: A. R. Forbes, *Gaelic Names of Beasts etc.* (Oliver & Boyd, 1905), p. 289.

167 'sown when the tide': Frazer, *The Golden Bough*, p. 34.

168 'the skins of seals': Ibid., p. 35.

168 '*Deoch*': Forbes, *Gaelic Names of Beasts etc.*, pp. 289, 266.

168 But how and when: Aristotle, *Meteorology*; Roland Gehrels and Antony Long, 'Sea level is not level', *Geography* 93, 1 (Spring 2008), 11–16.

168 'which, by its Respiration': Apollonius, Antonio Galateo, *De situ elementorum* (1558).

169 Wanting to preserve itself: David Edgar Cartwright, *Tides: A Scientific History* (CUP, 1999).

170 'At certain moments': Paolo Palmieri, 'Re-examining Galileo's Theory of Tides', *Archive for History of Exact Sciences*, Vol. 53, No. 3/4 (November 1998), 223–375.

170 For Kepler, long celebrated: Ernan McMullin, 'Kepler: Moving the Earth', *HOPOS: The Journal of the International Society for the History of Philosophy of Science*, Vol. 1, No. 1 (Spring 2011), 3–22.

170 'If the earth': Cartwright, *Tides*, p. 31.

171 'Do you think': In Bertrand Claude, *Les Fondateurs de l'Astronomie moderne*, p. 154.

173 'pushed up': Quoted in Ron Naylor, 'Galileo's Tidal Theory', *Isis*, Vol. 98, No. 1 (March 2007), 1–22.

173 'a process of expansion': Galileo's tidal theories are fully analysed in Palmieri, op. cit.

174 'If a broad Vessel': John Wallis, Letter from Oxford to Mr Boyle, 25 April 1666, *Royal Society Transactions*, 6 August 1666; 'An Essay of Dr John Wallis, Exhibiting His Hypothesis about the Flux and Reflux of the Sea, Taken from the Consideration of the Common Center of Gravity of the Earth and Moon', *Philosophical Transactions of the Royal Society* (1665–78), Vol. 1 (1665–6), 263–81.

177 When the moon was full: René Descartes, *The World or Treatise on Light* (1629–33), trans. Michael S. Mahoney, Chapter 12: 'On the Ebb and Flow of the Sea', http://www.princeton.edu/~hos/mike/texts/descartes/world/worldfr.htm; Patrick Suppes, 'Descartes and the Problem of Action at a Distance', *Journal of the History of Ideas*, Vol. 15, No. 1 (January 1954), 146–52; A. J. Snow, 'Newton's Objections to Descartes' Astronomy', *The Monist*, Vol. 34, No. 4 (October 1924), 543–57.

178 'Whether ye Earth': Richard S. Westfall, 'The Foundations of Newton's Philosophy of Nature', *The British Journal for the History of Science*, Vol. 1, No. 2 (December 1962), 171–82.

179 'I have often wondered': Philip E. B. Jourdain, 'Robert Hooke as a Precursor of Newton', *The Monist*, Vol. 23, No. 3 (July 1913), 353–84.

180 'all the surprising': Isaac Newton and Edmond Halley, 'The true Theory of the Tides, extracted from Mr Isaac Newton's Treatise, intitled, Philosophiae Naturalis Principia Mathematica; being a Discourse presented with that Book to the late King James, by Mr Edmond Halley', *Philosophical Transactions of the Royal Society* (1683–1775), Vol. 19 (1695–7), 445–57.

180 'a perfect stagnation': Cartwright, *Tides*, p. 262; Newton and Halley, op. cit.

8 Rock

187 the ice: J. W. Gregory, 'The Fiords of the Hebrides', *The Geographical Journal*, Vol. 69, No. 3 (March 1927), 193–212.

188 No more than 1,500 years: J. J. Lowe and M. J. C. Walker, 'Late glacial and early Flandrian environmental history of the Isle of Mull, Inner Hebrides, Scotland', *Earth and Environmental Science Transactions of The Royal Society of Edinburgh* 77(1) (1986), 1–20.

189 When all the fresh water: K. Walton, 'Vertical Movements of Shorelines in Highland Britain: An Introduction', *Transactions of the Institute of*

British Geographers, No. 39, Special Number on the Vertical Displacement of Shorelines in Highland Britain (October 1966), 1–8.

189 All over the west: S. B. McCann, 'The Main Post-Glacial Raised Shoreline of Western Scotland from the Firth of Lorne to Loch Broom', *Transactions of the Institute of British Geographers*, No. 39, Special Number on the Vertical Displacement of Shorelines in Highland Britain (October 1966), 87–99; it may be the sea level is also now rising, thanks to thermal expansion, at about the same rate.

190 'dwindled': From G. M. Hopkins 'Moonrise', with thanks to Seán Hewitt for alerting me to this.

192 Over a good proportion: J. Terrence et al., 'Zircon U-Pb Geochronology Links the end-Triassic Extinction With the Central Atlantic Magmatic Province', *Science* (May 2013), 24;340(6135):941–5; B. van de Schootbrugge et al., 'End-Triassic calcification crisis and blooms of organic-walled "disaster species"', *Palaeogeography, Palaeoclimatology, Palaeoecology* 244 (2007), 126–41.

192 Geologists have calculated: D. J. Beetling and R. A. Berner, 'Biogeochemical constraints on the Triassic–Jurassic boundary carbon cycle event', *Global Biogeochemical Cycles* 16(3) (2002), 10–11. Figures rounded up; Jessica H.

Whiteside, Paul E. Olsen, Timothy Eglinton, Michael E. Brookfield and Raymond N. Sambrotto, 'Compound-specific carbon isotopes from Earth's largest flood basalt eruptions directly linked to the end-Triassic mass extinction', *PNAS*, Vol. 107, No. 15 (2010), 6721–5.

195 Again and again: Weimu Xu et al., 'Orbital pacing of the Early Jurassic carbon cycle, black shale formation and seabed methane seepage', *Sedimentology* 64 (2017), 127–49.

197 My copy: Timothy A. M. Ewin, *British Mesozoic Fossils*, 8th edition (Natural History Museum, 2018).

200 Philip Henry Gosse: The outstanding biography is by Ann Thwaite, *Glimpses of the Wonderful: The Life of Philip Henry Gosse 1810–1888* (Faber & Faber, 2002).

201 'marching soberly': P. H. Gosse, *The Aquarium: An Unveiling of the Wonders of the Deep* (1854), p. 28.

201 'of the Gospel net': Ibid., p. 43.

202 'submarine gardens': Edmund Gosse, *Father and Son: A Study of Two Temperaments* (1907; Penguin, 1949), pp. 110–11.

203 'a stable resting place': P. H. Gosse, *Omphalos: An Attempt to Untie the Geological Knot* (1857), p. 9.

203 'Sometimes the whole': Ibid., p. 93.

204 'a mighty array of evidence': Ibid., p. 51.

204 'He who made': Ibid., p. 13.
204 'hatched a scheme': Ibid., p. 21.
205 'In this weed-fringed': Ibid., pp. 216–17.
205 'It may be objected': Ibid., p. 348.
205 'The law of creation': Ibid., p. 338.

9 Sacrifice

210 They fished down there: Brian T. Wygal and Stephan M. Heidenreich, 'Deglaciation and Human Colonization of Northern Europe', *Journal of World Prehistory*, Vol. 27, No. 2 (August 2014), 111–44.
211 In the northern temperate zones: Hein B. Bjerck, 'Colonizing the so-called margins. The development of marine relations and the colonization of coastal north-west Europe', *The Irish Naturalists' Journal*, Vol. 29 (2008), 35–44.
211 The world was warming: Christoper Tolan-Smith, 'The social context of landscape learning and the Late Glacial-Early Postglacial recolonization of the British Isles' in M. Rockman and J. Steele (eds), *Colonization of Unfamiliar Landscapes* (Routledge, 2003), pp. 116–29.
211 There was one: A. D. Lacaille, *The Stone Age in Scotland* (OUP, 1954), pp. 229–39.
212 Eat the shore: Adapted from Nicky Milner, 'Mesolithic consumption practices: food for thought', *Journal of Nordic Archaeological Science* 16 (2009), 49–64.

213 Often with them: Catherine Dupont et al., 'Beg-an-Dorchenn (Plomeur, Finistère): une fenêtre ouverte sur l'exploitation du littoral par les peuples mésolithiques du VIe millénaire dans l'Ouest de la France', *Bulletin de la Société préhistorique française*, T. 107, No. 2 (Avril–Juin 2010), 227–90.
213 To the sea-vertebrates: M. J. Schoeninger et al., 'Stable nitrogen isotope ratios of bone collagen reflect marine and terrestrial components of prehistoric human diet', *Science* 220 (1983), 1381–3; R. J. Schulting and M. P. Richards, 'The use of stable isotopes in studies of subsistence and seasonality in the British Mesolithic' in R. Young (ed.), *Mesolithic Lifeways: Current Research from Britain and Ireland* (School of Archaeological Studies. University of Leicester, 2000), pp. 55–65.
213 These were the sea people: Vladimir Lozovski, 'Late Mesolithic–Early Neolithic human adaptation to environmental changes at an ancient lake shore: The multi-layer Zamostje 2 site, Dubna River floodplain, Central Russia', *Quaternary International* 324 (2014), 146–61.
214 For about 300 years: Michael Rex Wilkinson, 'The study of fish remains from British archaeological sites', PhD Thesis, University of

Sheffield, September 1981.

214 Finger to finger: C. Mieklejohn, Deborah C. Merrett, R. Nolan, Michael P. Richards and Paul A. Mellars, 'Spatial relationships, dating and taphonomy of the human bone from the Mesolithic site of Cnoc Coig, Oronsay, Argyll, Scotland', *Proceedings of the Prehistoric Society*, Vol. 71 (2005), 85–105.

215 Quantities of: Paul Mellars and Martha V. Andrews, *Excavations on Oronsay: Prehistoric Human Ecology on a Small Island* (Edinburgh University Press, 1987), p. 113.

215 Overfishing was already: https://www.cam.ac.uk/ research/features/what-limpets-can-tell-us-about-life-on-mesolithic-oronsay; J. B. Jackson et al., 'Historical overfishing and the recent collapse of coastal ecosystems', *Science* 293(5530) (2001) 629–37; Marcello A. Mannino and Kenneth D. Thomas, 'Depletion of a Resource? The Impact of Prehistoric Human Foraging on Intertidal Mollusc Communities and Its Significance for Human Settlement, Mobility and Dispersal', *World Archaeology*, Vol. 33, No. 3 (February 2002), Ancient Ecodisasters, 452–74.

216 With no gradual transition: Michael P. Richards, Rick J. Schulting and Robert E. M. Hedges, 'Sharp shift in diet at

onset of Neolithic', *Nature*, Vol. 425 (2003), 366.

216 The protein punch: Geoffrey N. Bailey, 'Shell middens as indicators of postglacial economies: a territorial perspective', in P. A. Mellars, *The Early Postglacial Settlement of Northern Europe* (Duckworth, 1978), pp. 37–63.

216 New genetic evidence: Anna Szécsényi-Nagy, Guido Brandt, Wolfgang Haak, Victoria Keerl, János Jakucs, Sabine Möller-Rieker, Kitti Köhler et al., 'Tracing the genetic origin of Europe's first farmers reveals insights into their social organization', *Proceedings of the Royal Society B: Biological Sciences*, Vol. 282, No. 1805 (2015), 20150339; Zuzana Hofmanová, Susanne Kreutzer, Garrett Hellenthal, Christian Sell, Yoan Diekmann, David Díez-del-Molino, Lucy van Dorp et al., 'Early farmers from across Europe directly descended from Neolithic Aegeans', *Proceedings of the National Academy of Sciences of the United States of America*, Vol. 113, No. 25 (2016), 6886–91; Lara Cassidy et al., 'Neolithic and Bronze Age migration to Ireland and establishment of the insular Atlantic genome', *Proceedings of the National Academy of Sciences of the United States of America*, Vol. 113, No. 2 (2016), 368–73.

216 They brought: Bernardo Chessa et al., 'Revealing the History of

Sheep Domestication Using Retrovirus Integrations', *Science*, New Series, Vol. 324, No. 5926 (24 April 2009), 532–6.

216 brought by boat: David W. G. Stanton, Jacqueline A. Mulville and Michael W. Bruford, 'Colonization of the Scottish islands via long-distance Neolithic transport of red deer (Cervus elaphus)', *Proceedings of the Royal Society B: Biological Sciences*, Vol. 283, No. 1828 (2016), 20160095.

216 The genetic origins: Laura M. Shannon, Ryan H. Boyko, Marta Castelhano, Elizabeth Corey, Jessica J. Hayward, Corin McLean, Michelle E. White et al., 'Genetic structure in village dogs reveals a Central Asian domestication origin', *Proceedings of the National Academy of Sciences of the United States of America*, Vol. 112, No. 44 (2015), 13639–44.

216 Milk and cheese: Lucy J. E. Cramp et al., 'Immediate replacement of fishing with dairying by the earliest farmers of the north-east Atlantic archipelagos', *Proceedings of the Royal Society B: Biological Sciences*, Vol. 281, No. 1780 (7 April 2014), 1–8.

216 Reliance on: Rick J. Schulting and Michael P. Richards, 'The wet, the wild and the domesticated: the Mesolithic–Neolithic transition on the west coast of Scotland',
European Journal of Archaeology, Vol. 5, No. 2 (2002), 147–89; Nicky Milner and Oliver E. Craig, 'Mysteries of the middens: change and continuity across the Mesolithic-Neolithic transition', *Land and People: Papers in Memory of John G. Evans* (Oxbow Books, 2009), pp. 169–80; J. Thomas, 'Thoughts on the "repacked" Neolithic revolution', *Antiquity* 77 (2003), 67–74.

217 From about 3000 BC: B. A. S. Davis, S. Brewer, A. C. Stevenson and J. Guiot, 'The temperature of Europe during the Holocene reconstructed from pollen data', *Quaternary Science Reviews* 22 (15–17) (2003), 1701–16.

217 'rapid demographic growth': Sean S. Downey, W. Randall Haas Jr and Stephen J. Shennan, 'European Neolithic societies showed early warning signals of population collapse', *Proceedings of the National Academy of Sciences of the United States of America*, Vol. 113, No. 35 (30 August 2016), 9751–6.

217 These Neolithic teeth: J. Montgomery et al., 'Strategic and sporadic marine consumption at the onset of the Neolithic: increasing temporal resolution in the isotope evidence', *Antiquity*, Vol. 87, No. 338 (2013), 1060–72.

218 'It is feared': The Marine List, LL, No. 11,770, London, 12 December 1851.

220 'was called': Norman Macleod, *Reminiscences of a Highland Parish* (1867), p. 327; intriguingly, the 'sea of knives' is part of Egyptian mythology: Donald B. Redford, 'The Sun-disc in Akhenaten's Program: Its Worship and Antecedents, I', *Journal of the American Research Center in Egypt*, Vol. 13 (1976), 47–61.

220 'The plaided boatman': Walter Scott, Prologue to Joanna Baillie, *The Family Legend*, 2nd edition (1810).

220 This is the place: This rock is covered only at the highest of spring tides. Another, nearer Lismore and called Liath Sgeir, is thought by some to have been the rock in question as it is covered at a third of a flood tide. (With thanks to Iain Thornber for this information.)

221 At some time: J. P. (John Patterson) Maclean, *A History of the Clan MacLean from Its First Settlement at Duard Castle, in the Isle of Mull* (R. Clarke & Co., 1889), p. 73.

222 Such wickedness: With thanks to Amanda Moffett for these details. https://www.scotclans. com/lady-rock-off-mull/

222 'entertained': 'A Seneachie', *An Historical and Genealogical Account of the Clan Maclean* (Laing & Forbes, 1838), p. 28.

222 'The better to accomplish': Ibid., p. 30.

224 'so that the boatmen': Baillie, *The Family Legend*, p. vii.

224 In several of the versions: Roddy Regan, 'The Lady, the Rock and the Legend', *The Kist: The Magazine of The Natural History and Antiquarian Society of Mid-Argyll*, Iss. 93 (Spring 2017), 3–15.

224 'Maclean stood': Baillie, *The Family Legend*, p. v: 'The story, from which I have taken the plot, was put into my hands in the year 1805, by the Hon. Mrs. Damer. Anne Damer, a sculptor, was the daughter of Henry Conway and Lady Caroline Campbell, daughter of the 4th duke of Argyll and widow of Lord Aylesbury. The story as Anne Gamer had it had been told by her mother and her mother's forebears.'

225 'the crafty': 'A Seneachie', *An Historical and Genealogical Account*, p. 31.

225 Only many years: *A Diurnal of Remarkable Occurrents In Scotland A.D. M.D.XIII-A.D.M.D.LXXV* (Bannatyne Club, Edinburgh, 1833) (1523), p. 8.

225 His nickname: Maclean, *A History of the Clan Maclean*, p. 65; there is another but false etymology suggesting that his name comes from his mother who was of the Clan Chattan.

225 It marks a man: Ephraim Nissan, 'The Importance of Being Hairy: A Few Remarks on the Queen of Sheba, Esau, and the Andromeda Myth', *La Ricerca Folklorica*, No. 70, Comunità di pratica, sport e spazi urbani (2015), 273–83 quoting Robert Dankoff, 'Baraq and Burāq', *Central Asiatic Journal* 15(2) (1971),

Harrassowitz, Wiesbaden,
102–17. 'Long hair is a mark
of shamans in particular, and
of culture heroes generally. It is
safe to conclude that baraq
[hairy] was a favourite
descriptive word for Turkic
shamans and shamanic animals
especially, and for other more
or less religiously regarded
culture heroes as well, in
various times and places.'

225 Tristan and Isolde: See, for
example, Wendy Doniger, *The
Woman Who Pretended to Be
Who She Was: Myths of Self-
Imitation* (OUP, 2004), p. 60.

226 The oldest rites: J. P. Mallory,
In Search of the Indo-Europeans
(Thames & Hudson, 1989).
p. 128.

226 The fertility gods: Ibid., p. 139.

227 'Sacrificial killing': Walter
Burkert, *Homo Nectans: The
Anthropology of Ancient Greek
Sacrificial Ritual and Myth*,
trans. Peter Bing (University of
California Press, 1983), p. 3.

227 'Sacrifice is an act': Ibid.,
pp. 135, 296.

228 The killing: Ibid., p. 296.

228 In America: Ibid., pp. 64–5.

228 In Stone Age Germany: Ibid.,
pp. 14, 65.

228 In Genesis: Genesis 22.

228 Iphigenia: In several versions,
the girl is replaced with a deer.
In the earliest, Aeschylus'
Agamemnon lines 228–41, the
sacrifice of the innocent girl is
remembered in full and pitiful
detail.

229 'a goat or sheep': John
Abercromby, 'Traditions,
Customs, and Superstitions of

the Lewes', *Folklore*, Vol. 6, No.
2 (June 1895), 162–71.

230 'As soon as': Ibid.

230 'obtained from': A suggestion
made by Paul Bibire in D. U.
Stiùbhart, 'Some heathenish
and superstitious rites: a letter
from Lewis, 1700', *Scottish
Studies* (2006), 203–24.

230 Or the name: Stiùbhart, 'Some
heathenish and superstitious
rites', op. cit.

230 'some heathenish': Ibid.

231 'people in maritime': Alexander
Carmichael, *Carmina Gadelica:
Hymns and incantations, with
illustrative notes on words, rites
and customs, dying and obsolete*,
Vol. 1 (Oliver & Boyd, 1900),
pp. 162–3.

231 How to relate: Regan, 'The
Lady, the Rock and the
Legend', op. cit., 3–4, 13. All
that these stray fragments can
establish is to confirm the
ancient connection between
the sacrificed woman and the
grains from which food is
made. There is some
connection in inherited
memory between the sacrificed
woman and grains in the
tradition that she took refuge
in the mills at Kilmory in
North Knapdale, or at Taynish
on Loch Sween. Or that the
later owners of the mills had
first received them as reward
for saving her. Both mills are in
fact later than the story, but
such connections are migratory
in time and space.

232 It was not to spill: Burkert,
Homo Nectans, pp. 4–5.

233 Maclean guilt: Ibid., p. 65.

233 'War can be': Ibid.
233 In recent: M. E. C. Stewart, 'Bunrannoch Deserted Medieval Village', Unpublished manuscript MS/593/1, National Monuments Record of Scotland, Edinburgh 1966, quoted in Gavin MacGregor, 'Legends, Traditions or Coincidences: Remembrance of Historic Settlement in the Central Highlands of Scotland', *International Journal of Historical Archaeology*, Vol. 14, No. 3 (June 2010), 398–413.
234 'in an uncivilised': D. McAra, 'Parish of Fortingall', in J. Sinclair (ed.), *The Statistical Account of Scotland* (1795), pp. 449–60.
234 'The tradition': MacGregor, 'Legends, Traditions or Coincidences', op. cit.

10 Survival

236 'socializing': B. Stapleton, 'Malthus: the origins of the principle of population?' in M. Turner (ed.), *Malthus and His Time* (St Martin's Press, 1986), p. 22; see also Glenn Davis Stone's fascinating blog: https://fieldquestions.com/2013/10/20/overpopulation-and-the-small-farmers-of-oakwood/.
236 the average difference: John Komlos, 'On English Pygmies and Giants: the Physical Stature of English Youth in the late-18th and early-19th Centuries', *Research in Economic History* 25 (2005), 149–68.
236 'The sons and daughters': T. R. Malthus, *An Essay on the Principle of Population, as it affects the future improvement of society, with remarks on the speculations of Mr Godwin, M. Condorcet, and other writers* (J. Johnson, 1798), extract in *The Monthly Review* (September 1798), 4.
237 'the necessary result': Quoted by Malthus in *An Essay on the Principle of Population*, Chapter 8, online at https://historyhome.co.uk/peel/social/prin8.htm.
237 'the period when': Ibid.
238 a 'check': Gareth Dale, 'Adam Smith's Green Thumb and Malthus's Three Horsemen: Cautionary Tales from Classical Political Economy', *Journal of Economic Issues*, Vol. 46, No. 4 (December 2012), 859–79.
239 'The number of organisms': T. C. R. White, 'The role of food, weather and climate in limiting the abundance of animals', *Biological Reviews* 83 (2008), 227–48.
239 This connection: James W. Wood, 'Theory of Preindustrial Population Dynamics Demography, Economy, and Well-Being in Malthusian Systems', *Current Anthropology*, Vol. 39, No. 1 (February 1998), 99–135.
240 'stress hormones': Shelley A. Adamo, 'The effects of the stress response on immune function in invertebrates: An evolutionary perspective on an ancient connection', *Hormones*

and Behavior, Vol. 62, Iss. 3 (August 2012), 324–30.

240 'brood neglect': See, for example, S. Wanless and M. P. Harris, 'Kittiwake attendance patterns during chick rearing on the Isle of May', *Scottish Birds* 15 (1989), 156–61.

240 The annual rainfall: At Loch Arienas at the centre of Morvern, it is 3,319.8 mm a year or within a whisker of eleven feet; in Lismore it is 1,680.9 mm or sixty-six inches. The annual rainfall in the bay, halfway between the two, may be about eight feet or nearly a hundred inches. John Harrison and George Clark, 'The Lochaber Raingauge Network', https://rmets.onlinelibrary. wiley.com/doi/pdf/10.1002/j. 1477-8696.1998.tb06342.x.

240 'The whole of': J. Sinclair (ed.), *The Statistical Account of Scotland* (1795), XXI, p. 264.

240 For every grain: Robert A. Dodgshon, *From Chiefs to Landlords: Social and Economic Change in the Western Highlands and Islands, c.1493– 1820* (Edinburgh University Press, 1998), p. 15.

241 Most of the arable: From MS.La.11.623, 'Second Report to the Commissioners and Trustees for Improving Fisheries and Manufactures in Scotland' by Richard Neilson (1755), http://www.moidart. org.uk/datasets/neilson1755. htm.

241 'in caverns': Eric Richards, *The Highland Clearances*, 3rd edition (Birlinn, 2007), p. 93.

241 'the prevalence of destitution': John Macleod, 'Parish of Morvern', *New Statistical Account* (1843), p. 194.

241 the West Highlands: Richards, *Highland Clearances*, pp. 87, 89.

242 'if you could': Quoted in ibid., p. 46.

242 'Here is a melancholy': Edmund Burt, *Burt's Letters from the North of Scotland* (1754), ed. Andrew Simmons (Birlinn, 1998), p. 74.

242 'man-sties': Richards, *Highland Clearances*, p. 217.

242 'come out from': Quoted in ibid., p. 47.

242 'liable to fluxes': Burt, *Burt's Letters*, p. 183.

242 'they sit brooding': Ibid., p. 207.

242 'a set of people': Richards, *Highland Clearances*, p. 91.

242 'left to Providence's care': Thomas Pennant, *Tour in Scotland 1769*, Vol. I (1771; Birlinn, 2000), p. 353.

243 'the starving season': Burt, *Burt's Letters*, p. 204.

243 proverbial wisdom: A. R. Forbes, *Gaelic Names of Beasts etc.* (Oliver & Boyd, 1905), entry for limpet, p. 370.

243 The goats' kids: Sinclair (ed.), *The Statistical Account of Scotland*, p. 266.

243 The spoons they used: Burt, *Burt's Letters*, pp. 74, 83–4.

243 'Potatoes': John Macleod, 'Parish of Morvern', New *Statistical Account*, p. 187

243 'I do not remember': Burt, *Burt's Letters*, p. 213.

244 'Not far from Fort William':
Ibid., p. 214.

244 'Whatever his other': Tim
Robinson, *Stones of Aran,
Pilgrimage* (Faber & Faber,
2008), p. 189.

245 Exhausted hunger: Robert A.
Dodgshon and E. Gunilla
Olsson, 'Productivity and
Nutrient Use in Eighteenth-
Century Scottish Highland
Townships', *Geografiska
Annaler*. Series B, Human
Geography, Vol. 70, No. 1,
Landscape History (1988),
39–51.

245 'terrible time': http://
tobarandualchais.co.uk/en/
fullrecord/53965/4; School of
Scottish Studies, recorded 16
January 1974; Track ID:
53965.

245 'The old people': Norman
Macleod, *Reminiscences of a
Highland Parish* (1867; 2nd
edition, 1887), pp. 136–7.

246 'Great Map': Available online
at maps.nls.uk/geo/roy.

248 Turf walls: Dr Johnson: 'We
were driven once, by missing a
passage, to the hut of a
gentleman, where, after a very
liberal supper, when I was
conducted to my chamber, I
found an elegant bed of Indian
cotton, spread with fine sheets.
The accommodation was
flattering; I undressed myself,
and felt my feet in the mire.
The bed stood upon the bare
earth, which a long course of
rain had softened to a puddle.'
(*A Journey to the Western Islands
of Scotland* (1775; Penguin,
1984), pp. 105–6.

250 'in the face of the rock': John
Macleod, 'Parish of Morvern',
New Statistical Account, p. 185;
also described in 1800 in a
Notebook belonging to Sir
John MacGregor Murray
available online at https://
editions.curioustravellers.ac.uk/
doc/0055.

250 In times of dearth: Dodgshon,
From Chiefs to Landlords.

251 What remains: Mark Thacker,
*Ardtornish Castle: a buildings
archaeology study* (The Scottish
Medieval Castles & Chapels
C-14 Project, 2016).

251 They could command: For the
size of English contingents in
1415, see M. Burtscher, *The
FitzAlans: Earls of Arundel and
Surrey, Lords of the Welsh
Marches (1267–1415)* (Little
Logaston, 2008), pp. 106–7.

251 'in great numbers': Quoted in
James Petre, 'Donald Balloch,
the "Treaty of Ardtornish-
Westminster" and the
MacDonald raids of 1461–3',
Historical Research, Vol. 88,
Issue 242 (November 2015),
599–628.

253 The dependence: Joseph
Murphy, 'Place and Exile:
Imperialism, Development and
Environment in Gaelic Ireland
and Scotland', No. 17 SRI
Papers (Online) (June 2009); J.
MacInnes, 'Gaelic poetry and
historical tradition', in Michael
Newton (ed.), *Dùthchas Nan
Gàidheal: Selected Essays of John
MacInnes* (Birlinn, 2006),
pp. 3–33.

255 'The combination': Richards,
Highland Clearances, pp. 84–5.

255 'highly cultivated genealogical awareness': *West Highland Free Press*, 7 September 2002, 'Sorley Maclean: "Why Marx and Blake look down with equal admiration …"', http://www. whfp.com/1582/top2.html.

256 'Well, I am': School of Scottish Studies SA1982/150–7.

258 'Again and again': Sorley Maclean, 'Glen Eyre', in *Spring Tide and Neap Tide: Selected Poems 1932–72* (Canongate, 1977), p. 70.

258 '*Mo bheatha*': Sorley Maclean, 'Gleann Aoighre', in *Reothairt is Contraigh: Taghadh de Dhàin 1932–72* (Canongate, 1977), p. 71.

11 Belief

261 *Bi glic*: J. F. Campbell, *Popular Tales of the West Highlands*, Vol. 1 (Abela Publishing Ltd, 2009), p. 275.

262 'contributed to the': Edward H. Miller and Allan J. Baker, 'Antiquity of Shorebird Acoustic Displays,' *The Auk*, Vol. 126, No. 2 (April 2009), 454–9.

262 'many beautiful songs': Stuart A. Harris-Logan, 'Nam Bithinn Mar Eun ("If I were a Bird") Re-accessing the paralinguistic dimension of traditional Scots Gaelic storytelling', *eSharp*, Iss. 10: Orality and Literacy, 3–4, quoting Alexander Carmichael, *Carmina Gadelica: Hymns and incantations, with illustrative notes on words, rites and customs, dying and obsolete*, Vol. 1 (Oliver & Boyd, 1900), pp. 60–1.

263 '*A chaomhag*': Campbell, *Popular Tales*, p. 82.

263 'not because': Claude Lévi-Strauss, *Totemism*, trans. Rodney Needham (Beacon, 1963), p. 89.

263 '*bonnes à penser*': Claude Lévi-Strauss, *Le totémisme aujourd'hui* (PUF, 1962), p. 128.

264 'with much affected': Carmichael, *Carmina Gadelica*, pp. 171–2, slightly adapted. The St Kildans themselves used to drink the gannet eggs raw.

265 'he found': John Macleod, 'Parish of Morvern', *New Statistical Account* (1843), p. 174.

266 There was no illusion: A. R. Forbes, *Gaelic Names of Beasts etc.* (Oliver & Boyd, 1905), p. 236.

266 'Evil comes': J. G. Campbell, *The Gaelic Otherworld*, ed. Ronald Black (Birlinn, 2005), p. 272.

266 'prayed in the sea': Adomnán, 'Columba's Deeds', trans. Robert Crawford, *The Book of Iona* (Birlinn, 2016), Kindle edition.

269 'are spoken': Campbell, *The Gaelic Otherworld*, pp. xlii–xliii.

269 'This is not': Ibid., p. xliv, quoting Angela Bourke, *The Burning of Bridget Cleary* (Pimlico, 1999), p. 37.

270 The sign that: Arthur Mitchell, 'Various Superstitions in the North-West Highlands and Islands of Scotland, Especially in Relation to Lunacy', *Proceedings of the Society of*

Antiquaries of Scotland, Vol. IV (1862), 289.

270 'that five years ago': R. Black, 'Life of J. G. Campbell', in Campbell, *The Gaelic Otherworld*, p. 655.

270 Unbaptised children: Campbell, *The Gaelic Otherworld*, p. 94.

271 'She was buried': Mitchell, 'Various Superstitions', op. cit., 282.

272 Colkitto then: David Stevenson, *Highland Warrior: Alasdair MacColla and the Civil Wars* (1980; Birlinn, 2014), pp. 71–2.

272 'foaming sea': https://www.faclair.com/ròid.

273 'a smothered': Reverend Alexander Stewart (Nether Lochaber), *The Natural History, Legends, and Folk-lore of the West Highlands* (Kindle Locations 3852–68).

274 Between here and there: Reverend Ian Carmichael, *Lismore in Alba* (D. Leslie, 1948).

275 The *ròd*: Campbell, *The Gaelic Otherworld*, p. 288.

276 Hairy Donald: Ibid., p. 176.

276 Would he be expelled: Alexander Carmichael, 'Some Unrecorded Incidents of the Jacobite Risings (Continued)', *The Celtic Review*, Vol. 6, No. 24 (April 1910), 334–48.

277 'It was very stormy': Norman Macleod, *Reminiscences of a Highland Parish* (1867; 2nd edition, 1887), pp. 303–5.

278 'He lived': Ibid., p. 306.

279 'She was one': Eleanor Hull, 'Legends and Traditions of the Cailleach Bheara or Old Woman (Hag) of Beare', *Folklore*, Vol. 38, No. 3 (30 September 1927), 225–54.

280 'I have seen': Ibid.

12 Three steps to the modern

283 The popularity: Reverend Thomas Brown, *Annals of the Disruption*, Vol. I (Maclaren & Macniven, 1877), online at ecclegen.com/browns-annals-part-3-2/; L. A. Ritchie, 'The Floating Church of Loch Sunart', *Records of the Scottish Church History Society* 22 (1985), 159–73.

283 'The tide had': Brown, *Annals of the Disruption*.

283 'Lament at its': Alice Oswald, 'Interview with Water', Lecture as Oxford Professor of Poetry, June 2020, https://www.english.ox.ac.uk/article/alice-oswald-professor-of-poetry-lecture-now-online.

284 'rich, cultured': Philip Gaskell, *Morvern Transformed: A Highland Parish in the Nineteenth Century* (CUP, 1968), p. 41.

284 Energetic, resourceful: Ibid., pp. 57–80.

285 'varying in duration': Herbert Spencer, *An Autobiography* (2 vols, D. Appleton and Company, 1904), I, p. 576.

285 'Outline of a System': Ibid., II, p. 184.

285 'The ultimate result': Ibid., p. 5.

285 'the increase': Ibid., p. 9.

287 'favoured races': Charles Darwin, *On the Origin of Species by Means of Natural*

Selection, or the Preservation of Favoured Races in the Struggle for Life (John Murray, 1859).

287 'I have but': Spencer, *An Autobiography*, II, p. 32.

287 'occurred to me': Ibid., p. 34.

287 He kicked himself: Ibid., I, pp. 448–52.

287 'I was able': Ibid., II, p. 37.

288 'I once discovered': Ibid., p. 47.

288 His working papers: Ibid., p. 79.

288 'The coast': Ibid., pp. 77–8.

288 'Doubtless many': Herbert Spencer, *The Principles of Biology*, Vol. I (D. Appleton and Company, 1864), p. 445.

289 'organisms which': Ibid.

289 'Applying alike': Ibid., p. 354.

289 'This survival': Ibid., pp. 444–5.

289 'dreadful': Darwin to Charles Lyell, 25 February 1860 (Darwin–Lyell MSS, American Philosophical Society Library), quoted in Derek Freeman et al., 'The Evolutionary Theories of Charles Darwin and Herbert Spencer', *Current Anthropology*, Vol. 15, No. 3 (September 1974), 211–37.

291 'a philosopher': George Steiner, *Martin Heidegger* (1968; University of Chicago Press, 1991), p. xix.

291 'caught up': Ibid., p. 112.

292 Both visions: Ibid., p. 31.

292 By emphasising: Ibid., p. 38.

293 'real concreteness': Ibid., pp. xix, 21, 85.

293 In music being: Ibid., p. 43.

294 'thought must descend': Ibid., p. 54.

294 'being-with': Ibid., p. 91.

294 Concern for them: Ibid., p. 92.

294 'I care therefore': Ibid., p. 101.

294 'Knowing is not': Ibid., p. 86.

294 'a bracing awareness': Ibid., p. 107.

295 'a freedom': Ibid., p. 106.

295 We take and use: See, for example, Sasha Alexander, James Aronson, Oliver Whaley and David Lamb, 'The relationship between ecological restoration and the ecosystem services concept', *Ecology and Society*, Vol. 21, No. 1 (March 2016).

296 'I do not want': Louis MacNeice, 'Wolves' (October 1934), *Collected Poems* (Faber & Faber, 1966), p. 29.

Conclusion: The last pool

306 An ice boulder: Graham Harman, *Object-Oriented Ontology: A New Theory of Everything* (Pelican, 2018), pp. 66–9, 258–9.

307 'wonder is': Plato, *Theaetetus*, 155c–d.

307 'puzzlement': Plato, *Meno*, 84c.

313 Should one: Julian Cremona, *Seashores: An Ecological Guide* (The Crowood Press, 2014), pp. 72–9.

314 'migrating in': Stephen J. Hawkins et al., 'From the *Torrey Canyon* to Today: A 50-Year Retrospective of Recovery from the Oil Spill and Interaction with Climate-Driven Fluctuations on Cornish Rocky Shores', Abstract #138 for 2017 International Oil Spill Conference.

315 The boom-bust: Ibid.

316 They are long-livers: Stuart R. Jenkins and Richard G. Hartnoll, 'Food supply, grazing activity and growth rate in the limpet *Patella vulgata* L.: a comparison between exposed and sheltered shores', *Journal of Experimental Marine Biology and Ecology* 258 (2001), 123–39.

316 Those in the middle: Christopher D. G. Harley, Mark W. Denny, Katharine J. Mach and Luke P. Miller, 'Thermal Stress and Morphological Adaptations in Limpets', *Functional Ecology*, Vol. 23, No. 2 (April 2009), 292–301.

316 If it wants: H. D. Jones and E. R. Trueman, 'Locomotion of the limpet *Patella vulgata* L.', *Journal of Experimental Biology* 5a (1970), 201–316.

318 The trails left: Valerie M. Connor, 'The Use of Mucous Trails by Intertidal Limpets to Enhance Food Resources', *Biological Bulletin*, Vol. 171, No. 3 (December 1986), 548–64.

318 Some limpets: John Stimson, 'The Role of the Territory in the Ecology of the Intertidal Limpet *Lottia gigantea* (Gray)', *Ecology*, Vol. 54, No. 5 (September 1973), 1020–30; Christopher D. McQuaid and Pierre W. Froneman, 'Mutualism between the Territorial Intertidal Limpet *Patella longicosta* and the Crustose Alga *Ralfsia verrucosa*', *Oecologia*, Vol. 96, No. 1 (1993), 128–33.

319 Limpets feel: Ross A. Coleman, Mark Browne and Timothy Theobalds, 'Aggregation as a Defense: Limpet Tenacity Changes in Response to Simulated Predator Attack', *Ecology*, Vol. 85, No. 4 (April 2004), 1153–9.

319 Each organism needs: Steven D. Gaines and Jane Lubchenco, 'A Unified Approach to Marine Plant– Herbivore Interactions. II. Biogeography', *Annual Review of Ecology and Systematics* 13 (1982), 111–38; Mark P. Johnson et al., 'Spatial Structure on Moderately Exposed Rocky Shores: Patch Scales and the Interactions between Limpets and Algae', *Marine Ecology Progress Series* 160 (1997), 209–15.

320 diagram: Adapted from David Raffaelli and Stephen Hawkins, *Intertidal Ecology* (Chapman & Hall, 1996), p. 95.

BIBLIOGRAPHY

Most of the references in this book are to individual papers mentioned in the endnotes. This is a list of the books I have found most useful.

Map and Guides

Explorer 383 1:25,000, *Morvern & Lochaline, Kingairloch*, Ordnance Survey 2015

Heather Buttivant, *Rock Pool: Extraordinary Encounters Between the Tides*, September Publishing 2019

David Erwin and Bernard Picton, *Guide to Inshore Marine Life*, Immel 1987

Ray Gibson, Benedict Hextall, Alex Rogers, *Photographic Guide to Sea & Shore Life of Britain & North-west Europe*, Oxford 2001

Julie Hatcher and Steve Trewhella, *The Essential Guide to Beachcombing and the Strandline*, Wild Nature Press 2015

Julie Hatcher and Steve Trewhella, *The Essential Guide to Rockpooling*, Wild Nature Press 2019

Stephen J. Hawkins and Hugh D. Jones, *Rocky Shores*, Immel 1992

Peter J. Hayward, *Seashore*, Collins 2004

Peter J. Hayward, *Shallow Seas*, William Collins 2016

Peter J. Hayward and John S. Ryland, *Handbook of the Marine Fauna of North-West Europe*, Oxford University Press 2017

Paul Sterry and Andrew Cleave, *Collins Complete Guide to British Coastal Wildlife*, HarperCollins 2012

David Thomas, *Seaweeds*, Natural History Museum 2002

Douglas P. Wilson, *Life of the Shore and Shallow Sea*, Ivor Nicholson and Watson 1935

C. M. Yonge, *The Sea Shore*, 1949, Bloomsbury 1990

Biology

John Archer-Thomson and Julian Cremona, *Rocky Shores*, Bloomsbury 2019

Guido Chelazzi and Marco Vannini, *Behavioural Adaptation to Intertidal Life*, Plenum 1988

Julian Cremona, *Seashores: An Ecological Guide*, Crowood 2014

D. B. Dusenbery, *Sensory Ecology*, W. H. Freeman 1992

Cristina Eisenberg, *The Wolf's Tooth*, Island Press 2010

J. D. Fish and S. Fish, *A Student's Guide to the Seashore*, 3rd edn Cambridge University Press 2011

Stephen Jay Gould, *The Structure of Evolutionary Theory*, Harvard University Press 2002

O. Larink and W. Westheide, *Coastal Plankton*, edited by K. H. Wiltshire and M. Boersma, AWI Handbooks on Marine Flora and Fauna 2006

Colin Little and J. A. Kitching, *The Biology of Rocky Shores*, Oxford University Press 1996

R. C. Newell, *The Biology of Intertidal Animals*, 3rd edn Hyperion 1979

David Raffaelli and Stephen Hawkins, *Intertidal Ecology*, Chapman & Hall 1996

Philosophy

Justin Broackes (ed.), *Iris Murdoch, Philosopher*, Oxford University Press 2012

Fritjof Capra, *The Web of Life: A New Scientific Understanding of Living Systems*, 1996, Flamingo 1997

Melanie Challenger, *How to Be Animal*, Canongate 2021

Peter J. Conradi, *Iris Murdoch: A Life*, HarperCollins 2001

Guy Davenport, *Seven Greeks*, New Directions 1995

Wolfram Eilenberger, *Time of the Magicians: The Invention of Modern Thought 1919–1929*, Allen Lane 2020

Graham Harman, *Object-Oriented Ontology: A New Theory of Everything*, Pelican 2018

G. S. Kirk, J. E. Raven and M. Schofield, *The Presocratic Philosophers: A critical history with a selection of texts*, Cambridge University Press 1983

Iris Murdoch, *The Sovereignty of Good*, Routledge & Kegan Paul 1970

Iris Murdoch, 'On "God" and "Good"', in *Existentialists and Mystics*, 1997, Penguin 1999

Rudiger Safranski, *Martin Heidegger: Between Good and Evil*, Harvard University Press 1999

Erin Schrödinger, *What Is Life?*, Cambridge University Press 1967

George Steiner, *Martin Heidegger*, 1978, University of Chicago Press 1991

Rocks and Tides

Hugh Aldersey-Williams, *Tide*, Penguin 2017

Ronald Blythe, *The Time by the Sea*, Faber 2013

Bibliography

David Edgar Cartwright, *Tides: A Scientific History*, Cambridge University Press 1999

Alan Cook, *Edmond Halley: Charting the Heavens and the Seas*, Clarendon Press 1998

Timothy A. M. Ewin, *British Mesozoic Fossils*, 8th edn Natural History Museum 2018

Con Gillen, *Geology and Landscapes of Scotland*, 2nd edn Dunedin 2013

J. Hardisty, *The British Seas*, Routledge 1990

Gosse

Edmund Gosse, *The Naturalist of the Sea-shore: The Life of Philip Henry Gosse*, Heinemann 1896

Edmund Gosse, *Father and Son: A Study of Two Temperaments*, 1907, Penguin 1949

P. H. Gosse, *The Aquarium: An Unveiling of the Wonders of the Deep*, 1854, Forgotten Books 2012

P. H. Gosse, *Omphalos: An Attempt to Untie the Geological Knot*, 1857, Amazon 2019

P. H. Gosse, *Evenings at the Microscope; or, researches among the minuter organs and forms of animal life*, 1859

P. H. Gosse, *A History of the British Sea-Anemones and Corals*, London 1860

P. H. Gosse, *A Year at the Shore*, London 1865

Ann Thwaite, *Glimpses of the Wonderful: The Life of Philip Henry Gosse 1810–1888*, Faber 2002

Darwin

Charles Darwin, *A Monograph on the Sub-Class Cirripedia, With Figures of All the Species. The Lepadidae; or, Pedunculated Cirripedes*, Ray Society 1851

Charles Darwin, *On the Origin of Species by Means of Natural Selection, or the Preservation of Favoured Races in the Struggle for Life*, 2nd edn John Murray 1860

Charles Darwin, *The Descent of Man and Selection in Relation to Sex*, 1871

Daniel C. Dennett, *Darwin's Dangerous Idea*, Penguin 1995

Jonathan Smith, *Charles Darwin and Victorian Visual Culture*, Cambridge University Press 2006

Rebecca Stott, *Darwin and the Barnacle*, Faber 2003

Spencer

Herbert Spencer, *The Principles of Biology*, Vol. I, London and Edinburgh 1864

Herbert Spencer, *An Autobiography*, 2 vols, London and New York 1904

Poetry and Literature
Joanna Baillie, *The Family Legend*, 1805, 2nd edn Edinburgh 1810
Robert Crawford, *The Book of Iona*, Birlinn 2016
T. S. Eliot, *The Use of Poetry and the Use of Criticism*, Faber 1933
A. F. Falconer, *Shakespeare & the Sea*, Constable 1964
Gwen Harwood, 'The Sea Anemones' in *Mappings of the Plane: New Selected Poems*, Carcanet 2009
Hermione Lee, *Virginia Woolf*, Chatto & Windus 1996
Ewen MacCaig (ed.), *The Poems of Norman MacCaig*, Polygon 2009
Sorley Maclean, *Reothairt is Contraigh: Taghadh de Dhàin 1932–72/Spring Tide and Neap Tide: Selected Poems 1932–72*, Canongate 1977
Louis MacNeice, *Collected Poems*, Faber 1966
Steve Mentz, *At the Bottom of Shakespeare's Ocean*, Continuum 2009
Tim Robinson, *Setting Foot on the Shores of Connemara and other writings*, Lilliput 1996
R. L. Stevenson, *Kidnapped*, 1886, Dent, Children's Illustrated Classics 1960
David Thomson, *The People of the Sea*, 1954, Canongate Classics edition 1996

Anthropology
Angela Bourke, *The Burning of Bridget Cleary*, Pimlico 1999
Walter Burkert, *Homo Necans: The Anthropology of Ancient Greek Sacrificial Ritual and Myth*, trans. Peter Bing, University of California Press 1983
J. F. Campbell, *Popular Tales of the West Highlands*, 2 vols, Abela Publishing Ltd 2009
J. G. Campbell, *The Gaelic Otherworld*, ed. Ronald Black, Birlinn 2005
John Lorne Campbell, *A Very Civil People*, ed. Hugh Cheape, Birlinn 2000
Alexander Carmichael, *Carmina Gadelica: Hymns and incantations, with illustrative notes on words, rites and customs, dying and obsolete*, Oliver & Boyd 1928–71
Rev. Ian Carmichael, *Lismore in Alba*, D. Leslie 1948
Wendy Doniger, *The Woman Who Pretended to Be Who She Was: Myths of Self-Imitation*, Oxford University Press 2004
A. R. Forbes, *Gaelic Names of Beasts etc.*, Oliver & Boyd 1905
James Frazer, *The Golden Bough: A Study in Magic and Religion*, 1890, Cosimo 2009
Janet Hooper, *A Landscape Given Meaning: An Archaeological Perspective on Landscape History in Highland Scotland*, PhD thesis Glasgow 2002
Claude Lévi-Strauss, *Totemism*, trans. Rodney Needham, Beacon 1963
Claude Lévi-Strauss, *Le totémisme aujourd'hui*, PUF 1962
Tim Robinson, *Stones of Aran*, Pilgrimage, Faber 2008
Rev. Alexander Stewart, writing as 'Nether Lochaber', *The Natural History, Legends, and Folk-lore of the West Highlands*

Bibliography

History and Archaeology
Rev. Thomas Brown, *Annals of the Disruption*, Edinburgh 1877
Edmund Burt, *Burt's Letters from the North of Scotland*, 1754, ed. Andrew Simmons, Birlinn 1998
Robert A. Dodgshon, *From Chiefs to Landlords: Social and Economic Change in the Western Highlands and Islands: c.1493–1820*, 1998
Alexander Fenton, *The Shape of the Past I*, John Donald 1985
Philip Gaskell, *Morvern Transformed: A Highland Parish in the Nineteenth Century*, Cambridge University Press 1968
James Hunter, *The Making of the Crofting Community*, John Donald 1976
A. D. Lacaille, *The Stone Age in Scotland*, London 1954
John MacAskill, *Scotland's Foreshore*, Edinburgh University Press 2018
J. P. MacLean, *A History of the Clan Mac Lean from Its First Settlement at Duard Castle, in the Isle of Mull*, R. Clarke & Co. 1889
John MacLeod, *Parish of Morvern, New Statistical Account*, 1843
Norman MacLeod, *Reminiscences of a Highland Parish*, 1867, 2nd edn London 1887; new edition with notes and introduction by Iain Thornber published as *Morvern: A Highland Parish*, Birlinn 2018
J. P. Mallory, *In Search of the Indo-Europeans*, Thames & Hudson 1989
T. R. Malthus, *An Essay on the Principle of Population, as it affects the future improvement of society, with remarks on the speculations of Mr. Godwin, M. Condorcet, and other writers*, London: J. Johnson, 1798, extract in *The Monthly Review*, September 1798
Paula Martin (ed.), *Exploring Morvern*, 2 vols, Morvern Heritage Society 2004, 2010
Paul Mellars, *The Early Postglacial Settlement of Northern Europe*, Duckworth 1978
Paul Mellars and Martha V. Andrews, *Excavations on Oronsay: Prehistoric Human Ecology on a Small Island*, Edinburgh University Press 1987
Thomas Pennant, *Tour in Scotland 1769*, Vol. I 1771, Birlinn 2000
Faith Raven, *Ardtornish*, privately printed, 2019
Eric Richards, *The Highland Clearances*, 3rd edn Birlinn 2007
M. Rockman and J. Steele (eds), *Colonization of Unfamiliar Landscapes*, Routledge 2003
'A Seneachie', *An Historical and Genealogical Account of the Clan MacLean*, Laing & Forbes 1838
J. Sinclair, *The Statistical Account of Scotland*, Edinburgh 1795
David Stevenson, *Highland Warrior: Alasdair MacColla and the Civil Wars*, 1980, Birlinn 2014
M. Turner (ed.), *Malthus and His Time*, St Martin's Press 1986

ACKNOWLEDGEMENTS

This book comes with many thanks to all those who have helped, welcomed and looked after me when at the bay. Above all the members of the extended Raven family – Faith, Anna, Norrie, Hugh, Jane, Jane and Mandy. And to those who live and work at Ardtornish: Robin Bell, Simon Boult, Janet Cameron, Isobel Carmichael, Allan Davidson, Alan Kennedy, James Laurie, Ross Mackay, Kat and Kenny McLaughlin, Jennie Robertson and James and Annemie Shanks.

To my sisters Juliet and Rebecca and my dear friends Tom Hammick, Charlie Boxer, Aurea Carpenter and Andrew Palmer for their steady and welcome draughts of enthusiasm and wisdom. To Liam Ashmore for telling me that any relationship with rock pools would be meaningless without taking Heidegger into account. And for Sarah, of course, for first bringing me to the world of the bay and discovering its treasures with me.

To Janet Hooper, James Westland, Nigel Leask and Iain Thornber for their invaluable guidance and information. To Roddy Murray and Annie Macsween for making sure that the passages in Gaelic were not hopelessly scrambled. Thank you to Tim Gates of Althon, outfall engineers of Norwich, Gilbert Cox of Rockbond Special Concretes in Essex, Tony Bennett of the Crown Estate and Lyndsey McLaren of the Mull Aquarium for their exceptional professional expertise.

Acknowledgements

All thanks to Rosie Nicolson for making the beautiful maps and diagrams from my rough old sketches. And once again, a brimming bowl of thanks to Kate Boxer for her stupendous inhabiting of the creatures and people that adorn this book. Thank you also to Colin Gale of Artichoke Printmaking Studios for making the plates of Kate Boxer's images so beautifully.

And as ever to George Capel and Zoe Pagnamenta, to all at HarperCollins, especially book-improvers supreme David Milner, Jo Thompson, Iain Hunt and Arabella Pike, and at FSG, above all Jonathan Galassi, for their long and sustained encouragement.

INDEX